Ultimate Adventure Atlas of Earth

MAPS · GAMES · ACTIVITIES
and more for hours of extreme fun!

Rebecca Hirsch
& Sally Isaacs

WASHINGTON, D.C.

TABLE OF CONTENTS

This atlas highlights adventurous places and things to do all around the world. Extreme plants, animals, and weather are also featured to highlight natural wonders. With colorful maps, amazing pictures, and tons of fun information, it explores cool things about a range of features of each continent. It also looks at adventures in oceans and in the sky. Before trying any of these adventures, always follow health and safety guidelines concerning fitness, clothing, equipment, food, and travel to specific countries or locations.

EUROPE

SOUTH AMERICA

NORTH AMERICA

ADVENTURE TOPICS

In each chapter, double-page spreads focus on:

- Landforms
- Climates
- On Location
- Habitats
- Plants
- Animals
- Adventures

HOW TO USE THIS ATLAS

TOPIC ICON
Heading icons and titles define the overall topic of each spread.

You can experience adventures on all seven continents of the world and also in the oceans and in the sky. Our adventurous trip starts in North America and takes you around the globe to discover extreme landscapes, climates, wildlife, and thrills and spills. So buckle up and follow Aunt Bertha's tips to experience the the ultimate adventures of a lifetime!

TITLE
This book is a collection of double-page articles. The headings and subheadings provide a summary and flavor for each spread.

INTRODUCTION
The main text provides an overview of the landscape, climates, wildlife, or adventures you can experience on the continent. It highlights unique features and mentions well-known examples.

ADVENTURE FEATURES
Each story has a title, location, and descriptive text. Most stories also have an accompanying photograph.

ANIMALS

AWESOME ANIMALS
Extreme and EXOTIC

Australia and Oceania are packed with unusual animals. Red kangaroos—the world's largest marsupials (pouched mammals)—use their powerful legs to hop through Australia's deserts and grasslands. The giant weta—the world's heaviest insect—inhabits New Zealand, as do flightless birds such as the rare kakapo and the shy kiwi. Beautiful birds of paradise can be found on tropical islands and on the Australian mainland. Poisonous snakes and spiders are widespread.

5 PATCHWORK PLATYPUS
Australia

The egg-laying platypus looks like it was patched together from other animals. It has a bill and webbed feet like a duck, a body like an otter, and a tail like a beaver. Males have poisonous stingers on their back legs.

DID YOU KNOW?

The box jellyfish is the most venomous marine animal known. Its powerful sting stuns or kills prey instantly. Each tentacle can reach ten feet (3 m) in length and is covered with about 5,000 stinging cells.

ADVENTURE ATTRACTIONS

SALTY DESERT POOLS
The Simpson Desert is Australia's harshest and hottest desert. Seasonal salt lakes teem with fish and are a breeding ground for large numbers of waterbirds.

JELLYFISH LAKE
This saltwater lake in Palau is packed with golden jellyfish. The animal's sting is so mild that people can swim among them without getting hurt.

MEGAPODE FIELDS
On the beach at night in the Solomon Islands, female megapodes (flightless birds) dig about three feet (1 m) into the sand to bury their eggs. The volcanic soil is warmed from below, providing an ideal temperature for the eggs to incubate.

112

FUN FACTS
Did You Know?, Record Breaker, and Strange But True panels highlight weird, wonderful, and wacky facts about each topic.

ADVENTURE ATTRACTIONS
Three major landscape, climate, habitat, wildlife, or adventure features are listed and described here and appear on the map at the end of each chapter.

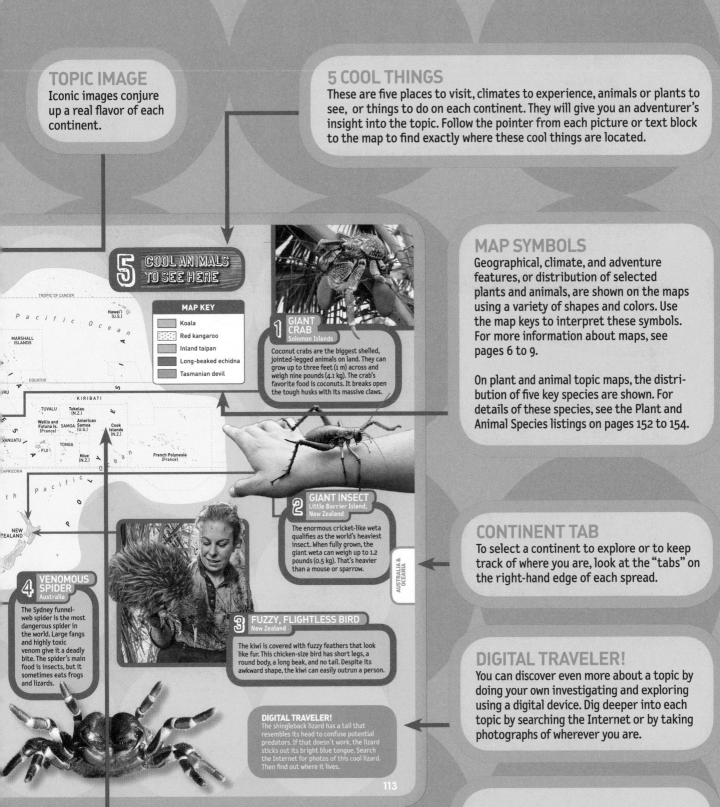

TOPIC IMAGE
Iconic images conjure up a real flavor of each continent.

5 COOL THINGS
These are five places to visit, climates to experience, animals or plants to see, or things to do on each continent. They will give you an adventurer's insight into the topic. Follow the pointer from each picture or text block to the map to find exactly where these cool things are located.

5 COOL ANIMALS TO SEE HERE

MAP KEY
- Koala
- Red kangaroo
- Inland taipan
- Long-beaked echidna
- Tasmanian devil

1 GIANT CRAB
Solomon Islands

Coconut crabs are the biggest shelled, jointed-legged animals on land. They can grow up to three feet (1 m) across and weigh nine pounds (4.1 kg). The crab's favorite food is coconuts. It breaks open the tough husks with its massive claws.

2 GIANT INSECT
Little Barrier Island, New Zealand

The enormous cricket-like weta qualifies as the world's heaviest insect. When fully grown, the giant weta can weigh up to 1.2 pounds (0.5 kg). That's heavier than a mouse or sparrow.

4 VENOMOUS SPIDER
Australia

The Sydney funnel-web spider is the most dangerous spider in the world. Large fangs and highly toxic venom give it a deadly bite. The spider's main food is insects, but it sometimes eats frogs and lizards.

3 FUZZY, FLIGHTLESS BIRD
New Zealand

The kiwi is covered with fuzzy feathers that look like fur. This chicken-size bird has short legs, a round body, a long beak, and no tail. Despite its awkward shape, the kiwi can easily outrun a person.

DIGITAL TRAVELER!
The shingleback lizard has a tail that resembles its head to confuse potential predators. If that doesn't work, the lizard sticks out its bright blue tongue. Search the Internet for photos of this cool lizard. Then find out where it lives.

113

AUSTRALIA & OCEANIA

MAP SYMBOLS
Geographical, climate, and adventure features, or distribution of selected plants and animals, are shown on the maps using a variety of shapes and colors. Use the map keys to interpret these symbols. For more information about maps, see pages 6 to 9.

On plant and animal topic maps, the distribution of five key species are shown. For details of these species, see the Plant and Animal Species listings on pages 152 to 154.

CONTINENT TAB
To select a continent to explore or to keep track of where you are, look at the "tabs" on the right-hand edge of each spread.

DIGITAL TRAVELER!
You can discover even more about a topic by doing your own investigating and exploring using a digital device. Dig deeper into each topic by searching the Internet or by taking photographs of wherever you are.

MAP
To find locations mentioned on each page, check out the maps! Then look for climate and habitat patterns, wildlife distribution, and location of adventures.

MEASUREMENTS
In the text, measurements are given first in U.S. units and then in metric units. The following abbreviations are used: ft = feet, mi = miles, m = meters, km = kilometers, F = Fahrenheit, C = Celsius, mph/kph = miles/kilometers per hour.

HOW TO USE MAPS

Maps tell visual stories about the world, but you have to learn how to read them to understand what they are illustrating. The maps in this book show the shape, size, and position of continents, regions, and countries. They also show the distribution of weather patterns (climate), natural vegetation (habitats), and selected plants, animals, and adventures. All maps are shown with north at the top.

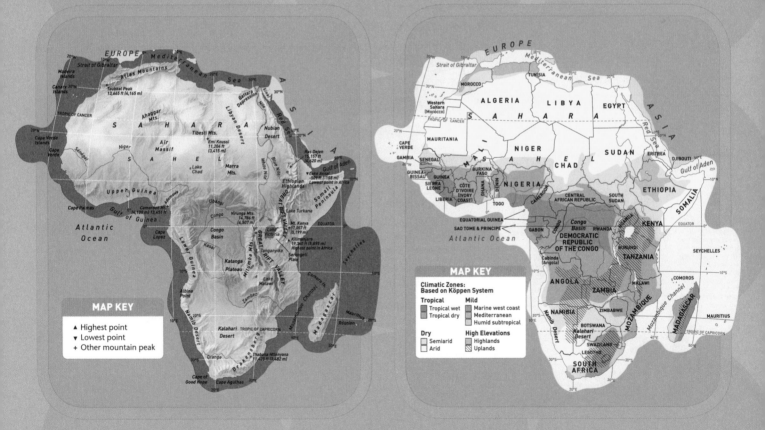

LANDFORM MAPS

The Equator marks the midpoint between Earth's Poles. Lines of latitude indicate distances north or south of the Equator. Lines of longitude indicate distances east or west. They start at the prime meridian.

HABITAT MAPS

These maps show areas of natural vegetation. Within each habitat area, there may be many differences, or variation, due to height above sea level and closeness to mountains and coasts. Climate maps are similar.

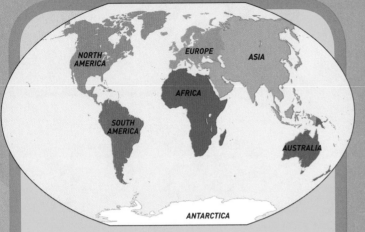

CONTINENTS

Earth's land area is mainly made up of seven giant landmasses known as continents. People have divided the continents into smaller political units called countries. Australia is a continent and also a single country. Antarctica is a continent with no countries. The five other continents include almost 200 independent countries.

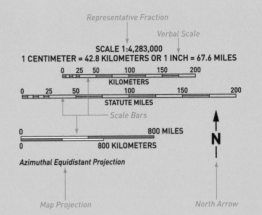

SCALE AND DIRECTION

The scale on a map may be shown as a fraction or comparison in words. A bar scale is a line or bar with measurements that compare distances on the map with those in the real world. Maps may include an arrow or compass rose to indicate north. If north is top, east is to the right, west to the left, and south is bottom.

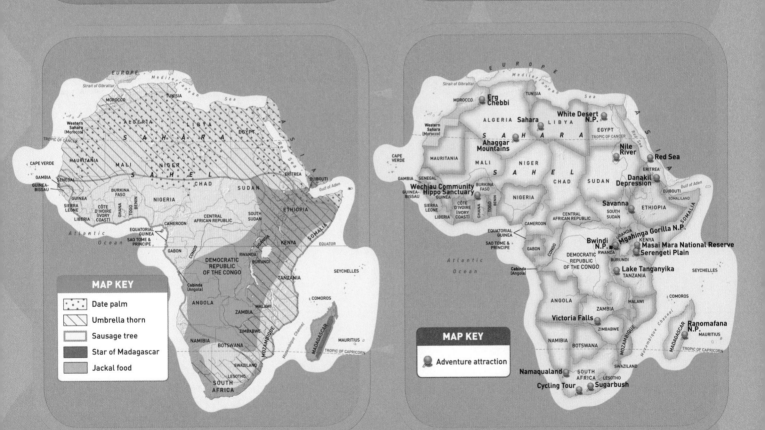

PLANT MAPS

Text blocks feature a selection of species that reflect the unique plant life of each continent. Maps show the distribution of five of these species. There are millions more species in the world. Animal maps are similar.

ADVENTURE MAPS

These maps show the countries of the continents and where our featured adventures are located. There are adventures to be had at many more locations, and new adventures are being created all the time.

WORLD MAP

150°W 120°W 90°W 60°W 0°

ARCTIC

Greenland
(Denmark)

ARCTIC CIRCLE

ICELAND

Alaska
(U.S.)

CANADA

UNITED
KINGDOM   DENMARK

IRELAND   NETH.
                 GERMANY
                 BELG.

FRANCE   SWITZ.
                 ITALY

PORTUGAL

UNITED STATES

ATLANTIC

OCEAN

SPAIN

30°N

TUNISIA

MOROCCO

TROPIC OF CANCER

Western
Sahara
(Morocco)

ALGERIA

Hawai'i
(U.S.)

MEXICO

MAURITANIA

MALI   NIGER

BAHAMAS

CUBA

BELIZE

HAITI

JAMAICA

GUATEMALA   HONDURAS

EL SALVADOR   NICARAGUA

COSTA RICA

PANAMA

DOMINICAN REP.

ST. KITTS & NEVIS
ANTIGUA & BARBUDA

ST. LUCIA — DOMINICA
GRENADA — BARBADOS
ST. VINCENT & THE GRENADINES
TRINIDAD AND TOBAGO

CAPE
VERDE

SENEGAL
GAMBIA
GUINEA-
BISSAU   GUINEA

SIERRA LEONE

LIBERIA

BURKINA
FASO   NIGERIA

BENIN
TOGO
GHANA

VENEZUELA

GUYANA

French Guiana
(France)

PACIFIC

COLOMBIA

SURINAME

CÔTE D'IVOIRE
(IVORY COAST)

EQ.
GUINEA

EQUATOR

ECUADOR

SAO TOME
AND
PRINCIPE

OCEAN

BRAZIL

PERU

French Polynesia
(France)

BOLIVIA

PARAGUAY

TROPIC OF CAPRICORN

30°S

ARGENTINA   URUGUAY

CHILE

60°S

ANTARCTIC CIRCLE

COUNTRIES OF THE WORLD

This is a political map of the world. It shows
country boundaries and country names. It also
shows the world's oceans.

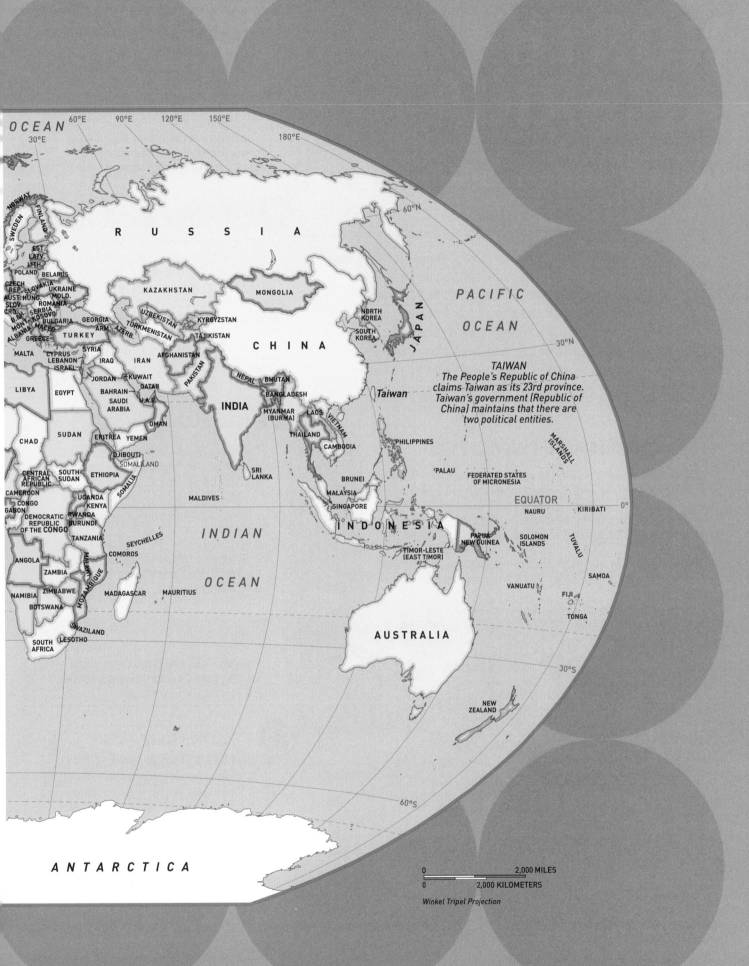

TAIWAN
The People's Republic of China claims Taiwan as its 23rd province. Taiwan's government (Republic of China) maintains that there are two political entities.

0 2,000 MILES
0 2,000 KILOMETERS

Winkel Tripel Projection

NORTH AMERICA

Wild, rugged, and WONDERFUL

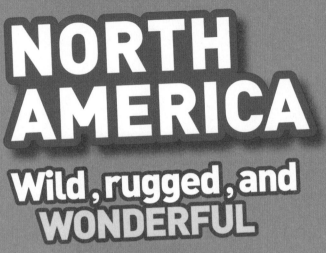

For an adventurer, this continent has everything—high mountains, raging rivers, volcanoes, deserts, lakes, glaciers, rugged coastlines, and tropical islands. The amazing wildlife ranges from giant sequoia trees and prickly cacti to grizzly bears, wild cats, and poisonous insects. You can go white-water rafting, skydiving, scuba diving, surfing, motor racing, skiing—any extreme sport you want!

AUNT BERTHA'S ADVENTURE TRAVEL TIPS

One of the most exciting ways to see the continent is to fly over it in a lightweight aircraft. The best time to fly is at sunrise.

In summer, the swamps in the southern U.S. are infested with mosquitoes and horseflies. Protect yourself with bug repellent!

In the northern Arctic region, it can be so cold that your breath freezes instantly. Bundle up with your warmest winter clothes!

People enjoying a hair-raising and body-soaking wild, white-water raft trip on the Adams River, British Columbia, Canada.

ADVENTURE HOT SPOTS

LANDFORMS
Saddle up a horse and hit the trails in the Great Smoky Mountains in the southeastern United States.

CLIMATES
Greenland is so far north that even the summers are cold. Kayak among giant icebergs—floating masses of ice.

GRAND CANYON
Fly in a helicopter over this deep gorge that cuts through the landscape of the southwestern United States.

HABITATS
The frigid, packed ice of northern Canada is home to more than 40 percent of Earth's polar bears.

PLANTS
Trek through temperate rain forests of the Pacific Northwest to see giant conifer trees.

ANIMALS
Snorkel or sail along the coasts of the islands of the Bahamas to watch turtles, sea snakes, and sharks.

YELLOWSTONE PARK
Try to imagine the active volcano that sits below what was the first national park in the United States.

ADVENTURES
For a hair-raising view of Panama's cloud forest, take a ride through the treetops on a zip line!

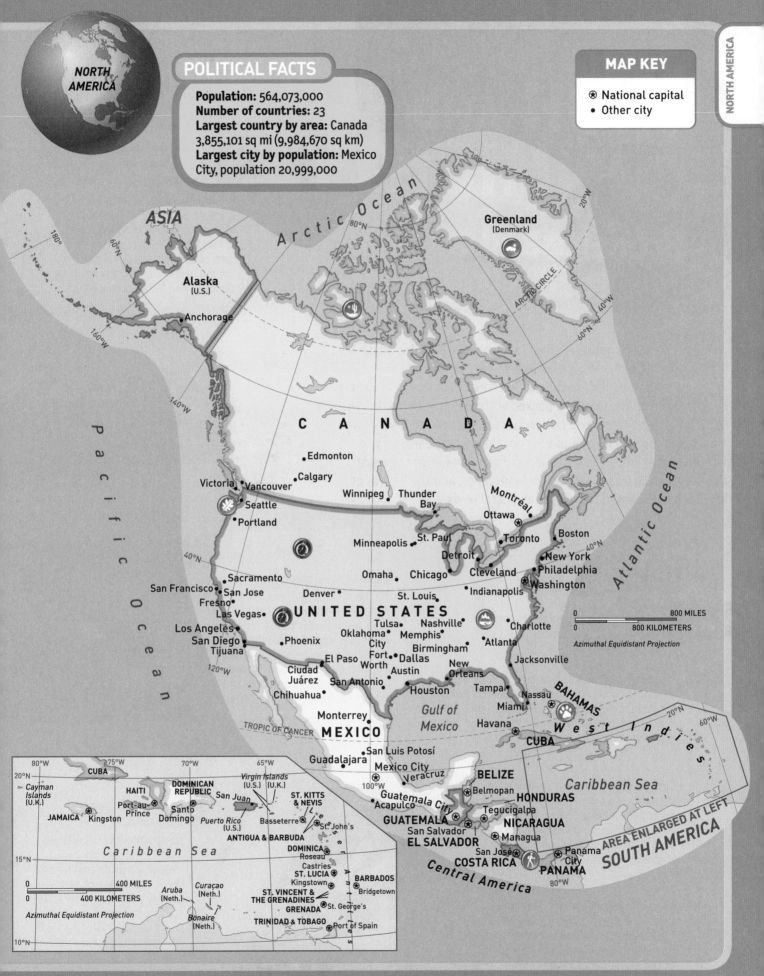

NORTH AMERICA

POLITICAL FACTS

Population: 564,073,000
Number of countries: 23
Largest country by area: Canada
3,855,101 sq mi (9,984,670 sq km)
Largest city by population: Mexico
City, population 20,999,000

MAP KEY

⊛ National capital
• Other city

ASIA

Arctic Ocean

Alaska
(U.S.)
• Anchorage

Greenland
(Denmark)

ARCTIC CIRCLE

C A N A D A

Atlantic Ocean

• Edmonton
• Calgary

Victoria • Vancouver
Winnipeg • Thunder Bay
Montréal
• Seattle
Ottawa ⊛
• Portland
St. Paul
Toronto • Boston
Minneapolis •
Detroit • • New York
Pacific Ocean
Omaha • Chicago
Cleveland • Philadelphia
Sacramento •
• • St. Louis • Indianapolis ⊛ Washington
San Francisco • San Jose
Denver •
Fresno •
U N I T E D   S T A T E S
Las Vegas •
Tulsa • Nashville
• Charlotte
Los Angeles •
Oklahoma Memphis •
San Diego • Phoenix
City Birmingham • Atlanta
Tijuana •
El Paso Fort Dallas
• Worth • Austin Jacksonville •
Ciudad
Juárez San Antonio • Houston New Orleans
Chihuahua • Tampa •
Monterrey Gulf of Mexico Nassau
M E X I C O Miami • BAHAMAS
TROPIC OF CANCER Havana ⊛ West Indies
San Luis Potosí •
Guadalajara • CUBA
Mexico City
Veracruz BELIZE Caribbean Sea
Guatemala City Belmopan ⊛
Acapulco • HONDURAS AREA ENLARGED AT LEFT
GUATEMALA ⊛ Tegucigalpa SOUTH AMERICA
San Salvador NICARAGUA
EL SALVADOR ⊛ Managua
San José Panama
COSTA RICA ⊛ • City
Central America PANAMA

800 MILES
800 KILOMETERS
Azimuthal Equidistant Projection

Inset map (Caribbean)

CUBA
Cayman Islands (U.K.)
HAITI
DOMINICAN REPUBLIC
Virgin Islands (U.S.) (U.K.)
San Juan
ST. KITTS & NEVIS
JAMAICA
Kingston
Port-au-Prince
Santo Domingo
Puerto Rico (U.S.)
Basseterre ⊛
St. John's ⊛
ANTIGUA & BARBUDA
DOMINICA
Roseau
Castries
ST. LUCIA
Kingstown ⊛
BARBADOS
Bridgetown ⊛
Aruba (Neth.)
Curaçao (Neth.)
ST. VINCENT & THE GRENADINES
GRENADA
St. George's ⊛
Bonaire (Neth.)
TRINIDAD & TOBAGO
Port of Spain ⊛
Caribbean Sea

400 MILES
400 KILOMETERS
Azimuthal Equidistant Projection

11

HIGH AND MIGHTY

From ice and snow to SANDY DESERTS

North America stretches from the Atlantic Ocean to the Pacific Ocean. In between, you'll find big and beautiful landforms. The towering Rocky Mountains in the west are packed with peaks, waterfalls, canyons, and narrow passes. East of the Rockies are thousands of small lakes and the enormous Great Lakes of the northeastern United States and southern Canada. In the south are huge caves, strange moonlike landscapes, and the islands of the Caribbean, home to lagoons and coral reefs.

ADVENTURE ATTRACTIONS

MONUMENT VALLEY

This region in the southwestern United States is filled with isolated towers and flat-topped blocks of rock known as mesas and buttes. These create an eerie landscape ideal for extreme hiking.

GIANT RIVER

The Mackenzie River is Canada's longest river. It begins in a northwestern lake and flows north to the Arctic Ocean. It lies in a remote part of the country, and few Canadians have seen it. For about seven months each year, the river is frozen.

STRING OF ISLANDS

On a map, a long string of islands known as the Lesser Antilles forms a boundary between the Atlantic Ocean and the Caribbean Sea. The dramatic island landscapes form the backdrop to the movie series Pirates of the Caribbean.

1 SIMMERING VOLCANO
United States

In 1980, there was an explosive eruption at Mount St. Helens, in Washington State. Wind laden with stones from the blast destroyed forests on the mountain. Smoky ash covered the state and beyond. Today climbers hike to the crater rim.

2 UNDERGROUND CAVES
United States

Mammoth Cave National Park in Kentucky is the world's longest cave system, with more than 400 miles (644 km) of explored tunnels. Extreme cavers go potholing and swimming through tunnels. Animal watchers study bats, snakes, and frogs that live in the cave system.

3 CRYSTAL CAVERNS
Mexico

Deep below the Chihuahuan Desert, you can see huge selenite crystals that formed in the groundwater over a period of 600,000 years. The cave temperature can reach 118°F (48°C), so explorers need special suits to stay cool.

4 GIANT ICE FIELDS
Canada

Go ice exploring on the Athabasca Glacier in the Canadian Rockies. It is a massive river of ice that "flows" down the mountainside. Special buses drive across it, but you can hike it, explore crevasses, enter ice caves, and climb with crampons and ice axes.

5 UNDERWATER CAVE
Belize

The Great Blue Hole is a large submarine sinkhole off the coast of Belize. It is almost 1,000 feet (305 m) across and 400 feet (122 m) deep. It is filled with spectacular coral formations. The hole is popular with adventurers seeking scuba-diving thrills.

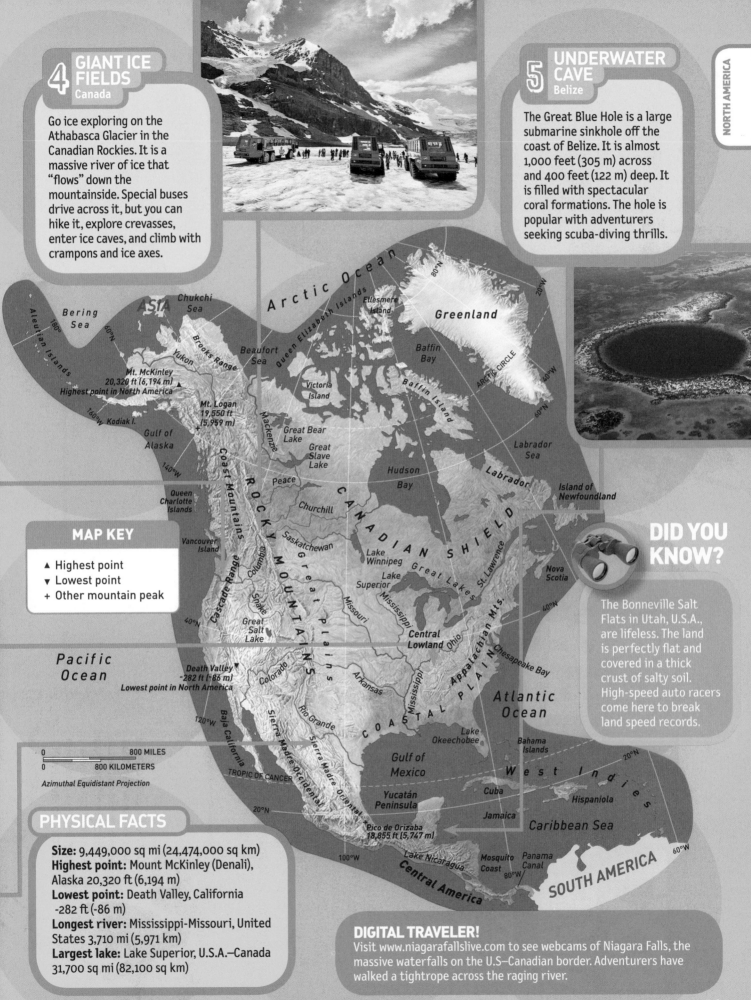

MAP KEY

▲ Highest point
▼ Lowest point
+ Other mountain peak

Mt. McKinley 20,320 ft (6,194 m) Highest point in North America

Mt. Logan 19,550 ft (5,959 m)

Death Valley -282 ft (-86 m) Lowest point in North America

Pico de Orizaba 18,855 ft (5,747 m)

0   800 MILES
0   800 KILOMETERS
Azimuthal Equidistant Projection

DID YOU KNOW?

The Bonneville Salt Flats in Utah, U.S.A., are lifeless. The land is perfectly flat and covered in a thick crust of salty soil. High-speed auto racers come here to break land speed records.

PHYSICAL FACTS

Size: 9,449,000 sq mi (24,474,000 sq km)
Highest point: Mount McKinley (Denali), Alaska 20,320 ft (6,194 m)
Lowest point: Death Valley, California -282 ft (-86 m)
Longest river: Mississippi-Missouri, United States 3,710 mi (5,971 km)
Largest lake: Lake Superior, U.S.A.–Canada 31,700 sq mi (82,100 sq km)

DIGITAL TRAVELER!
Visit www.niagarafallslive.com to see webcams of Niagara Falls, the massive waterfalls on the U.S–Canadian border. Adventurers have walked a tightrope across the raging river.

EXTREME WEATHER

From the icy north to the SIZZLING SOUTH

E xtreme weather hits all parts of the North American continent. In the Mojave Desert in the southwestern United States, the temperature can get as high as 130°F (54°C). In the Yukon in western Canada, it has gotten as low as -76°F (-60°C).

"Tornado Alley" in the middle of the United States sees violent storms, while parts of Central America get more than 160 inches (406 cm) of rain every year. Tropical rainstorms are common in the Caribbean and along the east and west coasts of Mexico.

ADVENTURE ATTRACTIONS

POWERFUL TIDES
The funnel-shaped Bay of Fundy in Nova Scotia, Canada, gets the world's highest tides—they can reach more than 50 feet (15 m). The water force is equal to more than 8,000 locomotives.

NORTHWEST PASSAGE
The sea route through the Arctic Ocean freezes each year in just a few hours. Boats can be stuck in the ice all winter.

HURRICANE COAST
Each year, hurricanes hit Florida, the Caribbean islands, and Central America, walloping the coasts with high winds, floods, and mudslides.

DIGITAL TRAVELER!
Pick a place with an extreme climate and track its weather on a meteorological website, such as weather.com. Then look at photos and videos made by the site's storm chasers.

5 EXTREME CLIMATES HERE

1 SUPER-SIZE SNOWFALL Canada
In Val-d'Or, Quebec, there are more snow days than anywhere else on the continent. Schools have closed as many as 103.5 days a year. Temperatures there can drop to -40°F (-40°C).

MAP KEY

Climatic Zones: Based on Köppen System

Tropical
- Tropical wet
- Tropical dry

Dry
- Semiarid
- Arid

Mild
- Marine west coast
- Mediterranean
- Humid subtropical

Continental
- Warm summer
- Cool summer
- Subarctic

Polar
- Tundra
- Ice cap

High Elevations
- Highlands

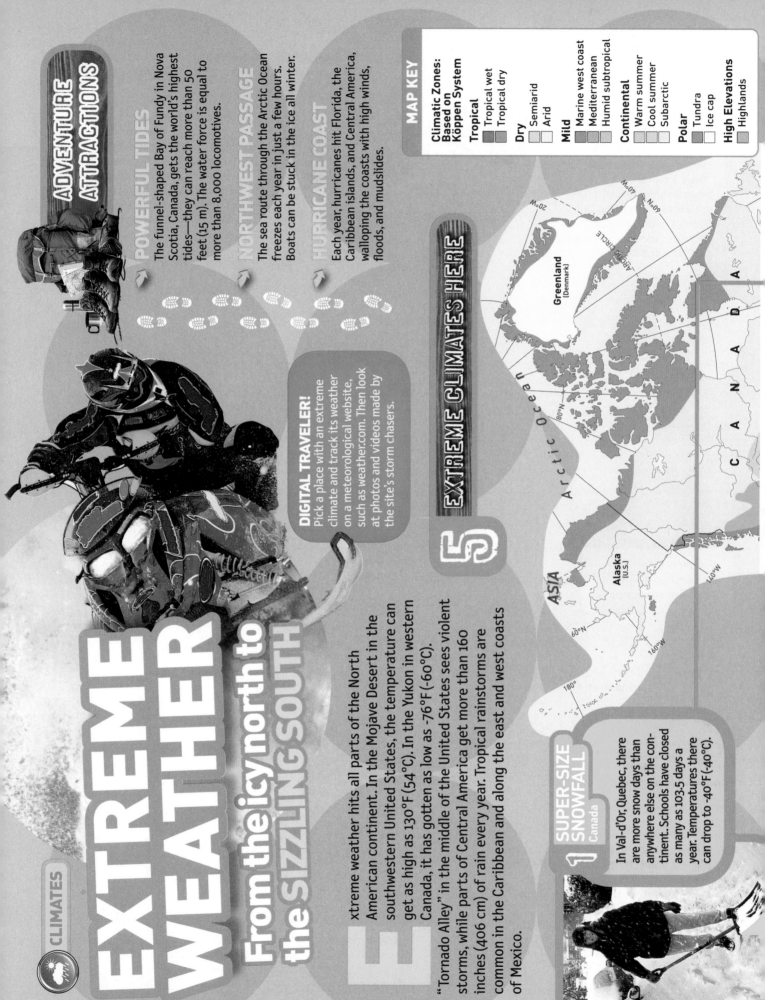

Greenland (Denmark)

Arctic Ocean

ARCTIC CIRCLE

ASIA

Alaska (U.S.)

C A N A D A

2 HABOOBS—DUST STORMS
United States

Huge walls of dust—about a half mile (0.8 km) high—can build up near Phoenix, Arizona, before thunderstorms strike. The black dust clouds cover skyscrapers and stop traffic. The storms are called *haboobs*, which is Arabic for "violent wind."

3 DEATH VALLEY
United States

Located in the Mojave Desert, this is the lowest and driest place on the continent and the hottest on the planet. Summer temperatures average 120°F (49°C).

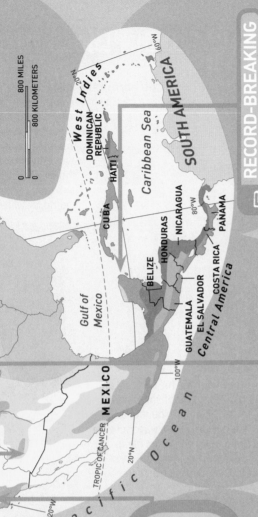

4 WICKED WIND
United States

A world-record wind, reaching 231 miles per hour (372 kph), hit the weather station on the summit of Mount Washington, New Hampshire, in 1934. The mountain has some of the world's most extreme weather. Even summer hikers are surprised by freezing winds.

5 RECORD-BREAKING RAIN
Mexico

During Hurricane Wilma in 2005, 64.3 inches (163.3 cm) of rain hit Isla Mujeres in one day. This set a rain record in the Northern Hemisphere.

STRANGE BUT TRUE

Some of the forests of Costa Rica are permanently covered in a fog or mist of clouds. Water constantly drips from leaves in the forest canopy, soaking the ground.

Atlantic Ocean

Great Lakes

UNITED STATES

West Indies

DOMINICAN REPUBLIC

HAITI

CUBA

Caribbean Sea

SOUTH AMERICA

NICARAGUA

PANAMA

COSTA RICA

HONDURAS

BELIZE

EL SALVADOR

GUATEMALA

Central America

Gulf of Mexico

MEXICO

TROPIC OF CANCER

Pacific Ocean

0 800 MILES
0 800 KILOMETERS

15

GRAND CANYON

Six million years IN THE MAKING

More than 275 miles (443 km) long, up to 18 miles (29 km) wide, and in places 1 mile (1.6 km) deep, this steep-sided canyon cuts through the Arizona landscape in the United States. Over millions of years, the Colorado River eroded the underlying rock and continues to run through the canyon. Weather conditions are always changing depending on the season, location, and depth of the canyon. There are droughts, flash floods, thunderstorms, and even snowfalls and frost.

5 COOL PLACES TO SEE HERE

This "3-D" map of the Grand Canyon highlights the massive, twisting, river-cut channel through the southwestern U.S. Along the canyon are narrow gorges, waterfalls and rapids, steep rock faces, and caves. Adventurers have their choice of rock climbing, extreme hiking, horseback riding, or white-water rafting.

NORTH
AMERICA
United States
Grand
Canyon

1 COLORED WATERFALL
Havasu Falls

Brace yourself for the cold and colorful splash of the Havasu Falls. Calcium carbonate and magnesium in the water create the blue-green color. Camp overnight near the falls and hike from one refreshing pool to the next.

Sanup Plateau

Surprise Canyon

Shivwits Plateau

G r a n

Prospect Canyon

Toroweap Valley

Mohawk Canyon

DIGITAL TRAVELER!
Feel the thrill of the canyon by finding online videos of high-flying helicopter rides over the canyon, climbs down vertical rock walls, or white-water rafting on the mighty Colorado River.

3 RIVER RAPIDS
Page

In some places, the Colorado River is peaceful and calm. In others, it is rough and wild. Ride the river in an inflatable raft and expect anything! Camp along the way as you spend 3 to 14 days on the river.

2 NARROW CANYON PATH
Bright Angel Trail

Saddle up a mule and let it transport you down Bright Angel Trail. Catch some breathtaking views of the Colorado River. Stop to sleep under the stars, and head back up at sunrise.

Scale varies in this perspective.

Lake Powell

Paria Plateau

Marble Canyon

Echo Cliffs

Kanab Plateau

Kanab Creek Canyon

Tapeats Amphitheater

Great Thumb Mesa

Kaibab Plateau North Rim

d Canyon

National Canyon

Hindu Amphitheater

Bright Angel Canyon

Little Colorado Gorge

Coconino

Havasu Canyon

Plateau

South Rim

5 STEEP CLIFFS
South Rim

Be careful as you descend the steep, red-wall faces of Hermit Trail. The path is narrow, and the drop is thousands of feet. With little shade, summer temperatures can soar above 100°F (38°C).

Cataract Canyon

4 PYRAMID-SHAPED MOUNTAIN
North Rim

Rock climbers call Zoroaster Temple one of the world's best climbs. A round-trip climb of Zoroaster requires almost 30 miles (48 km) of hiking and a vertical elevation gain and loss of 20,000 feet (6,096 m). Trail-runners race in the foothills.

FORESTS TO DESERTS

Home to warblers, waders, and WILD THINGS

North America has almost every kind of habitat you can think of, from the freezing wilderness regions of Alaska and northern Canada to the hot rain forests of Central America and the lush islands of the West Indies. In between are cool coastal forests, warm grasslands, high mountains, arid deserts, and steamy wetlands. Together they provide homes for rich and varied plant and animal life and an endless variety of natural places for adventurers to visit.

MAP KEY

- ☐ Grasslands
- ☐ Coniferous forests
- ☐ Tropical broadleaf forests
- ☐ Temperate broadleaf forests
- ☐ Mediterranean forests and shrublands
- ☐ Boreal forests
- ☐ Rock and ice
- ☐ Tundra
- ☐ Mangroves
- ☐ Deserts and dry shrublands

5 PRAIRIE
United States

You won't find trees on South Dakota's prairie. Grasses and short shrubs grow here instead. Herds of bison roamed the prairie when it was home to Native Americans. You'll still see coyotes, prairie dogs, and rattlesnakes.

ADVENTURE ATTRACTIONS

INSECTS BY THE MILLIONS
Bosawás Biosphere Reserve in Nicaragua is one of the world's largest rain forests, with more than 150,000 kinds of insects and at least 100 kinds of birds.

BAT CAVE
Workers at Bat Cave Preserve in North Carolina, U.S.A., avoid the cave during the winter. They do not want to disturb the hibernating bats. Spiders, millipedes, and amphipods also live here. They have adapted to the dark cave and its sparse water supply.

ISLAND VARIETY
Andros Island is the largest and least populated island in the Bahamas. Animals from tiny hummingbirds to giant land crabs live in mangrove, swamp, and cave habitats.

DID YOU KNOW?

Pitch Lake, in Trinidad and Tobago, is filled with gooey asphalt. Remains of a prehistoric giant sloth and a mastodon's tooth have been found in the lake.

5 COOL PLACES TO SEE HERE

0 — 500 MILES
0 — 500 KILOMETERS

ASIA

Arctic Ocean

Beaufort Sea

Greenland
(Denmark)

Alaska
(U.S.)

ARCTIC CIRCLE

Labrador
Sea

Hudson'
Bay

CANADA

ROCKY MOUNTAINS

GREAT PLAINS

UNITED STATES

Appalachian Mts.

Atlantic
Ocean

Pacific Ocean

Gulf of
Mexico

TROPIC OF CANCER

BAHAMAS

West Indies

CUBA

MEXICO

HAITI

DOMINICAN
REPUBLIC

JAMAICA

Caribbean Sea

BELIZE

GUATEMALA HONDURAS

EL
SALVADOR NICARAGUA

COSTA RICA PANAMA

TRINIDAD &
TOBAGO

SOUTH AMERICA

1 BOREAL FOREST
Canada

Also known as snow forest, this habitat in Canada's far north is packed with towering pine and spruce trees. The forest stays healthy because of lightning fires. Birds thrive on insects that live in burned tree trunks. Blueberries and huckleberries thrive on burned-out forest floors, while forest animals thrive on the berries.

2 EVERGLADES WETLANDS
United States

The Florida Everglades—sometimes called "a river of grass"—include mangrove swamps, hardwood trees, and sawgrass marshes. It is the only place in the world where you can find alligators and crocodiles in the same water.

4 ROCK DESERT
Mexico

The Chihuahuan Desert, on the U.S.A.–Mexico border, is a vast habitat of rocky plains and mountains. Spiny cacti and short shrubs grow well here. It is home to such tiny creatures as desert millipedes, tarantulas, lizards, and snakes.

3 TROPICAL RAIN FOREST
Costa Rica

These jungles are some of the richest wildlife habitats in the world, with more than 2,500 kinds of plants, 100 mammal species, 400 bird species, 120 kinds of reptiles and amphibians, and tens of thousands of different insects (including 5,000 kinds of moths)!

DIGITAL TRAVELER!
Many beaches in the Bahamas are scattered with seashells—once the protective armor for tiny sea creatures. Take photos of your favorite shells or find some online and make postcards to send to your friends.

5 COOL PLANTS TO SEE HERE

DIGITAL TRAVELER!
In the United States, each state has a flower that represents it. Search the Internet to find the flowers of states starting with the letter M.

1 PREHISTORIC PINES
United States

Bristlecone pines are the oldest living things on Earth. Some are more than 5,000 years old. They grow in cool, dry, windy areas of the western U.S.A. at heights between 5,600 and 11,200 feet (1,707 and 3,414 m).

MAP KEY

	Giant hogweed
	Poison sumac
	Giant redwood
	Jones' pitcher plant
	Skunk cabbage

2 TOWERING TRUNKS
United States

In Sequoia National Park in California, the giant redwood trees are the largest in the world. They can grow to a height of 275 feet (84 m).

3 VICIOUS SPINES
Mexico

Barrel cacti in deserts in the southwestern U.S.A. and Mexico grow to ten feet (3 m) high and two feet (0.6 m) wide. They have long spines that can puncture skin and cause a "dirty wound" that can take months to heal.

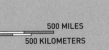

Map labels: ASIA, Arctic Ocean, Beaufort Sea, Alaska (U.S.), Greenland (Denmark), ARCTIC CIRCLE, Pacific Ocean, ROCKY MOUNTAINS, CANADA, Hudson Bay, Labrador Sea, GREAT PLAINS, UNITED STATES, Appalachian Mts., Atlantic Ocean, Gulf of Mexico, TROPIC OF CANCER, MEXICO, BAHAMAS, West Indies, CUBA, HAITI, DOMINICAN REPUBLIC, JAMAICA, Caribbean Sea, BELIZE, GUATEMALA, HONDURAS, EL SALVADOR, NICARAGUA, COSTA RICA, PANAMA, TRINIDAD & TOBAGO, SOUTH AMERICA

0 500 MILES
0 500 KILOMETERS

 **PLANTS**

TREES, CACTI, AND FUNGI

Tiny, tall, and everything IN BETWEEN

North America's plants can be pretty, prickly, or poisonous—sometimes all at once! The icy Arctic bursts into plant life as the short summer begins. Conifer forests span the continent with their towering evergreen trees. Mountain plants thrive on the ranges that run close to the northern Pacific and Atlantic coasts. Grasslands fill the interior, and plants such as cacti—adapted to hot, dry climates—are common in the southwest. Central America and the West Indies are rich in tropical plants, including lush rain forests.

5 POISON FRUIT TREE
The Bahamas

The *manchineel* tree grows on Caribbean islands as well as in Florida and Mexico. It is one of the world's most poisonous trees. The apple-like fruit is toxic, and so is the sap that drips from the trunk. Even raindrops that fall from the tree can burn the skin.

4 VENUS FLYTRAP
United States

This plant acts like a machine—with its hinges at the end of each leaf. The plant senses insects and snaps shut to absorb them. Venus flytraps are abundant in North and South Carolina.

ADVENTURE ATTRACTIONS

WET AND DECAYING LOWLANDS

The Hudson Bay Lowlands in northern Ontario, Canada, are more water than earth. They are rich in peat—decaying plant material. Peat traps water, forming bogs and frequently flooded wetlands.

DWARF TREE PARK

Dwarf trees grow on the mountain slopes of Cusuco National Park in Honduras. They are less than ten feet (3 m) high.

KELP FORESTS

Underwater jungles of giant kelp grow along the Pacific Coast from Alaska to Baja, California, and beyond. This kelp is a type of seaweed that grows to more than 148 feet (45 m) long at a rate of 2 feet (0.6 m) a day. It could be the fastest growing species in the world.

STRANGE BUT TRUE

"Mexican jumping beans" are actually the larvae of moths that ate their way inside seed pods of the *Sebastiana pavoniana* tree. Warm the beans in your hand, and they will jump. The larvae are trying to move the beans to a cooler place.

21

CREATURES OF THE CONTINENT

Flying in caves and swinging through TREES

North America's animals come in all shapes and sizes. Bears and arctic wolves prowl through the north of the continent, while monkeys swing through rain forests in the south. In between, lizards crawl through deserts; bats fly through caves; and turtles and other water animals swim in rivers, lakes, and oceans. As people built homes and businesses on the land, animal populations, such as bison and cougars, dwindled. National parks and preserves help save land for animals to live and grow—and for people to track and study them.

ADVENTURE ATTRACTIONS

MONKEY JUNGLE
At Gumbalimba Park in Roatán, Honduras, adventurers may find parrots or monkeys landing on their shoulders!

NATIONAL BISON RANGE
This land in Montana, U.S.A., was set aside to protect the American bison—a relative of the buffalo. The bison is the largest land mammal in North America. About 350 bison live in the range area.

TURTLE BEACH
Tortuguero National Park in Costa Rica protects hawksbill, loggerhead, leatherback, and Pacific green turtles. The turtles crawl out of the Caribbean to dig nests in the sand for their eggs.

1 GIANT HAIRY SCORPION
Mexico

Whether it lives in Mexico or the deserts of the U.S. southwest, this relative of the spider is a survivor! It can live on one meal per year and through a night in a freezer. Its sting can be painful and deadly.

2 RATTLESNAKE
Mexico

The eastern diamondback is North America's largest venomous snake. Adults can be eight feet (2.4 m) long and weigh up to ten pounds (4.5 kg). It lives in the southern U.S.A. and Mexico.

STRANGE BUT TRUE

The strange-looking axolotl can only be found in lakes and canals in the Xochimilco region of Mexico. If it loses a body part, it can grow it again. Scientists study it more than any other salamander.

5 COOL ANIMALS TO SEE HERE

5 ARCTIC WOLF
Canada

These wolves live in packs of seven to ten members on the northern edge of North America, including Canada and Alaska. They can stand subzero temperatures and up to five months of darkness each year.

MAP KEY

- Kodiak bear
- Star-nosed mole
- California condor
- Texas horned lizard
- Horseshoe crab

4 ALLIGATOR SNAPPING TURTLE
United States

Living in rivers, canals, and lakes of the southeastern U.S.A., this turtle is sometimes called the "dinosaur of the turtle world." It is the largest freshwater turtle on the continent.

3 HOWLER MONKEY
Guatemala

Common in coastal forests of southern Central America, the mantled howler is one of the largest monkeys of the region. Its howls can be heard over many miles. It is active by day and feeds mostly on leaves.

DIGITAL TRAVELER!

The incredibly slow three-toed sloth sleeps 16 to 18 hours a day in the treetops of Costa Rica's jungles. Go online to find facts about and photographs of three-toed sloths.

Map labels: ASIA, Bering Sea, Arctic Ocean, Beaufort Sea, Alaska (U.S.), Greenland (Denmark), ARCTIC CIRCLE, ROCKY MOUNTAINS, CANADA, Hudson Bay, Labrador Sea, GREAT PLAINS, Appalachian Mts., UNITED STATES, Atlantic Ocean, Pacific Ocean, Gulf of Mexico, BAHAMAS, TROPIC OF CANCER, West Indies, CUBA, DOMINICAN REPUBLIC, HAITI, JAMAICA, MEXICO, BELIZE, GUATEMALA, HONDURAS, EL SALVADOR, NICARAGUA, Caribbean Sea, COSTA RICA, PANAMA, SOUTH AMERICA

500 MILES / 500 KILOMETERS

23

5 COOL PLACES TO SEE HERE

Yellowstone is a plateau region surrounded by beautiful rocky mountains. It has been shaped by volcanic activity. It is rugged, wild, and great for adventurers.

NORTH AMERICA

Yellowstone National Park   United States

3 ANCIENT TREES
Specimen Ridge

See the largest concentration of petrified trees in the world. Some of the fossilized tree trunks still stand. Others are in underground forests that were buried by volcanic ash. You may also see bighorn sheep wandering on the ridge.

2 STEAMY SPRINGS
Mammoth Hot Springs

Take a walk on the boardwalks and feel the flowing hot water beneath you. This incredible natural plumbing system keeps more than 50 hot springs active. Rain and snow that have seeped into the earth are heated by underground volcanic activity.

1 THUNDERING HERDS
Lamar Valley

Get your camera ready, because you're likely to see herds of bison roaming by the roads and hiking trails. Don't be surprised if you also see grizzly bears, coyotes, antelope, and ospreys. Make sure to keep your distance!

5 GIANT GEYSER
Old Faithful

Check your watch and be sure you are near Old Faithful when it erupts. The thermal geyser erupts every 92 minutes—as it has done for the past 100 years. Watch from a bench at ground level or hike up to Observation Point. Boiling water shoots up 11 feet (3.4 m) in about 18 seconds.

Gallatin Range

MONTANA
WYOMING

Mammoth Hot Springs

Tower Fall   Specimen Ridge

Grand Canyon of the Yellowstone

MONTANA
WYOMING

Norris Geyser Basin

Central Plateau

Lower Geyser Basin

Midway Geyser Basin

Old Faithful

Shoshone Lake

IDAHO
WYOMING

Madison Plateau

Lewis Lake

Red Mountains

Pitchstone Plateau

N

Bechler Meadows

Scale varies in this perspective.

ON LOCATION

YELLOWSTONE NATIONAL PARK

4 PLUNGING CANYON
Grand Canyon of the Yellowstone

Take a hike beside the perilous plunge of this canyon. Over the last 14,000 years, the Yellowstone River has been carving a canyon that is 8,000 to 12,000 feet (2,438 to 3,658 m) deep. Iron compounds in the water change the rock colors from pink and lavender to yellow and orange.

Absaroka Range

Lamar Valley
Mirror Plateau

Yellowstone Lake

Absaroka Range

Heart Lake

Two Ocean Plateau

Atop an ACTIVE VOLCANO

One of the world's largest volcanoes sits beneath Yellowstone National Park. It last erupted 640,000 years ago, and it will erupt again. The thermal activity of this volcano gets hotter every year and causes the powerful geysers and hot springs that we see today. The U.S. Congress created Yellowstone as the country's first national park in 1872. Most of it is located in Wyoming, with parts in Idaho and Montana.

True or False

Coyotes live in Yellowstone National Park. Which of these statements about coyotes are true, and which are false? See page 149 for the answers.

A Coyotes eat mice, frogs, lizards, fish, snakes, berries, beavers, and birds.

B Coyotes weigh between 25 and 35 pounds (11.3 and 15.9 kg).

C Howling is one way that coyotes communicate their territorial boundaries or locate pack members.

D Coyotes live quite comfortably in big cities though people rarely see them.

E A coyote's paw print is smaller than the locator map shown top left.

DIGITAL TRAVELER!
Go to Yellowstone's website, www.nps.gov/yell/index.htm. Click on one of the park's photo galleries or webcams and become a virtual tourist.

BOLD ADVENTURES

Mountains, sky, and WATER

Fearless adventurers can find more than enough challenges in North America's most beautiful places. In the bone-chilling north, skiers, ice climbers, and dogsled racers find the thrills they need. The warm oceans in the south offer adventures for cliff divers, scuba divers, and surfers. Extreme thrill seekers on this continent may parachute into a cave, walk up a mountain on stilts, or plunge over waterfalls in a boat.

ADVENTURE ATTRACTIONS

DOGSLED COUNTRY
When winter hits Ely, Minnesota, U.S.A., adventurers race through the snow on sleds pulled by teams of strong dogs.

SOAR INTO CAVES
The bravest BASE jumpers head to the deep, dark Cave of Swallows in Mexico. From the cave opening, they leap toward the unseeable bottom 1,214 feet (370 m) below.

SURF INTO "JAWS"
Monster waves at a place called Jaws near Maui, Hawaii, can challenge even the best surfers. Waves can be 40 to 70 feet (12 to 21 m) high and move at speeds of about 30 miles per hour (48 kph). Instead of paddling out to catch the waves, surfers and their boards are towed out by boats.

MAP KEY

Adventure attraction

500 MILES

500 KILOMETERS

Greenland
[Denmark]

Northwest Passage

ARCTIC CIRCLE

Labrador
Sea

Arctic Ocean

Beaufort Sea

Hudson
Bay

Hudson Bay
Lowlands

C A N A D A

GRE

R O C K Y

Mackenzie River

Alaska
(U.S.)

ASIA

Bering
Sea

5 COOL THINGS TO DO HERE

1 ICE CLIMBING
Canada

Daring ice climbers in the Canadian Rockies head up frozen waterfalls. They poke ice axes into the ice and pull themselves upward. Sharp crampons on their boots help them inch their way to the top without falling.

Kelp Forests

Bay of Fundy

Ely

National Bison Range

Monument Valley

Bat Cave

Hurricane Coast

Andros Island

Gulf of Mexico

Cave of Swallows

Gumbalimba Park

Cusuco N.P.

Bosawás Biosphere Res.

Tortuguero N.P.

Lesser Antilles

TRINIDAD & TOBAGO

SOUTH AMERICA

West Indies

BAHAMAS   TROPIC OF CANCER

CUBA

HAITI

DOMINICAN REPUBLIC

JAMAICA

Caribbean Sea

BELIZE

GUATEMALA

EL SALVADOR

HONDURAS

NICARAGUA

COSTA RICA

PANAMA

MEXICO

Pacific Ocean

Atlantic Ocean

to Maui, Hawaii

DIGITAL TRAVELER!

Search online for a photo or video of cliff divers in Mexico or Hawaii. After you watch it, read to find the location and point it out on a globe.

2 CLIMB A ROCK WALL
United States

El Capitan in California, U.S.A., is twice as high as the Empire State Building. Climbers crawl up this steep granite tower. BASE jumpers parachute down from the top.

3 BUST A BRONCO
United States

At rodeos, cowboys try to stay on bucking bulls for eight seconds—but many fall off because it's harder than it sounds! Rodeos are popular throughout Texas and Arizona. Novices can try their hand at horseback riding, lassoing, and other cowboy skills.

4 KAYAK OVER WATERFALLS
Mexico

Only extreme risk takers try stunts like this one. They paddle kayaks to the top of a waterfall, such as La Tomata in Veracruz, and ride the falls down. One adventurer wore a camera on his helmet so others could watch up close.

5 GO FLYBOARDING
St. Kitts

Water pumped under high pressure from a craft through a hose linked to a special board can lift a person out of the water to do aerobatics. This new sport of flyboarding is full of spills and splashes.

RECORD BREAKER

U.S. athlete Ashrita Furman set a record for the greatest vertical height walked on stilts when he climbed 2,848 feet (868 m) up Mount Equinox in Manchester, Vermont, in 2008.

SOUTH AMERICA

From the high Andes to the base of the WORLD

Adventures are huge in South America. They match the features of the continent. Hikers head to the steamy Amazon rain forest in the north, with its dense mass of trees and undergrowth. Snaking through the forest is the mighty Amazon—home to the deadly anaconda and ferocious caiman. In the west, mountain climbers flock to the Andes. At the continent's southern tip, daring sailors head out to tackle high waves in the treacherous sea.

AUNT BERTHA'S ADVENTURE TRAVEL TIPS

Most of South America is south of the Equator, where the seasons are reversed in time to those north of this artificial line. Plan to ski in July and play on the beach in January.

The higher you go in the Andes, the thinner the air. To prevent altitude sickness, spend a few days at one level before moving higher. Drink lots of water, too.

South America has some of the strangest, largest, and deadliest animals on Earth. Look, but don't touch!

Backpackers at the Inca ruins of Machu Picchu, Peru. Many adventurous trails lead to these ruins.

ADVENTURE HOT SPOTS

LANDFORMS
Trek to some of the world's largest ice caps in Los Glaciares National Park in Argentina.

CLIMATES
Mount Cayambe near Quito, Ecuador, lies almost directly on the Equator. At night the temperature drops to 14°F (-10°C).

GALÁPAGOS ISLANDS
Sail to these remote islands and see the world's largest tortoises and other one-of-a-kind animals.

HABITATS
Take a jungle hike through Bolivia's Madidi National Park. It has possibly the world's richest variety of wildlife.

PLANTS
Deadly curare vines grow in Ecuador's Oriente rain forest. Tribal hunters crush the vines to make paralyzing poison darts.

ANIMALS
When you paddle in Brazil's swampy Pantanal, watch out for the yacare caiman, a relative of the crocodile.

MANÚ NATIONAL PARK
Listen for rustling leaves in this park in Peru. Numerous species of birds and monkeys are in the trees above you.

ADVENTURES
Sail around Cape Horn, where the Atlantic meets the Pacific. Hold on to your hat in the wildest winds ever.

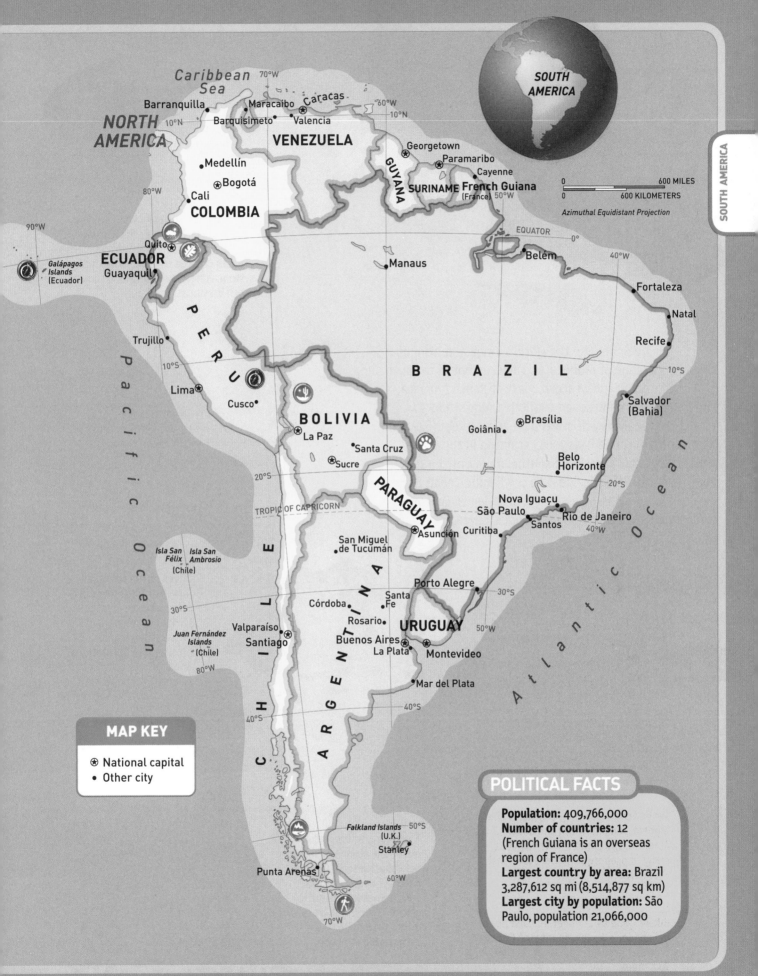

Caribbean Sea

70°W

60°W

Barranquilla

Maracaibo

Caracas

NORTH
AMERICA

10°N

Barquisimeto

Valencia

10°N

VENEZUELA

SOUTH
AMERICA

Medellín

Bogotá

Georgetown

Paramaribo

Cayenne

80°W

Cali

GUYANA

SURINAME French Guiana
(France) 50°W

COLOMBIA

0   600 MILES

90°W

0   600 KILOMETERS

EQUATOR

Quito

0°

Azimuthal Equidistant Projection

ECUADOR

Belém

40°W

Galápagos
Islands
(Ecuador)

Guayaquil

Manaus

P
E
R
U

Fortaleza

Natal

Trujillo

Recife

10°S

B R A Z I L

10°S

Lima

Cusco

Salvador
(Bahia)

BOLIVIA

La Paz

Santa Cruz

Brasília

Goiânia

Sucre

20°S

Belo
Horizonte

20°S

PARAGUAY

Nova Iguaçu

TROPIC OF CAPRICORN

São Paulo

Rio de Janeiro

Asunción

Curitiba

Santos

40°W

Isla San
Félix

Isla San
Ambrosio
(Chile)

San Miguel
de Tucumán

C
H
I
L
E

A
R
G
E
N
T
I
N
A

Porto Alegre

30°S

30°S

Córdoba

Santa
Fe

Juan Fernández
Islands
(Chile)

Valparaíso

Rosario

URUGUAY

80°W

Santiago

Buenos Aires

La Plata

Montevideo

50°W

Mar del Plata

40°S

40°S

MAP KEY

⊛ National capital

• Other city

Falkland Islands
(U.K.)

50°S

Stanley

Punta Arenas

60°W

POLITICAL FACTS

Population: 409,766,000
Number of countries: 12
(French Guiana is an overseas
region of France)
Largest country by area: Brazil
3,287,612 sq mi (8,514,877 sq km)
Largest city by population: São
Paulo, population 21,066,000

70°W

Pacific Ocean

Atlantic Ocean

ANDES AND AMAZON
High peaks and LAKES

The Andes are the world's longest continental range of mountains. They run north to south along the western coast of South America, spanning seven countries. More than 50 peaks reach more than 20,000 feet (6,096 m) high. A region called Patagonia, starting in the south Andes, stretches across the southern part of the continent from the Atlantic Coast to the Pacific Coast. It includes mountains, deserts, and grasslands. This big continent also has amazing volcanoes, caves, waterfalls, and islands.

ADVENTURE ATTRACTIONS

ENORMOUS RIVER
Extreme adventurers head to the Amazon to discover hidden villages and catch monster river creatures, such as a 400-pound (181-kg) fish, the arapaima.

TOP OF THE CONTINENT
Cerro Aconcagua in Argentina is the highest peak in North and South America. The climb seems easy, but many unprepared climbers have lost their lives.

AVENUE OF VOLCANOES
Bikers cycle by 11 major volcano peaks in Ecuador's Andes Mountains. Cotopaxi is one of the world's highest active volcanoes.

5 MARBLE CAVE
Chile
The changing blue colors and swirling shapes of Marble Cave will take your breath away. Crashing waves and melting glaciers created this one-of-a-kind cave system along a lake shore. You can only reach it by boat.

DID YOU KNOW?

The Catahuasi Canyon of Peru is the deepest canyon in the Americas. At 11,597 feet (3,535 m), it is almost twice as deep as the Grand Canyon in North America.

90°W

Galápagos Islands

4 VALLEY OF THE MOON
Argentina
Adventurers who study dinosaur fossils head to Ischigualasto Provincial Park. It is nicknamed Valley of the Moon because of its bizarre rock formations. Some of these are called the Mushroom, the Worm, the Sphinx, and the Submarine.

3 PEAKS AND ICEBERGS
Chile

Towering granite peaks pierce the skyline of Torres Del Paine National Park. Hikers trek or cycle past gushing waterfalls and icy glacial lakes. Kayakers on Grey Lake paddle by icebergs as big as houses.

PHYSICAL FACTS

Size: 6,880,000 sq mi (17,819,118 sq km)
Highest point: Cerro Aconcagua, Argentina 22,831 ft (6,959 m)
Lowest point: Laguna del Carbón, Argentina -344 ft (-105 m)
Longest river: Amazon 4,000 mi (6,437 km)
Largest lake: Lake Titicaca, Bolivia-Peru 3,200 sq mi (8,288 sq km)

5 COOL PLACES TO SEE HERE

1 WATER TOWER
Venezuela

Angel Falls in Venezuela is the highest uninterrupted waterfall in the world—20 times higher than Niagara Falls. Water plunges over the edge of Auyantepui Mountain more than 2,600 feet (792 m).

MAP KEY

▲ Highest point
▼ Lowest point
+ Other mountain peak

2 HIGHEST LAKE
Bolivia

On the border of Peru and Bolivia, Lake Titicaca is the world's highest navigable lake. People live on floating island villages built out of strong reeds. After about 25 years, lake water starts to seep through the reeds. The people build a new island and let the first one sink to the bottom of the lake.

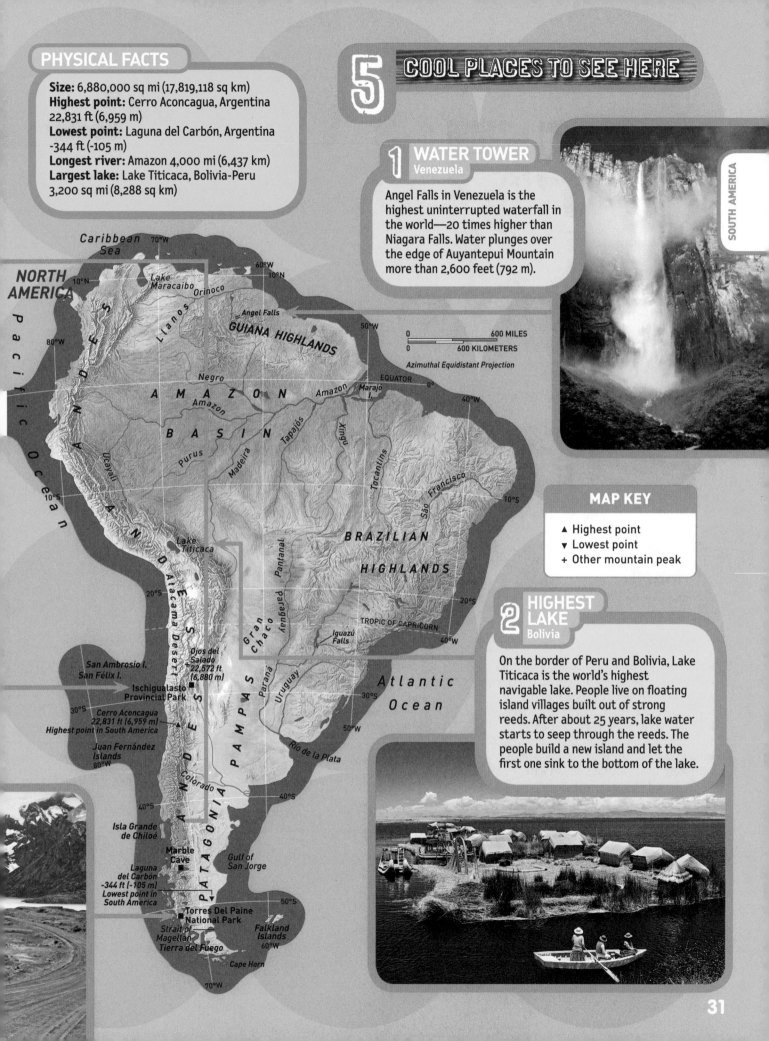

Map labels

Caribbean Sea
NORTH AMERICA
Pacific Ocean
Lake Maracaibo
Orinoco
Llanos
Angel Falls
GUIANA HIGHLANDS
Negro
AMAZON BASIN
Amazon
Amazon
Marajó
EQUATOR
Purus
Madeira
Tapajós
Xingu
Tocantins
São Francisco
Ucayali
ANDES
Lake Titicaca
Atacama Desert
BRAZILIAN HIGHLANDS
Pantanal
Paraguay
Gran Chaco
Iguazú Falls
TROPIC OF CAPRICORN
San Ambrosio I.
San Félix I.
Ischigualasto Provincial Park
Ojos del Salado 22,572 ft (6,880 m)
Cerro Aconcagua 22,831 ft (6,959 m) Highest point in South America
Juan Fernández Islands
Paraná
Uruguay
PAMPAS
Colorado
Río de la Plata
Atlantic Ocean
Isla Grande de Chiloé
Marble Cave
Laguna del Carbón -344 ft (-105 m) Lowest point in South America
PATAGONIA
Gulf of San Jorge
Torres Del Paine National Park
Strait of Magellan
Tierra del Fuego
Falkland Islands
Cape Horn

600 MILES
600 KILOMETERS
Azimuthal Equidistant Projection

5 EXTREME CLIMATES HERE

1 LIGHTNING STORMS
Venezuela

Lightning storms pop through the sky continuously for up to 10 hours almost every night over Lake Maracaibo. Sailors have used the lightning for centuries to guide them on their voyages.

2 ULTIMATE RAINFALL
Colombia

Central Colombia may be the wettest place on Earth. Towns in that region get more than 40 feet (12 m) of rain each year. It rains almost every day!

3 MELTING ICE FIELDS
Chile

Patagonian ice fields in Chile and Argentina stretch over the southernmost part of the Andes. As they melt, they flow into the ocean. In recent years, they have melted so fast that sea levels have risen at an alarming rate. Since 2000, they have melted enough to cover the entire United States with more than 1 inch (2.5 cm) of water.

4 ENDLESS RAINBOWS
Argentina

Weather watchers in Argentina and Chile get to see rainbow shows all along a 1,000-mile (1,609-km) stretch of coastline. The rainbows are caused by frequent summer storms and the sun's low angle.

MAP KEY

Climatic Zones: Based on Köppen System

Tropical
- Tropical wet
- Tropical dry

Dry
- Semiarid
- Arid

Mild
- Marine west coast
- Mediterranean
- Humid subtropical

High Elevations
- Highlands
- Uplands

Caribbean Sea

NORTH AMERICA

VENEZUELA
GUYANA
French Guiana (France)
COLOMBIA
SURINAME
ECUADOR

A M A Z O N
B A S I N
B R A Z I L

PERU
BOLIVIA
Atacama Desert
TROPIC OF CAPRICORN
PARAGUAY
Pacific Ocean
URUGUAY
ARGENTINA
CHILE
PATAGONIA
Atlantic Ocean

70°W · 60°W · 10°N · 50°W · 80°W · 90°W · 0° · 10°S · 20°S · 30°S · 40°S · 50°S · 60°W

EXCITING EXTREMES

From wettest rain forest to driest DESERT

No matter where they go in South America, adventurers can find exciting weather. The Amazon rain forests are steamy and hot. The Andes peaks can be icy cold. There are bone-dry deserts in northern Chile. In southwestern Chile, Pacific winds blow across the land, bringing heavy rains before they reach the Andes. In the south, the land east of the Andes is very dry.

EQUATOR 0°
40°W
20°S

0 600 MILES
0 600 KILOMETERS

DIGITAL TRAVELER!
The city of Ushuaia in Tierra del Fuego is the world's closest city to the South Pole, but it is still 2,485 miles (3,999 km) away from it. Take a guess at today's weather in Ushuaia. Then go online to check your guess.

ADVENTURE ATTRACTIONS

DEADLY TIDAL WAVES
In Brazil, they call gigantic Amazon River waves *pororoca*, meaning "big roar." A powerful wall of water swoops in and destroys the trees, homes, and animals in its path.

EPIC SNOWFALL
Skiers and snowboarders head for the Andes to catch the extreme snowfalls that average a total of 33 feet (10 m) a year. The average snow depth in July is 32 inches (81.3 cm).

BONE-DRY DESERT
The Atacama Desert in Chile is one of the driest places on Earth. It receives less than four inches (10 cm) of rain every 1,000 years.

STRANGE BUT TRUE

Since there is very little rain in the Atacama Desert, local villagers make special nets to capture water from the fog in the air. As the fog condenses, it drips into containers, creating drinking water.

5 FIERCE SEAS
Drake Passage

Rough seas toss boats and ships around the Drake Passage. This 500-mile (805-km) passage separates the southern tip of South America from the islands off Antarctica.

This group of islands lies 575 miles (925 km) west of the coast of Ecuador, to which it belongs. The Galápagos are a national park, and visiting is restricted to protect the environment.

Galápagos Islands Ecuador

SOUTH AMERICA

2 LAND IGUANAS
North Seymour

Nearly 2,500 land iguanas live on this island with no human population. Use your camera to snap these lizards along with blue-footed boobies and frigate birds.

1 RED BEACHES
Rábida

Rábida is a small, rocky island with no human population. The beaches are red because of iron-rich lava from its volcanoes. Sea lions and flamingos hang out in the lagoons.

N

Pacific Ocean

Isla Marchena

Isla Pinta

Isla San Salvador

Isla Santa Cruz

Canal Isabela

Isla Fernandina

Isla Isabela

Bahía Isabel

Scale varies in this perspective.

5 VOLCANO ISLAND
Isabela

Paddle a kayak around the largest island in the Galápagos. It is made of six large volcanoes. Two of them lie directly on the Equator. Sixteen different kinds of whales swim off Isabela's shores.

GALÁPAGOS ISLANDS

Islands for CREATURES

SOUTH AMERICA

3 GIANT TORTOISES
Santa Cruz

This is one of the best places to stand face-to-face with a giant tortoise. They are the longest-living vertebrates on Earth—their average age is 100 years! They are also the world's largest tortoises. Some weigh 550 pounds (249 kg).

Isla San Cristóbal

Isla Española

Isla Santa María (Isla Floreana)

The Galápagos Islands are the place where the most extraordinary animals on the planet roam freely in their own private world. Only 4 of the 19 islands have humans living on them. In 1835, the scientist Charles Darwin visited the islands to study the animals. His reports on finches, tortoises, and small mammals became famous. The islands are a great place to hike, kayak, snorkel, and have encounters with giant tortoises, sea lions, and birds of all kinds.

4 DEVIL'S CROWN
Floreana

Snorkel out till you see some rocky spikes sticking out of the water. Below is Devil's Crown, an underwater volcano crater. It attracts all kinds of water creatures, such as sea lions, tiger-snake eels, eagle rays, and hammerhead sharks. Strong swimming skills are needed to handle the rough currents.

DIGITAL TRAVELER!
The Galápagos penguin is the only penguin species that lives near the Equator. Search the Internet for videos of Galápagos penguins. Then find out how tall these penguins can grow.

SWAMPS AND DESERTS

Homes for monkeys, snakes, and OWLS

S ome of the world's most incredible habitats are in South America. The Amazon rain forest is nearly as big as the whole continent of Australia. More than one-third of all species in the world live there. Brave adventurers love it! Some take their flashlights there at night to peer into tree trunks for insects, owls, and other creatures. South America has many other habitats, too. Deserts, mountains, and islands provide homes to lots of plants and animals. There are also huge ice caps.

🔦 DID YOU KNOW?

Scientists were surprised to learn that soil in the Atacama Desert is similar to soil on Mars. NASA scientists go to the desert to study the possibility of plant and animal habitats on Mars.

ADVENTURE ATTRACTIONS

→ **PATAGONIA ICE CAPS**
Giant ice fields, frozen wastes, and lakes of glacial meltwater cover this southwestern landscape shared by Argentina and Chile. Birdlife here includes condors and eagles. Red and gray foxes and cougars prey on small mammals and livestock. There is very little plant life here.

→ **DESERT IN A RAIN FOREST**
In the Central Suriname Nature Reserve, dark granite peaks loom over the rain forest. Most plants can't survive on these sunbaked rocks. However, strong-willed orchids have adapted to growing in the ground instead of on trees.

→ **PREHISTORIC MOUNTAINTOP**
Scientists risk their lives to inspect the wildlife on Mount Roraima, at about 8,000 feet (2,438 m) high in Guyana. They climb sheer cliffs and sleep in tents that dangle from the mountain.

5 COOL THINGS TO SEE HERE

1 RAIN FOREST CANOPY
French Guiana

High above the floor of rain forests, tree branches spread out and overlap to form a living layer, the canopy. Here live squirrel, howler, and white-faced saki monkeys. They spend their day feeding, resting, and sleeping in the canopy.

NORTH AMERICA

Caribbean Sea

VENEZUELA
COLOMBIA
GUYANA
SURINAME
French Guiana (France)
GUIANA HIGHLANDS
ECUADOR
EQUATOR
A N D E S
A M A Z O N   B A S I N

0   500 MILES
0   500 KILOMETERS

2 TROPICAL SWAMP
Brazil

The Pantanal is called the "biggest swamp in the world." It extends into parts of Paraguay and Bolivia. On a boat ride, be on the lookout for animals that are the biggest of their kind: giant river otters, capybaras, jaguars, and anacondas.

MAP KEY

- Grasslands
- Tropical broadleaf forests
- Temperate broadleaf forests
- Mediterranean forests and shrublands
- Rock and ice
- Tundra
- Mangroves
- Deserts and dry shrublands

BRAZILIAN HIGHLANDS

BRAZIL

Pantanal

PARAGUAY

URUGUAY

ARGENTINA

PAMPAS

PATAGONIA

BOLIVIA

Salar de Uyuni

PERU

ANDES

CHILE

Pacific Ocean

TROPIC OF CAPRICORN

Atlantic Ocean

3 PARCHED PLAINS
Argentina

Adventurers and gauchos ride horseback across the dry, flat plains called the Pampas. The camel-like animal, the guanaco, is also well suited for the Pampas. Its long neck aids it to see danger approaching. It can run quickly across the rocky plains. Burrowing owls swoop in to eat insects, rodents, and birds. Then these owls sleep underground.

5 SKY-HIGH FORESTS
Peru

Gnarled trees with thick layers of bark grow high in the Andes. They are called *Polylepis*, which means "multilayered." The Andean people make medicines from the plants in these forests. Animals use the trees for shelter, nesting sites, and food.

4 SALT FLATS
Bolivia

Four-wheel-drive vehicles race across the Salar de Uyuni, the world's largest dried salt lake. Pink South American flamingos live here. Other birds include the Andean goose and horned coot. Giant cacti are among the few plants that grow here.

DIGITAL TRAVELER!
Magellanic penguins live in colonies on Isla Martillo, Argentina. They hunt for seafood, including fish, squid, and krill. They also build nests and tend their chicks. Search the Internet to find out how these birds build their unique nests.

5 COOL PLANTS TO SEE HERE

1 POISONOUS BEAUTY
Venezuela

Don't touch the lovely angel's trumpet plant! Many people admire these plants of the Andes because of their pretty flowers and sweet fragrance. But the entire plant is poisonous. Victims become sick, dizzy, confused, and worse.

DIGITAL TRAVELER!

The bladderwort plant of South America is a small, aquatic killer. A tadpole that brushes against one of its bladderlike traps is easily captured. Search the Internet to find out how the victim is killed.

2 GIANT WATER LILY
Brazil

These water lilies are so large that a colony of them can cover an entire lake. They can grow to seven feet (2 m) across and are strong enough to support a human.

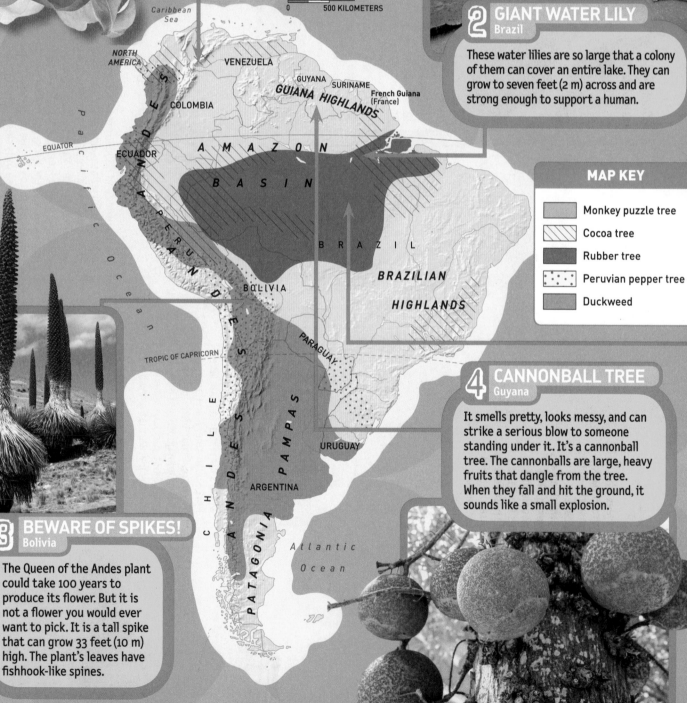

MAP KEY

- Monkey puzzle tree
- Cocoa tree
- Rubber tree
- Peruvian pepper tree
- Duckweed

0 — 500 MILES
0 — 500 KILOMETERS

Caribbean Sea

NORTH AMERICA

VENEZUELA

GUYANA   SURINAME   French Guiana (France)

GUIANA HIGHLANDS

COLOMBIA

Pacific Ocean

EQUATOR

ECUADOR

A M A Z O N   B A S I N

PERU

B R A Z I L

BRAZILIAN HIGHLANDS

BOLIVIA

PARAGUAY

TROPIC OF CAPRICORN

C H I L E

A N D E S

PAMPAS

URUGUAY

ARGENTINA

PATAGONIA

Atlantic Ocean

4 CANNONBALL TREE
Guyana

It smells pretty, looks messy, and can strike a serious blow to someone standing under it. It's a cannonball tree. The cannonballs are large, heavy fruits that dangle from the tree. When they fall and hit the ground, it sounds like a small explosion.

3 BEWARE OF SPIKES!
Bolivia

The Queen of the Andes plant could take 100 years to produce its flower. But it is not a flower you would ever want to pick. It is a tall spike that can grow 33 feet (10 m) high. The plant's leaves have fishhook-like spines.

 **PLANTS**

COCOA AND CANNONBALLS

Delicate and deadly PLANTS

South America's plants face many challenges. In the rain forest, many plants must survive constant wetness and annual flooding. Many must grow in the shade of the treetop canopy. Other plants survive on mountain ledges of the Andes or in the parched Atacama Desert. The continent's unusual places are homes to strange plants—from the duckweed that is smothering Lake Maracaibo to the bladderwort that traps and smothers its food.

DID YOU KNOW?

Since the 1600s, doctors have used quinine to treat a jungle disease called malaria. Quinine comes from the bark of cinchona trees in Ecuador and Peru.

5 RUBBER TREES
Brazil

Rubber trees grow in the rain forests. If the bark of a mature tree is cut, latex—a thick, white sap—leaks out. This can be collected and processed to make bouncy balls, tires, erasers, windshield wipers, balloons, and other flexible products.

ADVENTURE ATTRACTIONS

COASTAL RAIN FOREST
Paddle out to Cabo Orange National Park in Brazil to see where the Amazon rain forest meets the Atlantic Ocean. You'll see mangroves and marine forests.

WOOLLY CACTUS FIELDS
In Argentina's Los Cardones National Park, the cacti are quite a sight! Covered with wispy spines, they look almost huggable. But the spines are sharp! Even stranger, their flowers grow sideways.

WILDFLOWER DESERT
Not even bacteria can grow in most of Chile's Atacama Desert. However, near the coast, the ocean sends in enough fog for colorful wildflowers to grow.

AMAZING CREATURES

Giants of the animal KINGDOM

Millions of years ago, South America was separated from the rest of the continents. A unique collection of animals evolved there. Then volcanic lava connected it to Central America. Adventurers will find animals in South America that live nowhere else on Earth. More than 3,000 kinds of birds live on the continent. The Amazon rain forest and Amazon River are home to many of the largest, fastest, and most dangerous animals on the planet. Animals such as the jaguar became swimmers to adapt to the rains and floods of the region.

ADVENTURE ATTRACTIONS

JUNGLE ENCOUNTERS
In the Mamirauá Reserve in Brazil's Amazon rain forest, you can see crocodiles and dolphins in the river and monkeys and sloths in the trees.

FLAMINGO-FILLED LAKE
Flocks of pink Chilean flamingos live by Laguna Seca, a shallow lake in the Patagonia National Park.

CROCODILE CROWD
A group of crocodiles is called a "bask," and adventurers are sure to find a bask of caiman in Amacayacu National Natural Park in Colombia.

5 WORLD'S LARGEST SNAKE
Ecuador

The green anaconda is the world's heaviest snake and one of the longest. It can weigh 154 pounds (70 kg) and grow up to 22 feet (6.7 m) long. The snake overpowers its prey, including fish, birds, and small mammals, and squeezes it to death. It then swallows its prey whole.

4 FIRE ANTS
Brazil

Eighty thousand fire ants may live in an ant colony underground. If one of their mounds is disturbed, worker ants race to the surface and run up the legs and arms of the intruder. The ants sting, injecting a venom that causes pain, itching, and sometimes severe allergic reactions.

RECORD BREAKER

Goliath bird-eater tarantulas, the world's biggest spiders, lurk in the Amazon rain forest. Some have a leg span of 11 inches (28 cm). Their menu consists of frogs, rodents, bats, and birds.

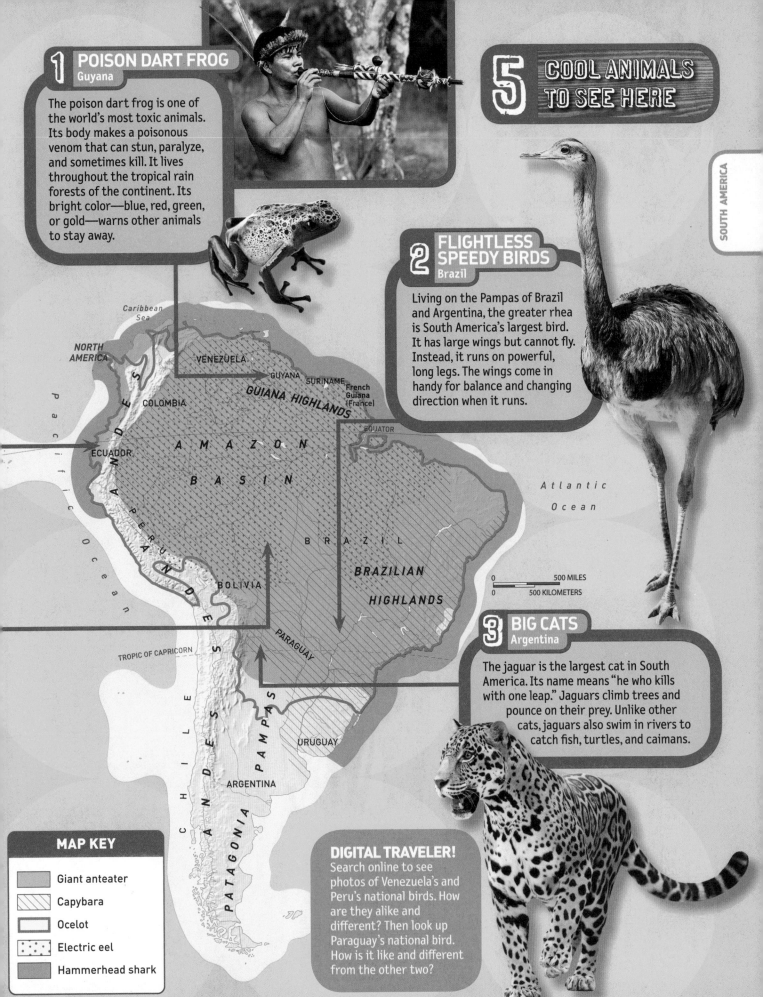

1 POISON DART FROG
Guyana

The poison dart frog is one of the world's most toxic animals. Its body makes a poisonous venom that can stun, paralyze, and sometimes kill. It lives throughout the tropical rain forests of the continent. Its bright color—blue, red, green, or gold—warns other animals to stay away.

5 COOL ANIMALS TO SEE HERE

2 FLIGHTLESS SPEEDY BIRDS
Brazil

Living on the Pampas of Brazil and Argentina, the greater rhea is South America's largest bird. It has large wings but cannot fly. Instead, it runs on powerful, long legs. The wings come in handy for balance and changing direction when it runs.

3 BIG CATS
Argentina

The jaguar is the largest cat in South America. Its name means "he who kills with one leap." Jaguars climb trees and pounce on their prey. Unlike other cats, jaguars also swim in rivers to catch fish, turtles, and caimans.

DIGITAL TRAVELER!
Search online to see photos of Venezuela's and Peru's national birds. How are they alike and different? Then look up Paraguay's national bird. How is it like and different from the other two?

MAP KEY

	Giant anteater
	Capybara
	Ocelot
	Electric eel
	Hammerhead shark

Caribbean Sea

NORTH AMERICA

VENEZUELA

GUYANA SURINAME French Guiana (France)

GUIANA HIGHLANDS

COLOMBIA

EQUATOR

ECUADOR

A M A Z O N B A S I N

P a c i f i c   O c e a n

P E R U

A N D E S

BOLIVIA

B R A Z I L

BRAZILIAN HIGHLANDS

Atlantic Ocean

PARAGUAY

TROPIC OF CAPRICORN

C H I L E

A N D E S

PAMPAS

URUGUAY

ARGENTINA

P A T A G O N I A

0   500 MILES
0   500 KILOMETERS

ON LOCATION

MANÚ NATIONAL PARK

Home to otters, caimans, macaws, and ORCHIDS

Manú National Park is in southern Peru. Adventurers will find a mind-boggling variety of plants and animals. Researchers have counted 800 bird species and 200 species of mammals, including 13 kinds of monkeys and 100 kinds of bats. The huge park covers land from the high Andes cloud forest to the tropical Amazon rain forest. Visitors travel by rafts and canoes on fast-flowing rivers and calm lakes.

2 RIVER SITES
Manú River Reserve

Fly by light aircraft close to the park and then climb onto a wooden raft and paddle on the Manú River. You'll be treated to the sight of river birds such as egrets, herons, and Orinoco geese. At sunset, you'll see parrots heading to their roosts for the night.

5 COOL PLACES TO SEE HERE

To adventurers, this wildlife reserve is a treasure trove. Many of the animals and plants are not well known, and there are trails and riverways known only to the local native Indian people.

SOUTH AMERICA

Peru

Manú National Park

1 OTTER HABITAT
Camungo Oxbow Lake

When paddling on this lake, you are likely to see giant otters. They are also called "river wolves." They have long bodies and strong tails that make them excellent swimmers. They have no fear of hunting fierce piranhas, anacondas, and alligators.

to Camungo Oxbow Lake

Río Pinquina

N

Río Manu (Manú River)

Río Providencia

Ríos Sotilija

A n d e

42

True or False

The Andean cock-of-the-rock is the national bird of Peru and a resident of Manú National Park. Which of these statements about this bird are true, and which are false? See page 149 for the answers.

A The Andean cock-of-the-rock lives only in the cloud forests of the Andes.

B Adult male and females of the species look alike.

C Male birds perform a bowing-and-jumping dance as they fight to win the attention of a female bird.

D From head to tail, an adult is about 20 inches (51.8 cm) long.

E Its diet consists mainly of fruit, but it will also eat lizards, frogs, and insects, including army ants.

DIGITAL TRAVELER!

Manú National Park has more kinds of amphibians than any other place in the world! Do an Internet search to see if you can figure out how many species live here. Then look for photos and names of Manú frogs.

Scale varies in this perspective.

3 NIGHTTIME TRAILS
Greenlands Robles Ecological Reserve

Brave adventurers, grab your flashlights and take a night walk through the jungle! Shine a light inside a tree trunk and see what spiders, insects, or other nocturnal creatures scurry out. You may also see a tapir, South America's largest land mammal.

4 CLOUD FOREST VIEWING
Acjanaco Pass

This road is the entrance to the park. It is located 11,483 feet (3,500 m) high and is a great place to look out over the cloud forest. Moisture in this part of the park forms low-hanging clouds. This area is known for beautiful orchids and a huge variety of frogs.

M o u n t a i n s

s

5 SHRIEKING-BIRD HANGOUT
Macaw Clay Lick

A clay lick is an area of soil that contains mineral-rich clay common in the rain forest. Parrots and macaws need the minerals to stay healthy. So, hundreds of the birds swoop to Manú Park to actually lick the clay. The colorful birds make so much noise that you may want to cover your ears!

DAREDEVIL ADVENTURES

Speed, power, and DANGER

MAP KEY

📍 Adventure attraction

With some of the world's longest rivers, the highest sand dunes, the deadliest fish, and the most dangerous roads, South America offers some big adventures. People test their courage here in extreme ways. They hang glide from mountaintops, sandboard down dunes, and jump from planes all for the fun of it. In the end, they just want to say, "I did it!"

1 MUDDY VOLCANO
Colombia

Just for the fun of it, adventurers climb a 50-foot (15-m) staircase up El Totumo Volcano. At the top, they step into a gooey pool of mud. They stretch out and soak in the crater.

5 COOL THINGS TO DO HERE

2 BOLD BIKING
Bolivia

They call it "The World's Most Dangerous Road" and "Death Road." One heart-racing bike tour starts with an uphill struggle to pedal to a summit. At the top, bikers take their feet off the pedals and coast downhill, steering around scary hairpin curves.

Caribbean Sea

NORTH AMERICA

VENEZUELA
Mt. Roraima
Kaieteur Fall
Central Suriname Nature Reserve
French Guiana (France)
COLOMBIA
GUYANA
SURINAME
GUIANA HIGHLANDS
Cabo Orange N.P.
Cotopaxi
EQUATOR
ECUADOR
AMAZON
Amacayacu N.N.P.
Mamirauá Reserve
Amazon River
Pororoca
PERU
BASIN
BRAZIL
Cerro Blanco
BRAZ
HIGHL
Atacama Desert
BOLIVIA
PARAGUAY
TROPIC OF CAPRICORN
Los Cardones N.P.
Cerro Aconcagua
PAMPAS
URUGUAY
ARGENTINA
Andes Skiing
Laguna Seca
Patagonia Ice Caps
PATAGONIA
Beagle Channel

Pacific Ocean

ANDES

CHILE

0   500 MILES
0   500 KILOMETERS

ADVENTURE ATTRACTIONS

SANDBOARDERS' DUNE

Cerro Blanco, in Peru's Sechura Desert, is one of the highest sand dunes in the world. It is about 3,860 feet (1,177 m) high. Sandboarders grease their boards, hike to the top, and race down the dune at heart-pounding speeds.

COLD CHALLENGE SWIM

Extreme swimmers plunge into Beagle Channel, where the water is typically below 41°F (5°C). They swim from Chile to Argentina, between the world's southernmost towns of Ushuaia and Puerto Williams. Part two of the challenge: to swim around Cape Horn.

DEATH-DEFYING WATERFALL

Kaieteur Falls in Guyana drops 741 feet (226 m)—about four times the height of Niagara Falls. There are no safety rails to stop the daredevils who perch themselves very close to the plunge.

3 HANG GLIDING
Brazil

Strap on a hang glider's harness and hang on tight! Step off a mountaintop and let the wind carry you on a motorless flight. Hang gliders soar over the city of Rio de Janeiro and get a bird's-eye view of the skyscrapers and beaches.

DIGITAL TRAVELER!
The Dakar Rally runs in South America every year. More than 500 cars, all-terrain vehicles, motorcycles, and trucks speed over mud and rocks to try to win the race. Search online for the rally route. Name the countries it covers.

4 SURFING MONSTER WAVES
Brazil

Every February and March, the Amazon River churns up monster waves called *pororocas*. Extreme surfers ignore snakes, piranhas, and crocodiles to ride these terrifying waves. If surfers are able to stay on their boards, they can ride one wave for hours.

Atlantic Ocean

ILIAN

ANDS

5 GET A BITE
Guyana

One of the world's most deadly fish is the black piranha that swims in the Rewa River of Guyana. For an extreme day of sport, adventurers try to catch these piranhas. The creatures are attracted to bloody meat, splashing water, and noise. Once you catch one, watch out for its teeth. They are sharp enough to cut through metal.

RECORD BREAKER

In 2014, skydivers set a new South American Sequential Formation Record. Seventy-four skydivers jumped from planes. They grabbed hands or feet and formed a human snowflake.

45

POLITICAL FACTS

Population: 743,852,000
Number of independent countries: 46
Largest country entirely in Europe by area:
Ukraine 233,030 sq mi (603,550 sq km)
Largest city by population: Moscow, Russia,
population 12,166,000

EUROPE

Arctic Ocean

Novaya Zemlya

Barents Sea

Murmansk

Arkhangel'sk

R U

Kirov

ARCTIC CIRCLE

Norwegian Sea

ICELAND

Reykjavík

Faroe Islands
(Denmark)

Shetland
Islands

Orkney Islands

N O R W A Y

S W E D E N

F I N L A N D

Helsinki

St. Petersburg

Yaroslavl'

Nizhniy
Novgorod

Tver'

Moscow

Ryazan'

Penza

Oslo

Stockholm

Göteborg

Tallinn
ESTONIA

Baltic Sea

Rīga LATVIA

LITHUANIA

Vitsyebsk

Smolensk

Bryansk

Kursk

SCOTLAND

Glasgow
Edinburgh

N. IRELAND
Belfast

North Sea

DENMARK

Copenhagen

Vilnius

Minsk

Kaliningrad
(Russia)

Kaunas

Gdańsk

B E L A R U S

Homyel'

IRELAND

Dublin

Liverpool Manchester

WALES

Cardiff ENGLAND

London

UNITED
KINGDOM

Birmingham

Kiel

The
Hague Amsterdam

NETH.

Hamburg

Berlin

POLAND

Warsaw

Kiev

Poltava

Kharkiv

Donets'k

Rostov

Brussels

BELGIUM

LUX.

GERMANY

Frankfurt

Bydgoszcz

Łódź

Wrocław

Prague

Kraków

L'viv

U K R A I N E

Vinnytsya

Dnipropetrovs'k

Atlantic Ocean

Paris

Nantes

FRANCE

*Bay of
Biscay*

Bordeaux

Lyon

Toulouse

Zürich
Bern

SWITZ.

LIECH.

CZECH REP.

Munich

Vienna

AUSTRIA

SLOVAKIA

Bratislava

Budapest

HUNGARY

MOLDOVA

Chișinău

ROMANIA

Odesa

Simferopol'

CRIMEA

Sevastopol'

Oporto

Bilbao

Valladolid

PORTUGAL

Madrid

Lisbon

S P A I N

Valencia

Seville Murcia

Málaga

Gibraltar
(U.K.)

ANDORRA

Zaragoza

Marseille

Barcelona

*Balearic Is.
(Spain)*

Milan
Turin Venice
Genoa

MONACO

Nice

*Corsica
(France)*

*Sardinia
(Italy)*

SAN
MARINO

I T A L Y

VATICAN
CITY Rome

Naples

SLOV.

Ljubljana

Zagreb

CROATIA

Sarajevo

BOSNIA &
HERZEGOVINA

MONTENEGRO

Podgorica

KOSOVO

Pristina

Tirana

ALBANIA

MACED.

Skopje

Belgrade Bucharest

SERBIA

BULGARIA

Sofia

Black Sea

Varna

Istanbul

Thessaloníki

G R E E C E

T U R K E Y

A S I A

*Mediterranean
Sea*

Palermo

Sicily

Messina

Catania

Athens

Crete

NORTHERN CYPRUS

Nicosia

CYPRUS

A F R I C A

Valletta

MALTA

0		400 MILES
0		400 KILOMETERS

Azimuthal Equidistant Projection

EUROPE

A commonly accepted division between Asia and Europe—marked here by a maroon, dashed line—is formed by the Ural Mountains, Ural River, Caspian Sea, Caucasus Mountains, and the Black Sea with its outlets, the Bosporus and Dardanelles.

Mixed and sweeping LANDSCAPES

Snowboarding in France.

Europe may be smaller than every continent except Australia, but it is home to 46 different countries. It is a large peninsula connected to Asia and bordered by islands. It is home to jagged coastlines, high mountains, and dark forests. These provide adventurers with a rich mix of challenges. A vast central plain supplies fertile farmland, and rivers form a transportation network.

AUNT BERTHA'S ADVENTURE TRAVEL TIPS

Most Europeans travel by public transportation. You can hop aboard a train, bus, subway, canal boat, ferry, or cable car.

Winter climate ranges from freezing cold in the north to warm and rainy in the south.

Watch out for unusual sports, ranging from bog snorkeling, cheese rolling, and tossing the caber to minigolf and boules.

A S I A

S S I A

Perm'

Ufa

Kazan'

Samara

Orenburg

Saratov

KAZAKHSTAN

Volgograd

Astrakhan'

Caspian Sea

Groznyy

GEORGIA

AZERBAIJAN Baku

ADVENTURE HOT SPOTS

LANDFORMS
Explore the lake region of Finland, where millions of years of glacial erosion have shaped highlands and valleys.

PLANTS
Follow trained pigs across southern France as they sniff out prized black truffle mushrooms.

CLIMATES
Climb above the 6,000-foot (1,829-m) mark in the Alps to discover a snowy wonderland.

ANIMALS
Visit a Norwegian fjord to see white-tailed eagles soar on eight-foot (2.4-m)-wide wings.

ICELAND
Get pulled in a sled by huskies over the massive glaciers that blanket southern Iceland.

LAKE DISTRICT
Plunge down natural rock slides in a tumbling mountain river in England's picturesque Lake District.

HABITATS
Explore the rivers, waterfalls, and forests of Croatia's Plitvice Lakes National Park and see bears, wolves, and rare birds.

ADVENTURES
Dive off the Contra Dam in Switzerland, the world's most famous bungee jump. It's not for the fainthearted.

MAP KEY
- ⊛ National capital
- • Other city
- ▫ Small country
- ▢ Disputed area

47

MOUNTAINOUS COUNTRY

Glaciers and craggy PEAKS

S tretching across the south of Europe near the Mediterranean Sea are the majestic Alps. These magnificent mountains are home to rocky peaks and deep valleys. In northern Europe, the ice age that ended about 10,000 years ago left a lasting mark. Melting glaciers sprinkled the land with watery marshes, odd boulders, glittering lakes, and deep fjords. In the west lies Iceland, a giant geological hot spot that is a wonderland of volcanoes, geysers, and glaciers.

ADVENTURE ATTRACTIONS

DEEP CAVE
Vrtoglavica Cave in Slovenia has the deepest single drop of any cave in the world—1,978 feet (603 m). The upper part of the deep cave is adorned with dangling icicles, posing a danger to cavers far below.

DRAMATIC DOLOMITES
The Dolomites mountain range in Italy is filled with knife-edged, pointed peaks. They are known as some of the most beautiful mountains in the world.

SNOW-CAPPED MOUNTAINS
The Pyrenees stretch between Spain and France. Dotted with glittering glacial lakes, these mountains are a great place for hiking or water skiing.

DIGITAL TRAVELER!
Along England's Jurassic coast, pounding waves and weather have exposed ancient fossils. Lyme Regis is one world-famous fossil site. Search the Internet for pictures of fossils discovered there.

5 COOL PLACES TO SEE HERE

1 ROCK TOWER
Norway

Climb to the top of Pulpit Rock and enjoy the scenery, but keep away from the edge. It's a 1,981-foot (604-m) drop from the flat rock to the deep fjord below. There are no safety railings!

2 GIANT PILLARS
Ireland

Climb the rocky pillars at Giant's Causeway. Legend says the curious columns were steps for ancient giants. Scientists say they were formed by an ancient volcano.

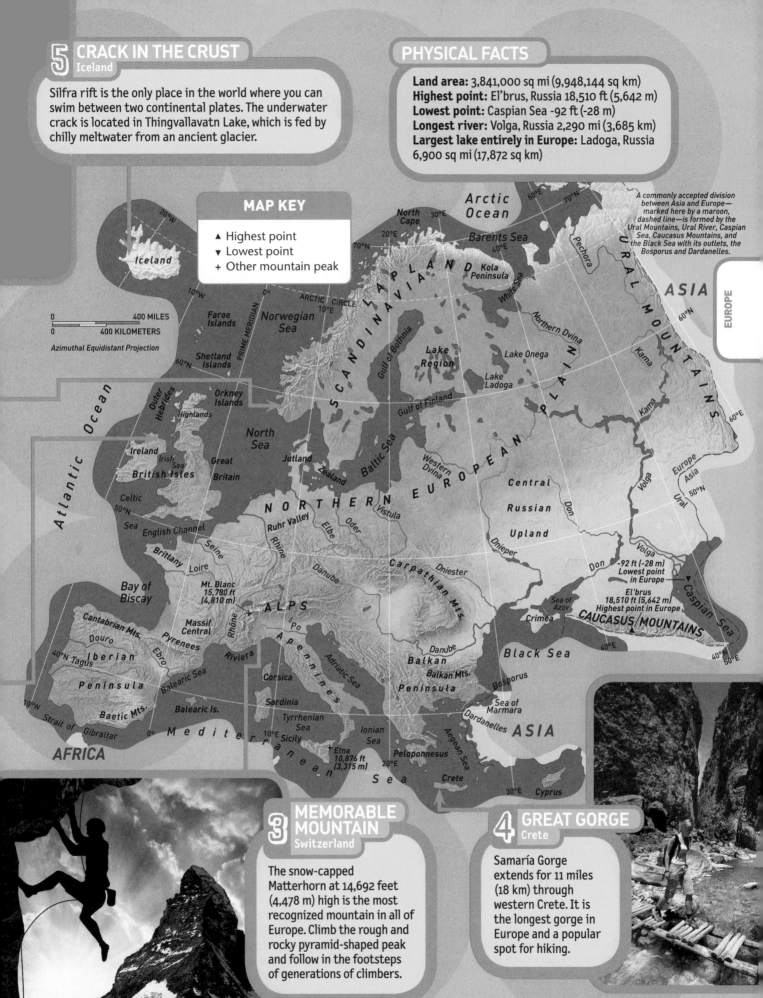

5 CRACK IN THE CRUST
Iceland

Silfra rift is the only place in the world where you can swim between two continental plates. The underwater crack is located in Thingvallavatn Lake, which is fed by chilly meltwater from an ancient glacier.

PHYSICAL FACTS

Land area: 3,841,000 sq mi (9,948,144 sq km)
Highest point: El'brus, Russia 18,510 ft (5,642 m)
Lowest point: Caspian Sea -92 ft (-28 m)
Longest river: Volga, Russia 2,290 mi (3,685 km)
Largest lake entirely in Europe: Ladoga, Russia 6,900 sq mi (17,872 sq km)

MAP KEY

- ▲ Highest point
- ▼ Lowest point
- + Other mountain peak

0 — 400 MILES
0 — 400 KILOMETERS
Azimuthal Equidistant Projection

A commonly accepted division between Asia and Europe—marked here by a maroon, dashed line—is formed by the Ural Mountains, Ural River, Caspian Sea, Caucasus Mountains, and the Black Sea with its outlets, the Bosporus and Dardanelles.

EUROPE

ASIA

Arctic Ocean
North Cape
Barents Sea
Kola Peninsula
White Sea
Pechora
URAL MOUNTAINS
Northern Dvina
Lake Onega
Lake Ladoga
Lake Region
Gulf of Bothnia
Gulf of Finland
Kama
Kama
Volga
NORTHERN EUROPEAN PLAIN
SCANDINAVIA
LAPLAND
Norwegian Sea
Faroe Islands
Shetland Islands
Orkney Islands
Outer Hebrides
Highlands
North Sea
Jutland
Zealand
Baltic Sea
Western Dvina
Central Russian Upland
Don
Europe
Asia
Ural
Iceland
Atlantic Ocean
Ireland
Irish Sea
Great Britain
British Isles
Celtic Sea
English Channel
Brittany
Seine
Loire
Rhine
Elbe
Oder
Vistula
Dnieper
Dniester
Carpathian Mts.
Danube
Don
Volga
Don
-92 ft (-28 m) Lowest point in Europe
El'brus 18,510 ft (5,642 m) Highest point in Europe
Sea of Azov
Crimea
CAUCASUS MOUNTAINS
Caspian Sea
Bay of Biscay
Mt. Blanc 15,780 ft (4,810 m)
ALPS
Massif Central
Rhône
Po
Apennines
Riviera
Cantabrian Mts.
Douro
Pyrenees
Ebro
Iberian Peninsula
Tagus
Baetic Mts.
Strait of Gibraltar
Balearic Sea
Balearic Is.
Corsica
Sardinia
Tyrrhenian Sea
Sicily
Etna 10,876 ft (3,315 m)
Ionian Sea
Adriatic Sea
Balkan
Balkan Mts.
Peninsula
Danube
Black Sea
Bosporus
Sea of Marmara
Dardanelles
ASIA
Aegean Sea
Peloponnesus
Crete
Cyprus
Mediterranean Sea
AFRICA

20°W, 20°E, 30°E, 50°E, 70°E, 70°N, 60°N, 50°N, 40°N, 10°W, 10°E, 0°, 60°E, 50°E, 40°E, 20°E, 30°E
ARCTIC CIRCLE
PRIME MERIDIAN

3 MEMORABLE MOUNTAIN
Switzerland

The snow-capped Matterhorn at 14,692 feet (4,478 m) high is the most recognized mountain in all of Europe. Climb the rough and rocky pyramid-shaped peak and follow in the footsteps of generations of climbers.

4 GREAT GORGE
Crete

Samaría Gorge extends for 11 miles (18 km) through western Crete. It is the longest gorge in Europe and a popular spot for hiking.

EXTREME WEATHER

From scorching heat to deep SNOW

Although most of Europe enjoys a mild climate, extreme weather is not hard to find. Many places—from sparkling ice caves to snow-capped mountaintops—have snow, ice, or permafrost year-round. In northern Europe, long, harsh winters bring frequent snowstorms. Short northern summers feature abundant sunshine. The summer sun hovers just above the horizon during the night. Across southern Europe, summertime can bring sizzling temperatures, setting off forest fires.

ADVENTURE ATTRACTIONS

ICE CAVE
The Eisriesenwelt in Austria is the largest ice cave in the world. Glittering ice formations fill the 26-mile (42-km)-long labyrinth.

POLAR NIGHT
In northern Finland and Russia, winter darkness can last for weeks, with the pale sun lingering just below the horizon throughout the day.

WIND CHANNEL
Trees in Provence, France, are forever bent from the fierce wind known as Le Mistral. The howling gusts can reach speeds of 62 miles per hour (100 kph).

5 HUMONGOUS HAIL
Germany

Catastrophic hailstorms are not uncommon in Munich. In 1984, hail the size of baseballs damaged about 70,000 homes in the city, along with 190 aircraft. The damage was estimated at more than $2 billion.

MAP KEY

Climatic Zones: Based on Köppen System

Dry
- Semiarid
- Arid

Mild
- Marine west coast
- Mediterranean
- Humid subtropical

Continental
- Warm summer
- Cool summer
- Subarctic

Polar
- Tundra

High Elevations
- Highlands

4 TORNADO TORRENT
United Kingdom

Each year the United Kingdom is hit by more than 50 tornadoes. Rarely are these severe, but they give the country the highest rate of twisters for its land area of any country in the world.

1 GHOSTLY SPECTRE
Scotland

Climb through the mist in the Scottish highlands, and you may see the ghostly figure of the Brocken spectre. This optical illusion is your shadow cast on the clouds and mists, surrounded by a rainbow of light.

5 EXTREME CLIMATES HERE

2 SHIVERING COLD
Russia

Experience bitter cold in the Ural Mountains. Near the village of Ust-Shchuger, on December 31, 1978, the thermometer dropped to -72.6°F (-58.1°C)—the lowest temperature ever recorded in Europe.

DIGITAL TRAVELER!

In 2014, isolated areas of Moldova, Albania, and Romania were buried under 15 feet (4.6 m) of snow. Search the Internet to see photos of the shivery, shovel-worthy snowfall.

3 HORRENDOUS HEAT
Greece

Summertime in Greece is always hot. In 1977, a heat wave baked the city of Athens and the nearby town of Elefsína, bringing temperatures to a broiling 118.4°F (48°C). Sweaty residents cooled off in swimming pools and at the beach.

STRANGE BUT TRUE

In the summer of 1816, days were so overcast that many farmers in Europe lost their crops. The gloomy "Year Without a Summer" was later traced to an 1815 volcanic eruption. Thick dust from the eruption had blocked sunlight.

Map labels

ARCTIC CIRCLE
Barents Sea
ASIA
NORWAY
SWEDEN
FINLAND
RUSSIA
Sea
Baltic Sea
ESTONIA
LATVIA
LITHUANIA
DENMARK
Kaliningrad (Russia)
BELARUS
GERMANY
POLAND
CZECH REP.
SLOVAKIA
AUSTRIA
LIECH.
SLOV.
HUNGARY
SAN MARINO
CROATIA
BOSN. & HERZG.
SERBIA
ROMANIA
MOLDOVA
ITALY
VATICAN CITY
MONTENEGRO
KOSOVO
MACED.
BULGARIA
ALBANIA
TURKEY
GREECE
MALTA
CYPRUS
UKRAINE
KAZAKHSTAN
Caspian Sea
Black Sea
GEORGIA
AZERBAIJAN
ASIA
ranean Sea

0 400 MILES
0 400 KILOMETERS

70°N
10°E
20°E
30°E
50°E
60°E
70°N
40°E
60°N
50°N
40°N
40°E
50°E
20°E
30°E

5 COOL PLACES TO SEE HERE

Iceland is known as the Land of Fire and Ice. The south of the country is marked by ice caps and volcanoes. There are also tiny offshore islands with large colonies of seabirds.

Iceland
Eyjafjallajökull Glacier

EUROPE

1 ACTIVE VOLCANO
Katla

Ride snowmobiles across Mýrdalsjökull glacier, but know that an active volcano sleeps beneath you. The volcano has erupted every 50 to 100 years and is now overdue. Each eruption spews poisonous ash, unleashes a flood of meltwater, and can even trigger tidal waves.

Scale varies in this perspective.

Seljalandsfoss

Tindfjallajökull

Laugavegurinn

Eyjafjallajökull

Sólheimajökull

Katla Volcano

Mýrdalsjökull

Höfðabrekkujökull

2 COLOSSAL CRATER
Eyjafjallajökull Glacier

Ride a jeep halfway up and then hike through the snow and ice to reach the one- to two-mile (1.6- to 3.2-km)-wide crater left by a 2010 volcanic eruption. Sky-high ash from the eruption halted air traffic in Europe for a week.

Hafursey

Mýrdalssandur

Atlantic Ocean

—Z→

3 GREAT GLACIER
Sólheimajökull

Scale this icy giant to discover sparkling ice sculptures, rugged ridges, and deep crevasses. Try your skill at climbing an ice wall. Bring warm clothing, ice axes, and spiky crampons to slip over your boots.

LAND OF FIRE AND ICE

Glaciers, volcanoes, and WATERFALLS

EUROPE

Slow-moving glaciers and fiery volcanoes have shaped southern Iceland. The Mýrdalsjökull and Eyjafjallajökull ice caps both sit atop active volcanoes. When a volcano erupts, it punches through the ice in a cloud of steam and ash and lets loose a glacial flood. Because of the forces of fire and ice, the rugged landscape is dotted with lava fields, hot springs, craters, canyons, and waterfalls.

5 SCENIC TRAIL
Laugavegurinn

Trek through a landscape of deep canyons, glassy lakes, and steaming hot springs. Take in spectacular views of colorful mountains and rugged glaciers. Stop in a hut for the night. Look up and you may see the Northern Lights.

4 TURNED AROUND WATERFALL
Seljalandsfoss

Visit a sparkling waterfall where water cascades 203 feet (62 m) down the sheer cliff wall. Hike behind the falls and look through a wall of water. Don't forget your waterproof camera!

DIGITAL TRAVELER!
There is a place in southern Iceland called Reynisfjara Beach. Search the Internet to find photos of its black sand and chunky rock columns. What colorful birds nest above the columns?

53

DIVERSE DWELLINGS

Creepy caves and mystical FORESTS

Europe's habitats are a mixed bag, from the snowy boreal forests of Denmark, Norway, Sweden, and Russia to the hot, dry Mediterranean basin in the south. There are steep alpine meadows filled with flowers, soggy and ever-changing wetlands, and remnants of the ancient forests that once covered much of the continent. These assorted habitats are packed with plants and provide a home for Europe's wildest animals.

5 TIDAL WETLANDS
Netherlands

The Wadden Sea is a vast tidal area and one of the largest wetlands in the world. Islands, channels, gullies, and flats change shape and location throughout the day. The adaptable plants that grow here must continually adjust to the shifting conditions.

4 ICY MOUNTAINTOPS
Austria

On rocky mountaintops in the Alps, no trees can survive the extreme cold. Yet the harsh mountaintops are home to spiky grasses and scratchy shrubs. These tough plants survive the icy conditions by growing low to the ground.

DIGITAL TRAVELER!
The diverse Mediterranean basin includes all of the countries that border the Mediterranean Sea. Choose one of these countries. Then use your digital device to discover some of the plants and animals that live there.

3 BIODIVERSITY HOT SPOT
Spain

The coast of southern Europe is rich in animal and plant life, with hundreds of bird, reptile, and mammal species and diverse sealife. Most of its 20,000 plant species are found nowhere else in the world.

Map labels: ICELAND, ARCTIC CIRCLE, Norwegian Sea, SCANDINAVIA, SWEDEN, North Sea, UNITED KINGDOM, IRELAND, DENMARK, Atlantic Ocean, NETH., NORTH, GERMANY, BELGIUM, LUX., CZECH REP., Bay of Biscay, FRANCE, LIECH., AUSTRIA, SWITZ., ALPS, SLOV., CROATIA, BOSNIA & HERZEGOVINA, PORTUGAL, ANDORRA, SPAIN, ITALY, Mediterranean, MALTA

5 COOL PLACES TO SEE HERE

1 PRIMEVAL FOREST
Poland

The Białowieza Forest is the last large remnant of the ancient forests that once covered much of Europe. Tall trees and rotting logs fill the forest. Bison roam here, as do wolves.

EUROPE

DID YOU KNOW?

The Bavarian Forest National Park in Germany is an ancient forest regrowing naturally after a massive thunderstorm uprooted thousands of spruce trees in 1983. Park officials decided not to replant but to let the forest recover without human help.

2 PITCH-BLACK CAVE
Romania

Movile Cave crawls with blind spiders, scorpions, and millipedes. These adaptable creatures thrive in darkness 80 feet (24.2 m) below ground. There is no light for plants to grow, but a thick scum of bacteria feeds on energy-rich gases and provides food for the creatures living in the cave.

Map labels: Barents Sea, LAPLAND, SCANDINAVIA, DENMARK, FINLAND, RUSSIA, EUROPEAN PLAIN, ASIA, Baltic Sea, ESTONIA, LATVIA, LITHUANIA, Kaliningrad (Russia), BELARUS, KAZAKHSTAN, ERN POLAND, UKRAINE, Carpathian Mts., SLOVAKIA, MOLDOVA, HUNGARY, ROMANIA, Caspian Sea, CAUCASUS MOUNTAINS, Black Sea, GEORGIA, SERBIA, AZERBAIJAN, MONTENEGRO, KOSOVO, BULGARIA, MACED., ALBANIA, TURKEY, ASIA, GREECE, Sea, CYPRUS

MAP KEY
- ☐ Grasslands
- ■ Coniferous forests
- ☐ Temperate broadleaf forests
- ☐ Mediterranean forests and shrublands
- ■ Boreal forests
- ☐ Rock and ice
- ☐ Tundra
- ☐ Deserts and dry shrublands

0   300 MILES
0   300 KILOMETERS

ADVENTURE ATTRACTIONS

CONIFER PARK
Oulanka National Park in Finland is home to bristly Scotch pines and silver birches. Reindeer herders graze their hungry animals in the forest.

SKY-HIGH MEADOWS
Trek high in the Pyrenees to see alpine meadows packed with springtime wildflowers. The vibrant blooms attract colorful butterflies.

DANUBE DELTA
Where the Danube River flows into the Black Sea is the largest marshland in Europe. The delta is home to about 300 species of birds and 45 kinds of fish.

TREES, SHRUBS, AND FLOWERS

From poisonous plants to weird FRUITS

Plants of all kinds dot the European landscape. Across the far north stretches a vast boreal forest, filled with pine, spruce, and birch trees that can stand up to long winters and thick snow. In more temperate regions, forests are home to such broadleaf trees as walnut, ash, elm, and chestnut. In Europe's northwest corner, heathlands and boggy meadows burst with colorful heather plants that thrive in the acidic soil. In the south grow shady oak trees and spiky shrubs adapted to the region's rainy winters, dry summers, and frequent wildfires.

ADVENTURE ATTRACTIONS

COLORFUL MOOR
In Dartmoor National Park in the United Kingdom, patches of purple heather and clumps of gorse with golden yellow flowers dot the rugged landscape.

LUSH LANDSCAPE
The hot, dry forests of southern France and Spain are thick with stands of wild olive and carob trees. On south-facing slopes grow grapevines.

ANCIENT FORESTS
Northern Portugal's ancient forests are home to about 2,000 plant species, including 40 species of orchid.

DIGITAL TRAVELER!
Spiky thistle, with its pink or purple flowers, is the proud symbol of Scotland. But how did a painful weed turn into a national emblem? Uncover the legend using the Internet.

---

2 UNDERCOVER FLOWER
Ukraine
The fly orchid is no great beauty. Its flower looks like a fly and smells, too. Bees, flies, and other insects are attracted to the sneaky blossom and unknowingly pollinate it.

---

5 COOL PLANTS TO SEE HERE

5 POWERFUL POISON
Hungary
The roots, seeds, and flowers of the wolfsbane plant are poisonous. This garden plant was once the source of a potent poison used to kill wolves, giving the plant its name. The poison was also rumored to be an ingredient in witch's brew.

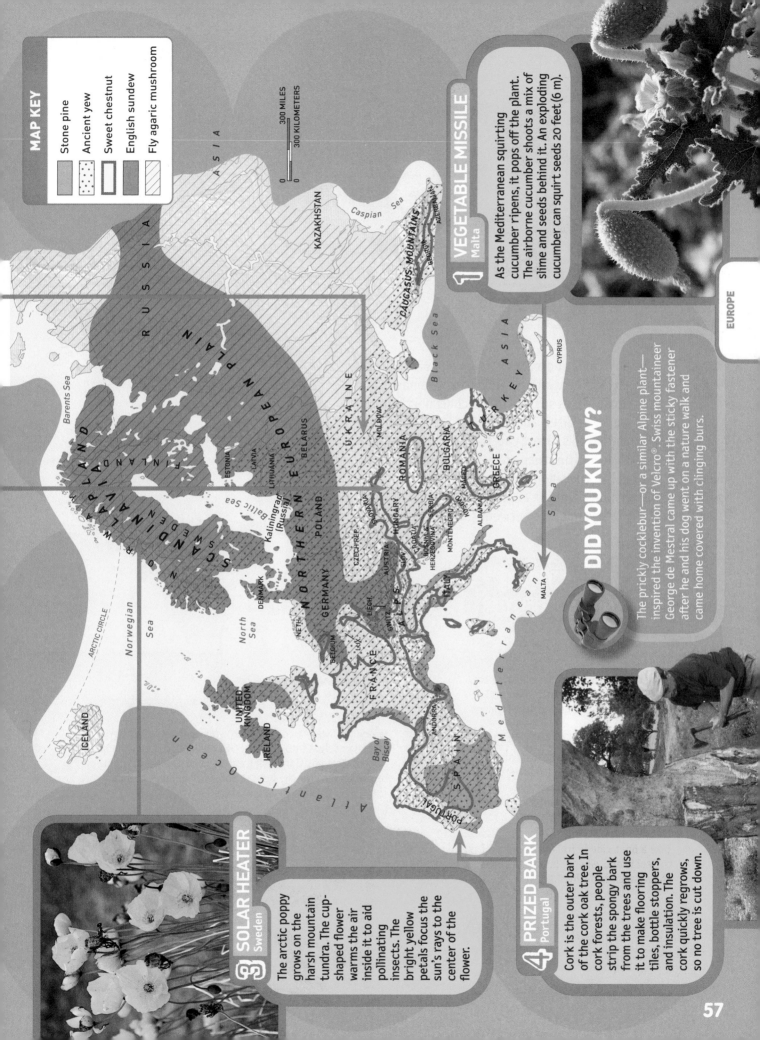

MAP KEY

- Stone pine
- Ancient yew
- Sweet chestnut
- English sundew
- Fly agaric mushroom

0 — 300 MILES
0 — 300 KILOMETERS

1 VEGETABLE MISSILE
Malta

As the Mediterranean squirting cucumber ripens, it pops off the plant. The airborne cucumber shoots a mix of slime and seeds behind it. An exploding cucumber can squirt seeds 20 feet (6 m).

DID YOU KNOW?

The prickly cocklebur—or a similar Alpine plant—inspired the invention of Velcro®. Swiss mountaineer George de Mestral came up with the sticky fastener after he and his dog went on a nature walk and came home covered with clinging burs.

3 SOLAR HEATER
Sweden

The arctic poppy grows on the harsh mountain tundra. The cup-shaped flower warms the air inside it to aid pollinating insects. The bright yellow petals focus the sun's rays to the center of the flower.

4 PRIZED BARK
Portugal

Cork is the outer bark of the cork oak tree. In cork forests, people strip the spongy bark from the trees and use it to make flooring tiles, bottle stoppers, and insulation. The cork quickly regrows, so no tree is cut down.

57

WILD ANIMALS

Creatures from the Arctic to the COASTS

Many kinds of creatures roam and visit Europe's diverse ecosystems. Wolverines, reindeer, and arctic foxes survive in the chilly north. In the warm Mediterranean region live wild horses and the world's rarest cat, the Iberian lynx. The Alpine ibex makes its home on the steep and rocky slopes of mountains. Fierce carnivores like the silent eagle owl and the speedy peregrine falcon hunt from the air. Each year, huge numbers of songbirds and wildfowl migrate between Europe, Asia, and Africa.

MAP KEY

- Chamois
- Eagle owl
- Saiga antelope
- Wolverine
- Marbled polecat

ICELAND · ARCTIC CIRCLE
Norwegian Sea
NORWAY · SCANDINAVIA · SWEDEN
Baltic Sea
UNITED KINGDOM
North Sea
IRELAND
DENMARK
Kaliningrad (Russia)
Atlantic Ocean
NETH.
NORTHERN
POLAND
BELGIUM
GERMANY
LUX.
CZECH REP.
LIECH.
Bay of Biscay
FRANCE
SLOVAKIA
SWITZ.
AUSTRIA
HUNGARY
ALPS
SLOV.
CROATIA
PORTUGAL
ANDORRA
BOSNIA & HERZEGOVINA
ITALY
MONTENEGRO
SPAIN
ALBANIA
Mediterranean
MALTA

ADVENTURE ATTRACTIONS

BIRD CLIFFS
At Iceland's westernmost point rise the Látrabjarg Cliffs. Colorful puffins and other seabirds nest here by the millions.

ANCIENT HORSELAND
In the Camargue—marshlands of southeastern France—gallop herds of white horses thought to be the descendants of ancient wild horses.

SEAL ISLAND
Take a boat ride in Ireland's Donegal Bay to Seal Island, where about 200 harbor and Atlantic seals live.

5 PRICKLY CRITTER
United Kingdom

Hedgehogs wear a coat of sharp spines. If threatened, they curl themselves into a bristly ball. Hedgehogs sometimes sleep in this position during the day and awaken at night to search for crunchy insects and small animals to eat. They often sneak into adventurers' tents!

DIGITAL TRAVELER!
Search the Internet for pictures of the saiga antelope. Why does the antelope have such a large nose? Take a guess, and then do a search to find the answer.

5 COOL ANIMALS TO SEE HERE

1 COLD-LOVING DEER
Russia

Reindeer survive winter with the help of thick, heat-trapping fur. Large, flat hooves act as snowshoes and are good for digging for food—lichens and plants hidden under the snow. Both male and female reindeer have antlers.

2 COOL CREATURE
Finland

The arctic fox can survive shivery temperatures as low as -58°F (-50°C). Furry soles and short ears help the fox stay warm. When icy winds blow, the fox wraps its tail around its body like a blanket.

3 FAST FLIER
Macedonia

One of the fastest animals in the world, the peregrine falcon hunts bats and other birds from above. When prey is spotted, this powerful predator can dive at speeds that can top 200 miles per hour (322 kph).

4 MISSING LYNX
Spain

The Iberian lynx, with ears sensitive to tiny sounds, is a stealthy predator that is rarely seen. It hunts for birds and mammals at night in cork oak woodlands and open scrubland.

STRANGE BUT TRUE

In Gran Paradiso National Park in northern Italy, Alpine ibex scale a nearly vertical rocky dam in a way that makes even thrill-seeking adventurers marvel. The mountain-loving goats climb the steep dam to lick the rocks for minerals and salts.

Map labels: Barents Sea, FINLAND, URAL MOUNTAINS, ASIA, RUSSIA, EUROPEAN PLAIN, LAND, ESTONIA, LATVIA, LITHUANIA, BELARUS, KAZAKHSTAN, UKRAINE, MOLDOVA, ROMANIA, Caspian Sea, CAUCASUS MOUNTAINS, SERBIA, KOSOVO, BULGARIA, MACED., GEORGIA, AZERBAIJAN, Black Sea, GREECE, TURKEY, ASIA, CYPRUS, Sea

0 300 MILES
0 300 KILOMETERS

THE LAKE DISTRICT

An adventure PLAYGROUND

Welcome to a land of rugged hills, clear lakes, and green forests. The Lake District spans just 900 square miles (2,331 sq km)—about one percent of the land area of Great Britain. However, plenty of stunning scenery is packed into this small space. The area is home to England's deepest lake and its highest peaks, known locally as fells. The peaks and valleys look a lot like they did at the end of the last ice age about 10,000 years ago, when retreating glaciers revealed a landscape of breathtaking beauty.

5 WATERFALL
Wast Water

Kayak down a waterfall at Skelwith Force or swim in Wast Water, the deepest of the area's lakes. Take a dip in cold, inky black water that plunges an icy 260 feet (79 m) to the bottom. Then take in the spectacular mountain views.

Bassenthwaite Lake

Ennerdale Water

C u m b r

Scafell Pike

Wast Water

Eskdale Valley

Scale varies in this perspective.

Irish Sea

True or False

The European kingfisher can sometimes be seen in the Lake District. Which of these statements about this bird are true, and which are false? See page 149 for the answers.

A The kingfisher is widespread in Great Britain, where it is common in woodlands and forests.

B As it waits and watches for swimming food, it often bobs its head up and down.

C When preying on fish, it whacks the fish's head onto a hard surface and then swallows it whole.

D It eats not only fish but also tadpoles and insect larvae.

E An adult kingfisher measures up to seven inches (17.8 cm) in length.

4 CRAGGY PEAKS
Langsdale Valley

Take a rugged walk through the scenic Langsdale Valley. Climb the steep peaks at about 2,300 feet (701 m) high and catch spectacular views. Go fell-running, then scramble back down into the valley below.

5 COOL PLACES TO SEE HERE

The Lake District has more outdoor activity centers than any other region of the United Kingdom. With lakes, streams, mountains, caves, cliffs, and forests, there are many places for extreme activities and adventures.

United Kingdom

The Lake District

EUROPE

1 MAJESTIC WATERS
Windermere

Sail or kayak the deep, quiet waters of Lake Windermere. Stop at a beach for a swim, but stay near the shore. The lake floor beneath the water drops away suddenly and deeply. The deep water is ice cold.

Derwent Water

Thirlmere

Ullswater

Haweswater Reservoir

ian Mountains

Langsdale Valley

The Old Man of Coniston

Coniston Water

Windermere

Grizedale Forest

N

2 MYSTICAL TRAIL
Grizedale Forest

Cycle the scenic roads beside the lakes for views of mountains. For an adrenaline-pumping bike ride, try the Black Trail in Grizedale Forest, with its daring jumps, tricky boardwalks, and steep descents.

3 SLIPPERY GORGE
Eskdale Valley

Scale rock faces and splash and slide down mountain streams through narrow gorges in the Eskdale Valley. Scramble over rocks, climb cascading waterfalls, and jump into swirling pools. Enjoy hidden places few people ever get to see.

DIGITAL TRAVELER!

Many places in the Lake District still carry names given by tenth-century Norse settlers. What are "tarns," "becks," and "thwaites"? Search the Internet to find the meanings of these ancient words.

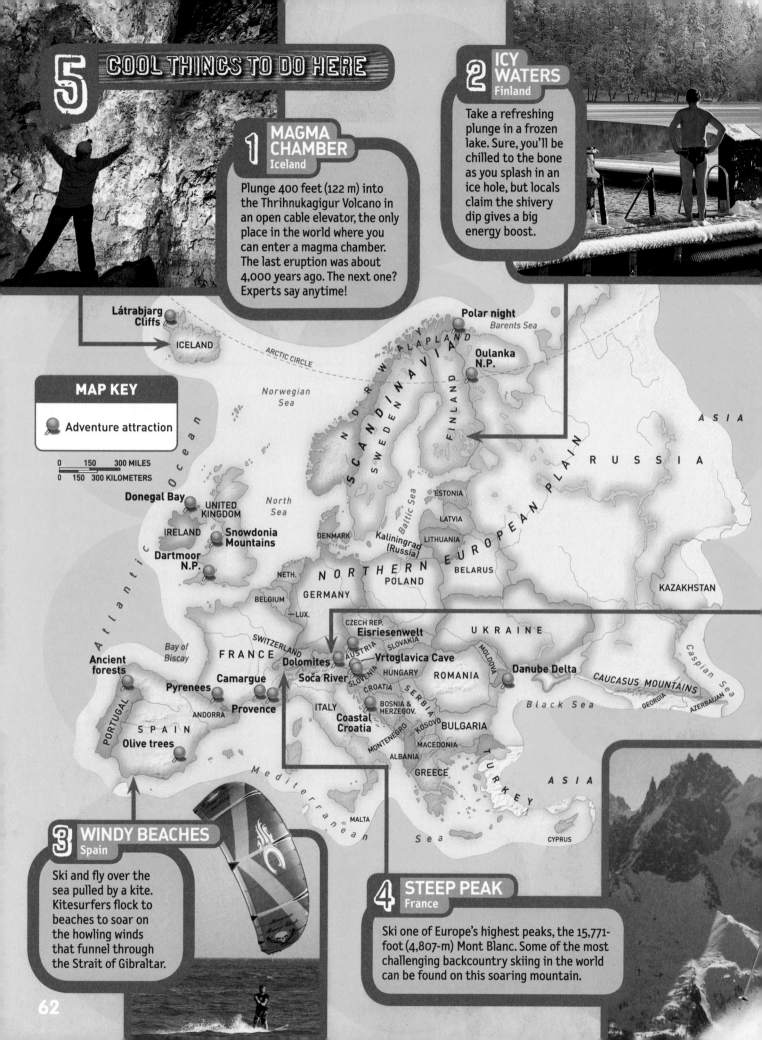

5 COOL THINGS TO DO HERE

1 MAGMA CHAMBER
Iceland

Plunge 400 feet (122 m) into the Thrihnukagigur Volcano in an open cable elevator, the only place in the world where you can enter a magma chamber. The last eruption was about 4,000 years ago. The next one? Experts say anytime!

2 ICY WATERS
Finland

Take a refreshing plunge in a frozen lake. Sure, you'll be chilled to the bone as you splash in an ice hole, but locals claim the shivery dip gives a big energy boost.

3 WINDY BEACHES
Spain

Ski and fly over the sea pulled by a kite. Kitesurfers flock to beaches to soar on the howling winds that funnel through the Strait of Gibraltar.

4 STEEP PEAK
France

Ski one of Europe's highest peaks, the 15,771-foot (4,807-m) Mont Blanc. Some of the most challenging backcountry skiing in the world can be found on this soaring mountain.

MAP KEY

🔍 Adventure attraction

0   150   300 MILES
0   150   300 KILOMETERS

Map labels:

Látrabjarg Cliffs
ICELAND
ARCTIC CIRCLE
Polar night
Barents Sea
Oulanka N.P.
Norwegian Sea
SCANDINAVIA
NORWAY
SWEDEN
LAPLAND
Finland
Atlantic Ocean
Donegal Bay
UNITED KINGDOM
North Sea
IRELAND
Snowdonia Mountains
Dartmoor N.P.
NETH.
BELGIUM
LUX.
GERMANY
DENMARK
Baltic Sea
Kaliningrad (Russia)
ESTONIA
LATVIA
LITHUANIA
BELARUS
POLAND
NORTHERN EUROPEAN PLAIN
RUSSIA
ASIA
KAZAKHSTAN
Ancient forests
Bay of Biscay
FRANCE
SWITZERLAND
Pyrenees
Camargue
Provence
ANDORRA
PORTUGAL
SPAIN
Olive trees
ITALY
Dolomites
Soča River
AUSTRIA
CZECH REP.
Eisriesenwelt
SLOVAKIA
SLOVENIA
Vrtoglavica Cave
HUNGARY
CROATIA
Coastal Croatia
BOSNIA & HERZEGOV.
MONTENEGRO
SERBIA
KOSOVO
ALBANIA
MACEDONIA
BULGARIA
ROMANIA
MOLDOVA
UKRAINE
Danube Delta
Black Sea
CAUCASUS MOUNTAINS
GEORGIA
AZERBAIJAN
Caspian Sea
GREECE
TURKEY
ASIA
Mediterranean Sea
MALTA
CYPRUS

EXTREME ADVENTURE

Swim in icy waters and fly over LAKES

5 LAKE ACHENSEE
Austria

Take a cable car ride to a mountain perch, where you can harness to a paraglider and jump off. Gently float back down through the picturesque valley to get magnificent views of the lake.

With its mosaic of mountains, islands, and jagged coastlines, Europe offers exciting options for extreme adventurers. The Mediterranean coasts are a thrilling location for surfers and kayakers. Europe's peaks offer high-flying sports, from skiing the Alps to zipping through Wales's Snowdonia mountains. Adrenaline junkies can go rally car racing, descend into an active volcano, plunge into an ice hole, or take a wet and wild ride on a roaring river.

ADVENTURE ATTRACTIONS

RECORD BREAKER

Italian skier Simone Origone set a world record when he reached speeds of 156.8 miles per hour (252.3 kph) on a slope near the village of Vars in the French Alps.

DIGITAL TRAVELER!
Search online for a video of "scree" running in Spain. After you watch, look up the meaning of scree. What are some other names for this extreme sport?

RIVER RAPIDS
Get soaked in Slovenia's Soca River. Raft, boat, or swim the emerald green river as it winds through wild canyons.

A-MAZE-ING WATERS
Croatia's coast offers sea kayakers sparkling blue water and a maze of more than 1,200 islands to explore.

HIGH-FLYING IN THE MOUNTAINS
The Snowdonia mountains are the site of the world's longest series of zip lines—five miles (8 km)—where you can reach a speed of 60 miles per hour (97 kph). Dangle over meadow and mountain in an amazing Welsh landscape.

ASIA
The biggest on EARTH

The continent of Asia covers almost one-third of the world's land area. It is Earth's largest continent. There are five subregions. Western Asia includes Saudi Arabia, Israel, Iraq, and other countries on the Arabian Peninsula and Persian Gulf. Central Asia has Kazakhstan and four other "stans." South Asia includes India, Nepal, Iran, Afghanistan, and others. China, North and South Korea, and Japan are in East Asia. Malaysia, Indonesia, and Vietnam are in Southeast Asia. Adventurers in Asia will find a continent of extremes—from the towering Himalaya to the vast desert of the Gobi.

AUNT BERTHA'S
ADVENTURE TRAVEL TIPS

Check the weather forecast before heading to the Gobi so you can pack the right clothes. Summer temperatures soar to 113°F (45°C). Winter temperatures drop to -40°F (-40°C).

Whether you are climbing Mount Fuji, Everest, or K2, try to reach the peak at sunrise. The view at that time is the most spectacular!

There are many adventurous ways to travel in Asia. People get around on rickshaws, tuk-tuks, camels, donkey-drawn carts, elephants, junks, and sampans. Pick your favorite and hop on!

In spring, adventurers can join in the colorful celebrations of the Hindu festival of Holi.

ADVENTURE
HOT SPOTS

LANDFORMS

One of the world's deepest canyons is Yarlung Zangbo in China and Tibet. The river that runs through it is fast flowing.

CLIMATES

A hot and dry wind in Kuwait's desert called the *shamal* causes whopping sandstorms.

MOUNT EVEREST

The world's highest mountain draws daring adventurers to its base camps and summit.

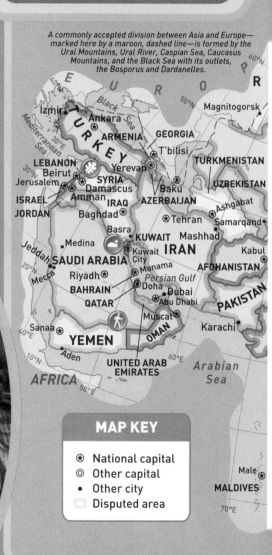

A commonly accepted division between Asia and Europe—marked here by a maroon, dashed line—is formed by the Ural Mountains, Ural River, Caspian Sea, Caucasus Mountains, and the Black Sea with its outlets, the Bosporus and Dardanelles.

MAP KEY

⊛ National capital
◎ Other capital
• Other city
▢ Disputed area

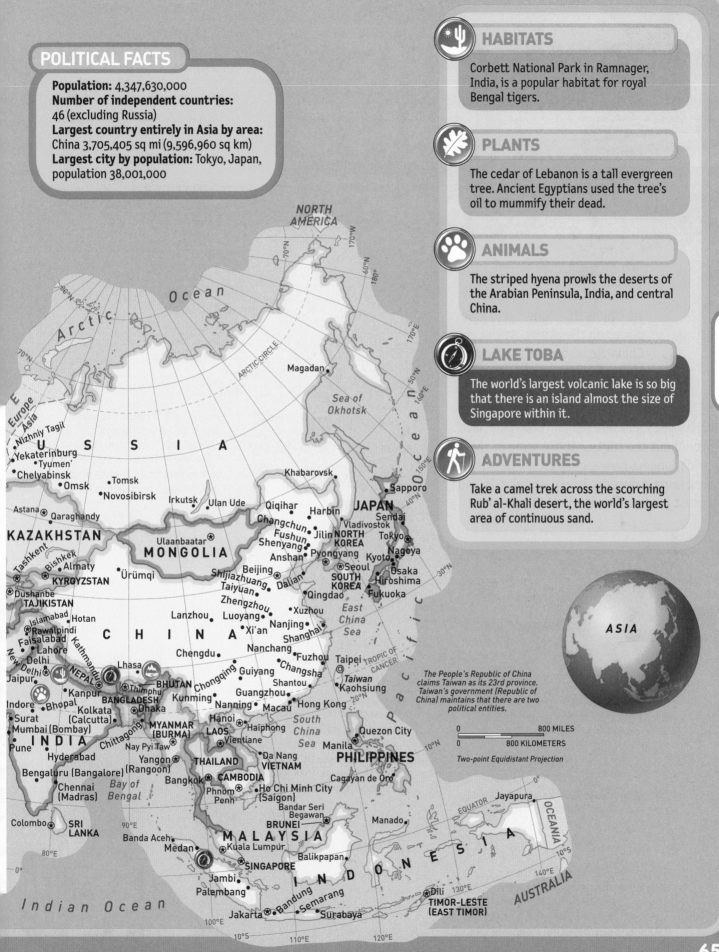

POLITICAL FACTS

Population: 4,347,630,000
Number of independent countries:
46 (excluding Russia)
Largest country entirely in Asia by area:
China 3,705,405 sq mi (9,596,960 sq km)
Largest city by population: Tokyo, Japan,
population 38,001,000

HABITATS

Corbett National Park in Ramnager,
India, is a popular habitat for royal
Bengal tigers.

PLANTS

The cedar of Lebanon is a tall evergreen
tree. Ancient Egyptians used the tree's
oil to mummify their dead.

ANIMALS

The striped hyena prowls the deserts of
the Arabian Peninsula, India, and central
China.

LAKE TOBA

The world's largest volcanic lake is so big
that there is an island almost the size of
Singapore within it.

ADVENTURES

Take a camel trek across the scorching
Rub' al-Khali desert, the world's largest
area of continuous sand.

ASIA

The People's Republic of China
claims Taiwan as its 23rd province.
Taiwan's government (Republic of
China) maintains that there are two
political entities.

0   800 MILES
0   800 KILOMETERS

Two-point Equidistant Projection

NORTH AMERICA

Arctic Ocean

Magadan

Sea of Okhotsk

RUSSIA

Nizhniy Tagil
Yekaterinburg
Tyumen'
Chelyabinsk
Omsk
Tomsk
Novosibirsk
Astana
Qaraghandy
KAZAKHSTAN
Tashkent
Bishkek
Almaty
KYRGYZSTAN
Dushanbe
TAJIKISTAN
Islamabad
Rawalpindi
Faisalabad
Lahore
New Delhi
Delhi
Jaipur
Kanpur
NEPAL
Kathmandu
Lhasa
Thimphu
BHUTAN
BANGLADESH
Dhaka
Indore
Bhopal
Kolkata
(Calcutta)
Surat
Mumbai (Bombay)
Pune
INDIA
Hyderabad
Bengaluru (Bangalore)
Chennai
(Madras)
Colombo
SRI LANKA
Chittagong
MYANMAR
(BURMA)
Nay Pyi Taw
Yangon
(Rangoon)
THAILAND
Bangkok
CAMBODIA
Phnom
Penh
LAOS
Vientiane
Hanoi
Haiphong
VIETNAM
Da Nang
Ho Chi Minh City
(Saigon)
Bandar Seri
Begawan
BRUNEI
MALAYSIA
Banda Aceh
Medan
Kuala Lumpur
SINGAPORE
Jambi
Palembang
Bandung
Jakarta
Semarang
Surabaya
INDONESIA
Indian Ocean

Irkutsk
Ulan Ude
MONGOLIA
Ulaanbaatar
Ürümqi
CHINA
Hotan
Lanzhou
Chengdu
Chongqing
Kunming
Nanning
Guangzhou
Macau
Hong Kong
South China Sea
Manila
PHILIPPINES
Quezon City
Cagayan de Oro
Manado
Balikpapan

Qiqihar
Harbin
Changchun
Fushun
Jilin
Shenyang
Anshan
Beijing
Shijiazhuang
Taiyuan
Zhengzhou
Luoyang
Xuzhou
Nanjing
Xi'an
Shanghai
Nanchang
Changsha
Guiyang
Shantou
Fuzhou
Taipei
Taiwan
Kaohsiung
East China Sea
TROPIC OF CANCER
Pacific Ocean

Khabarovsk
Sapporo
JAPAN
Sendai
Vladivostok
Tokyo
NORTH KOREA
Pyongyang
Nagoya
Kyoto
Seoul
SOUTH KOREA
Osaka
Hiroshima
Fukuoka
Qingdao
Dalian

Dili
TIMOR-LESTE
(EAST TIMOR)
Jayapura
OCEANIA
AUSTRALIA
EQUATOR

ARCTIC CIRCLE

Europe
Asia

Bay of Bengal

AT THE LIMITS

Earth's highest and lowest POINTS

DID YOU KNOW?

The world's first cities were developed in the land between the Tigris and Euphrates Rivers near the Persian Gulf. Archaeologists have uncovered city ruins that date back more than 5,500 years.

5 COOL PLACES TO SEE HERE

Asia claims the highest and lowest places on the planet. At the China-Nepal border, the tip of Mount Everest reaches 29,035 feet (8,850 m) above sea level. The shore of the Dead Sea between Israel and Jordan lies 1,388 feet (423 m) below sea level. Throughout the continent are some of the world's longest rivers, deepest gorges, biggest lakes, largest deserts, iciest wastelands, and densest jungles. This is a land of extremes!

1 HIDDEN CITIES
Turkey

As you walk through the jagged volcanic "fairy chimneys" in Cappadocia, Turkey, you may think you've landed on the moon. In medieval times, people built cave homes and churches here.

ADVENTURE ATTRACTIONS

DIGITAL TRAVELER!
Mount Fuji in Japan is really three volcanoes on top of one another. Use your digital device to find out the best months to climb there.

WORLD'S HIGHEST MOUNTAINS

The Himalaya are the core of Asia. The peaks are so high that some climbers wear oxygen masks to help them breathe in the thin air.

2 THE DEAD SEA
Jordan/Israel/West Bank

The shore of the Dead Sea is the lowest land area on Earth. Step into the water, and you'll float. The sea is about nine times saltier than the oceans. The high salt content is what allows you to float.

PARCHED DESERT

Sweeping across southern Mongolia and northern China, the Gobi covers an area two-thirds the size of Mexico.

FAN MOUNTAINS

The Fannsky Gory are favorite mountains for hiking in Tajikistan. The views from the mountains are spectacular, especially when you get to Iskander-Kul, a beautiful mountain lake.

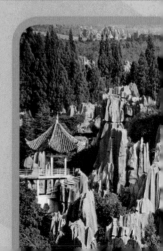

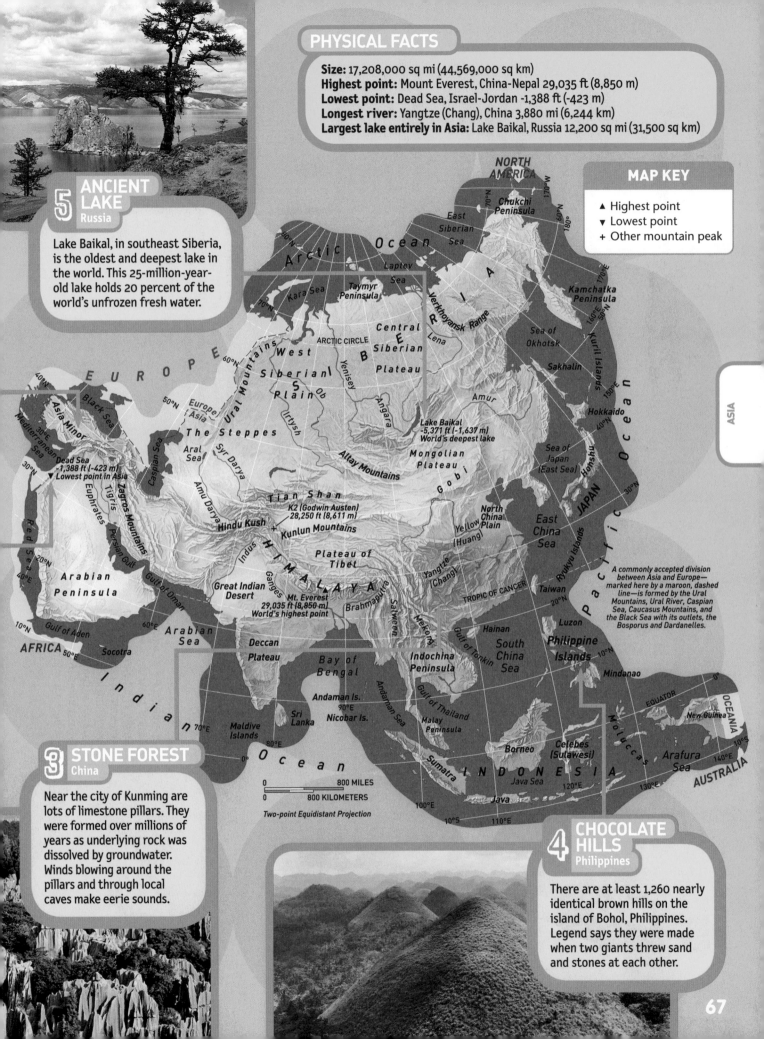

PHYSICAL FACTS

Size: 17,208,000 sq mi (44,569,000 sq km)
Highest point: Mount Everest, China-Nepal 29,035 ft (8,850 m)
Lowest point: Dead Sea, Israel-Jordan -1,388 ft (-423 m)
Longest river: Yangtze (Chang), China 3,880 mi (6,244 km)
Largest lake entirely in Asia: Lake Baikal, Russia 12,200 sq mi (31,500 sq km)

MAP KEY

▲ Highest point
▼ Lowest point
+ Other mountain peak

5 ANCIENT LAKE
Russia

Lake Baikal, in southeast Siberia, is the oldest and deepest lake in the world. This 25-million-year-old lake holds 20 percent of the world's unfrozen fresh water.

A commonly accepted division between Asia and Europe—marked here by a maroon, dashed line—is formed by the Ural Mountains, Ural River, Caspian Sea, Caucasus Mountains, and the Black Sea with its outlets, the Bosporus and Dardanelles.

NORTH AMERICA

Arctic Ocean

Chukchi Peninsula
East Siberian Sea
Laptev Sea
Kara Sea
Taymyr Peninsula
Verkhoyansk Range
Kamchatka Peninsula
Central Siberian Plateau
Lena
Sea of Okhotsk
ARCTIC CIRCLE
Kuril Islands
West Siberian Plain
Ob
Yenisey
Amur
Sakhalin
S I B E R I A
Hokkaido
E U R O P E
Ural Mountains
Irtysh
Angara
Lake Baikal -5,371 ft (-1,637 m) World's deepest lake
Sea of Japan (East Sea)
Europe Asia
The Steppes
Aral Sea
Mongolian Plateau
Honshu
JAPAN
Black Sea
Asia Minor
Caspian Sea
Syr Darya
Gobi
Altay Mountains
Sea of Japan (East Sea)
Mediterranean Sea
Amu Darya
Tian Shan
North China Plain
East China Sea
Dead Sea -1,388 ft (-423 m) ▼ Lowest point in Asia
Zagros Mountains
K2 (Godwin Austen) 28,250 ft (8,611 m)
Yellow Sea
Ryukyu Islands
Euphrates
Tigris
Hindu Kush + Kunlun Mountains
Yellow (Huang)
Taiwan
Red Sea
Persian Gulf
Indus
Plateau of Tibet
Yangtze (Chang)
Gulf of Oman
H I M A L A Y A
TROPIC OF CANCER
Arabian Peninsula
Great Indian Desert
Ganges
Mt. Everest 29,035 ft (8,850 m) World's highest point
Brahmaputra
Salween
Mekong
Hainan
Luzon
Gulf of Aden
Arabian Sea
Gulf of Tonkin
South China Sea
Philippine Islands
AFRICA
Socotra
Deccan Plateau
Bay of Bengal
Indochina Peninsula
Mindanao
I n d i a n
Andaman Is.
Nicobar Is.
Andaman Sea
Gulf of Thailand
Maldive Islands
Sri Lanka
Malay Peninsula
O c e a n
Celebes (Sulawesi)
Arafura Sea
Sumatra
I N D O N E S I A
Moluccas
New Guinea
OCEANIA
EQUATOR
Borneo
Java Sea
Java
AUSTRALIA
Pacific Ocean

0 — 800 MILES
0 — 800 KILOMETERS
Two-point Equidistant Projection

3 STONE FOREST
China

Near the city of Kunming are lots of limestone pillars. They were formed over millions of years as underlying rock was dissolved by groundwater. Winds blowing around the pillars and through local caves make eerie sounds.

4 CHOCOLATE HILLS
Philippines

There are at least 1,260 nearly identical brown hills on the island of Bohol, Philippines. Legend says they were made when two giants threw sand and stones at each other.

FROM ARCTIC TO EQUATOR

Hot, cold, wet, and DANGEROUS

When a continent stretches from a polar region to the Equator, you are going to find a huge variety of climates. Asia has extreme weather, including drenching monsoons in India and monster typhoons in the Philippines. Weather conditions can change in a heartbeat, setting off an avalanche down a mountainside or wiping out villages in a rainstorm.

DIGITAL TRAVELER!
Monster sandstorms can hit Saudi Arabia and cover its cities with darkness and sand. Go online to search for a video of a recent sandstorm in Saudi Arabia.

ADVENTURE ATTRACTIONS

LAND OF MONSOONS
Monsoons are winds that blow over the northern part of the Indian Ocean. In the summer, they bring drenching rain. Monsoon rains can wash away soil in monstrous floods.

RAGING RIVER
When the tide comes in on the Qiantang River in China, it can create the Silver Dragon—waves that can reach 29 feet (8.8 m) moving at a speed of 25 miles an hour (40 kph). Surfers come from all over the world to try to ride these waves.

UFOS OVER THE MOUNTAINS?
They look like unidentified flying objects from outer space. But they are really disk-shaped clouds called lenticular clouds that form over Nepal's Annapurna mountain and other towering peaks.

EXTREME CLIMATES HERE

1 BONE-CHILLING CITY
Russia

Yakutsk in Siberia is called the Coldest City on Earth. Winter temperatures drop below -70°F (-56.7°C). Plumbing pipes freeze, so most toilets are outhouses. People leave their cars running while they are parked. Otherwise the engines freeze, and the cars won't restart.

2 AVALANCHE!
Himalaya

An avalanche—a tumbling mass of snow and ice—is deadly as it barrels down a mountain. It can bury everything in its path. In April 2014, an avalanche on Mount Everest killed 16 mountain climbers and injured 9.

NORTH AMERICA

Arctic Ocean

MAP KEY

Climatic Zones: Based on Köppen System

Tropical
- Tropical wet
- Tropical dry

Dry
- Semiarid
- Arid

Mild
- Mediterranean
- Humid subtropical

Continental
- Warm summer
- Cool summer
- Subarctic

Polar
- Tundra

High Elevations
- Highlands

TSUNAMI HAZARD ZONE

พื้นที่เสี่ยงภัยคลื่นยักษ์

IN CASE OF EARTHQUAKE. GO TO HIGH GROUND OR INLAND

เมื่อเกิดแผ่นดินไหว ให้หนีขึ้นที่สูง
จากชายหาดและริมแม่น้ำโดยเร็ว

---

3 SIZZLING HEAT
Iran

The temperature in the Lut Desert is so hot that no creature can survive there. When a NASA satellite flew over the desert in 2005, it reported the hottest land surface temperature ever recorded: 159.3°F (70.7°C). That is hot enough to fry an egg!

---

4 RAINSTORMS
India

Heavy downpours fill rivers near Jammu, causing flooding. Homes are washed away, and fields of crops are destroyed. Neighboring regions of Pakistan suffer similar heavy rains.

---

5 KILLER WAVES
Thailand

People fear the deadly tsunamis that can follow an earthquake. In 2004, a 50-foot (15-m) wall of water rose out of the Indian Ocean at the speed of a jetliner, causing disasters in Indonesia, Sri Lanka, India, Thailand, and the Maldives.

STRANGE BUT TRUE

In 2009, people in Japan saw a rainstorm of frogs, tadpoles, and fish! No one is sure what caused the animals to fall from the sky. They may have been carried up by water spouts during a storm and then dumped out.

MOUNT EVEREST
Top of the WORLD

5 COOL PLACES TO SEE HERE

Risk-taking visitors fly over and ski down the slopes of Everest. Mountain climbers travel with local Sherpa guides.

Nepal China
Mount Everest

Pumori

Khumbu Glacier

Taboche

Ask extreme mountain climbers which mountain they would most like to climb and they will likely say, "Mount Everest!" Its summit, or highest point, is 29,035 feet (8,850 m) above sea level. Everest is part of the Himalaya. The safest months to climb are April and May, before monsoons soften the snow and create a greater risk of avalanches. The summit is snow-covered, and daytime temperatures may reach only -2°F (-19°C).

4 SHIFTING ICE
Khumbu Icefall

The icefall is a river of ice that forms at the head of Khumbu Glacier. As the glacier moves, huge gaps crack open in the ice. Sometimes parts of the icefall collapse, hurling blocks of ice toward climbers.

5 CAMP OF HOPES AND DREAMS
Base Camp

The Southern Face Base Camp is located 17,590 feet (5,361 m) above sea level. Climbers take eight to ten days to hike to the campsite. They spend a few days in tents here to get used to the altitude. Temperatures are freezing.

1 TOP OF THE WORLD!
Summit

The summit is so high that there is only one-third of the breathable oxygen that is at sea level. Climbers bring along bottles of oxygen to help them breathe. Winds can reach 100 miles an hour (161 kph). Most climbers head back down after about half an hour.

Mount Everest

Hillary Step

Knife Ridge

Lhotse

Nuptse

Scale varies in this perspective.

ASIA

Lhotse Glacier

Ama Dablam

Imja Khola Valley

DIGITAL TRAVELER!
Use your digital device to watch a video of climbers on Everest. What is most exciting to you?

2 A MOUNTAIN RIVER
Dudh Kosi

The Dudh Kosi River flows at the foot of Mount Everest at a wild and dangerous pace. Only daredevil boaters try to kayak through its waterfalls, whirlpools, and huge waves.

3 STEEP AND SCARY
Knife Ridge

Leading up to the summit are slippery ridges of snow and rock. Knife Ridge leads to the steep Hillary Step, named after Edmund Hillary who climbed this 40-foot (12-m) rock in 1953 without modern ropes.

71

ASIA'S ANIMAL HOMES

Jungles, caves, and MOUNTAINTOPS

5 COOL PLACES TO SEE HERE

You will find a huge variety of plants and animals throughout Asia. Each lives in a habitat that encourages its growth. These habitats range from high mountain cliffs, where snow leopards prowl, to grasslands and human-made animal sanctuaries that help elephants survive. Many of these habitats have become national parks and preserves. This helps save the plants and animals from extinction.

1 MOUNTAIN FOOTHILLS
India

Some of the world's most endangered animals live in the foothills of the Himalaya. The Manas Wildlife Sanctuary protects them. The animals include the one-horned rhinoceros, pygmy hog, elephant, sloth bear, and Bengal florican (a large, rare bird).

ADVENTURE ATTRACTIONS

GIANT WATER RESERVOIR
Minneriya tank in Sri Lanka is a lake that does not completely dry up in the very dry summers. More than 200 elephants gather here to drink their fill of water and graze on grass.

OLD TROPICAL JUNGLE
The jungle of Taman Negara National Park in Malaysia grew over hundreds of millions of years. Walk through the tree-tops across a long, swaying bridge to see some of the park's 300 species of birds.

TIGER FORESTS
Endangered tigers, fishing cats, and spotted deer live in the Sundarbans mangrove forests of Bangladesh.

2 WILDLIFE RESERVOIR
United Arab Emirates

The Dubai Desert Conservation Reserve protects animals and plants of the Arabian Desert. This desert habitat is home to the Arabian oryx—seen here with their long, curved horns—and sand gazelle. Both are types of antelope.

STRANGE BUT TRUE

Giant squid live deep in the Pacific Ocean off Asia. In 2012, three researchers went down in a submarine and waited for 400 hours. They finally saw a 43-foot (13-m) squid at a depth of 2,953 feet (900 m).

DIGITAL TRAVELER!
Search the Internet to find photos of ten animals that live in the Gobi. Print the pictures and arrange the animals by size.

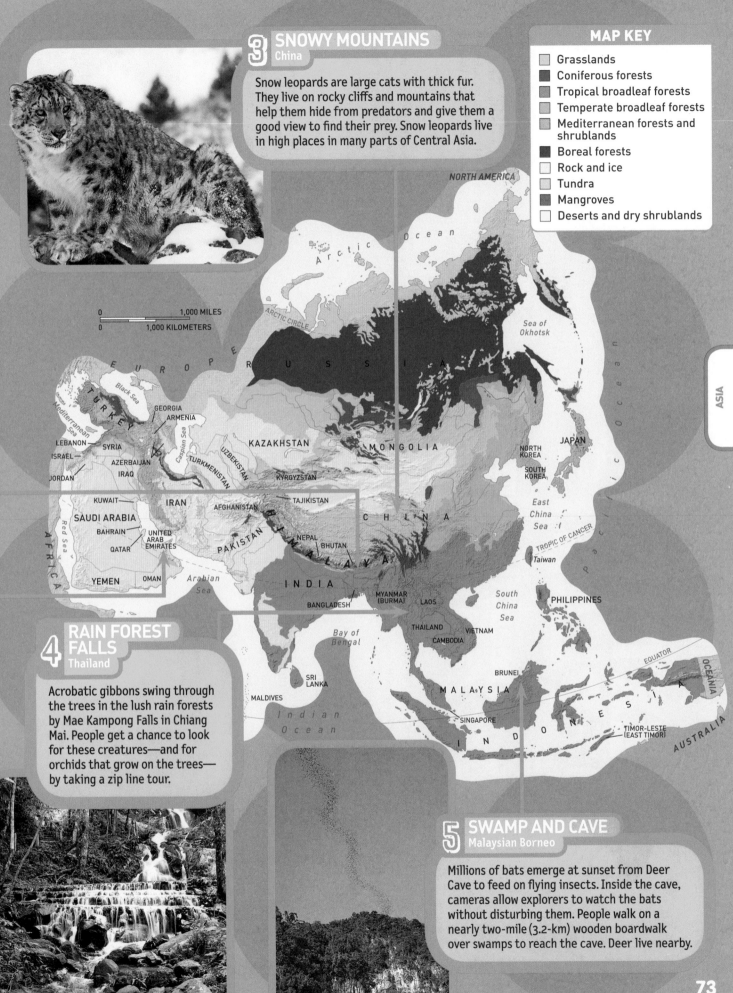

③ SNOWY MOUNTAINS
China

Snow leopards are large cats with thick fur. They live on rocky cliffs and mountains that help them hide from predators and give them a good view to find their prey. Snow leopards live in high places in many parts of Central Asia.

MAP KEY

- Grasslands
- Coniferous forests
- Tropical broadleaf forests
- Temperate broadleaf forests
- Mediterranean forests and shrublands
- Boreal forests
- Rock and ice
- Tundra
- Mangroves
- Deserts and dry shrublands

1,000 MILES
1,000 KILOMETERS

NORTH AMERICA

ASIA

Arctic Ocean

ARCTIC CIRCLE

E U R O P E

Black Sea

TURKEY

Mediterranean Sea

GEORGIA
ARMENIA

LEBANON
SYRIA
ISRAEL
AZERBAIJAN
JORDAN
IRAQ

Caspian Sea

KAZAKHSTAN

R U S S I A

M O N G O L I A

Sea of Okhotsk

NORTH KOREA

SOUTH KOREA

JAPAN

East China Sea

Pacific Ocean

UZBEKISTAN

TURKMENISTAN

KYRGYZSTAN

KUWAIT
SAUDI ARABIA
BAHRAIN
QATAR
UNITED ARAB EMIRATES

IRAN

AFGHANISTAN

TAJIKISTAN

C H I N A

TROPIC OF CANCER

AFRICA

Red Sea

YEMEN
OMAN

PAKISTAN

Arabian Sea

NEPAL
BHUTAN

H I M A L A Y A

I N D I A

BANGLADESH

MYANMAR (BURMA)

LAOS

Taiwan

PHILIPPINES

South China Sea

④ RAIN FOREST FALLS
Thailand

Acrobatic gibbons swing through the trees in the lush rain forests by Mae Kampong Falls in Chiang Mai. People get a chance to look for these creatures—and for orchids that grow on the trees— by taking a zip line tour.

Bay of Bengal

THAILAND

VIETNAM

CAMBODIA

SRI LANKA

MALDIVES

Indian Ocean

BRUNEI

M A L A Y S I A

SINGAPORE

EQUATOR

I N D O N E S I A

OCEANIA

TIMOR-LESTE (EAST TIMOR)

AUSTRALIA

⑤ SWAMP AND CAVE
Malaysian Borneo

Millions of bats emerge at sunset from Deer Cave to feed on flying insects. Inside the cave, cameras allow explorers to watch the bats without disturbing them. People walk on a nearly two-mile (3.2-km) wooden boardwalk over swamps to reach the cave. Deer live nearby.

EXTREME PLANTS

Trees, flowers, and FUNGI

F ew plants can survive in Asia's far north. A little south of the Arctic, evergreen trees are valuable for lumber. Central Asia is dry and covered mostly with grasses. Southeast Asia is warm and humid, good for growing tall bamboo plants and rubber and teak trees. The deserts of the dry southwest provide date and olive trees. Many people in Asia farm the land, growing rice and wheat.

ADVENTURE ATTRACTIONS

HIGH-ALTITUDE MOSS
The moss that grows on Mount Everest may be the highest-growing plant on Earth. Scientists think a fungus in the moss could be used to help other plants withstand cold weather in other places.

BIG, SMELLY FLOWERS
The world's largest flower is the corpse lily (*Rafflesia arnoldii*), shown far left. It grows in Taba Penanjung Nature Reserve, a rain forest in Sumatra, Indonesia. The flower smells like rotting dead animals to attract flies for pollination.

FOREST MUSEUM
The Gwangneung Forest in South Korea was once a king's forest. It is now a protected arboretum. There are plant gardens, a seed bank, and a forest museum.

5 COOL PLANTS TO SEE HERE

1 GLOWING MUSHROOM
Japan

This glow-in-the-dark mushroom is the oldest known glowing fungus. It grows on rotting wood in Japan, Taiwan, Sri Lanka, and other subtropical places. The mushroom glows for a few days as its cap fully forms.

MAP KEY

Durian fruit tree

Bat flower

Kudzu

Date palm

Cherry blossom tree

1,000 MILES
1,000 KILOMETERS

5 FASTEST GROWING TREE
China

The empress tree is the fastest growing tree on Earth. It can grow as much as 12 inches (30 cm) in three weeks and more than 19 feet (5.7 m) during its first year.

4 RAINBOW EUCALYPTUS
Philippines

Growing from Indonesia to the Philippines, these trees could stop traffic! The bark is striped in bright colors. The tree's outer layer peels off and leaves a bright green layer. As that layer ages, it turns blue, purple, pink, and orange.

3 DRAGON'S BLOOD TREE
Yemen

This umbrella-shaped tree of the Socotra islands produces a red sap that was thought to be dragon's blood. The sap is used as a medicine and paint dye.

2 BLACK PEPPER PLANT
India

Black pepper, a popular spice, starts as dried fruit on pepper vines. It has many uses as medicine as well as for cooking.

DIGITAL TRAVELER!
The national flower of Jordan is the black iris. Go online and find a photo of this flower. Then pick another country in Asia and search for its national flower.

RECORD BREAKER

The longest avenue of trees is the 22-mile (35.41-km) Nikko Cryptomeria Avenue in the city of Imaichi, Japan. The Japanese cedar trees were planted in the 1600s. More than 13,500 of the original 200,000 are still standing.

ASIA

FANTASTIC ANIMALS

Extra-extra LARGE

5 COOL ANIMALS TO SEE HERE

Many of Asia's animals are super-size. The Asian elephant is one of Earth's biggest mammals. The tiger is the biggest cat. The reticulated python is one of the world's longest snakes. Even typically small creatures are king-size in Asia. You can find gigantic jellyfish, moths, hornets, salamanders, and lizards. But Asia's animals come in small sizes, too. The rivers are teeming with tiny sealife. Small birds, bats, and other creatures live in the rain forests.

MAP KEY

- Sunda flying lemur
- Green peafowl
- Reticulated python
- Himalayan jumping spider
- Firefly squid

EUROPE • RU

Mediterranean Sea • TURKEY • Black Sea • ARMENIA • GEORGIA • Caspian Sea

LEBANON • SYRIA • AZERBAIJAN • TURKMENISTAN • KAZAKHSTAN • UZBEKISTAN • KYRGYZSTAN

JORDAN • IRAQ • IRAN • AFGHANISTAN • TAJIKISTAN

ISRAEL • SAUDI ARABIA • KUWAIT • BAHRAIN • QATAR • UNITED ARAB EMIRATES • PAKISTAN • H I

YEMEN • OMAN • INDIA

AFRICA • Arabian Sea

I n d i a n • SRI LANKA • MALDIVES

0 _____ 1,000 MILES
0 _____ 1,000 KILOMETERS

DID YOU KNOW?

The ghost beetle of Southeast Asia looks whiter in color than any other animal. Not only are its scales white, they are also extremely thin, giving the beetle a ghostlike appearance.

1 SAND CAT
Saudi Arabia

About the size of a large domestic cat, the sand cat lives in sandy and stony deserts, such as those of the Arabian Peninsula. It lives in burrows—often those abandoned by foxes, gerbils, and porcupines. The sand cat preys on a variety of rodents and birds but will also eat lizards and insects.

DIGITAL TRAVELER!

There are two types of camel—the one-humped dromedary and the two-humped bactrian. Go online to find out where each type lives and what camels are used for.

② GIANT HORNET
China

The Asian giant hornet is the world's largest hornet. It grows to the size of a human thumb with a three-inch (7.6 cm) wingspan. Its sting can be deadly to people who are allergic to it. The hornets live throughout eastern Asia. In Taiwan, people call them "tiger heads."

BORNEO'S ANIMAL KINGDOM
Adventurers ride boats along the muddy Kinabatangan River in Malaysian Borneo to spy on crocodiles, pythons, and orangutans.

PARK OF TINY DRAGONS
About 5,700 fierce-looking lizards—called Komodo dragons—live in Komodo National Park in Indonesia. The lizards are voracious meat-eaters and grow to ten feet (3 m) long.

AMPHIBIAN BASE
The Western Ghats of India are a mountain range with a unique collection of frogs, toads, and salamanders. The rare purple frog feasts on termites, which it sucks out of the ground with its tongue.

ASIA

③ JAPANESE GIANT SALAMANDER
Japan

This large amphibian lives in the cold streams and rivers of western Japan, where its brown and black skin camouflages it in the mud. It can be five feet (1.5 m) long and weigh 55 pounds (25 kg). It uses sensory organs on its body to feel its way around.

④ MIMIC OCTOPUS
Indonesia

When the mimic octopus wants to avoid an attack from its predators, it changes its color and shape. It can copy the look of more than 15 dangerous animals, including a stingray and the poisonous banded sea snake.

⑤ CUDDLY MAMMAL
China

The giant panda is closely related to bears, but it is a plant-eater, feeding mainly on bamboo shoots. The panda is protected and cared for at Bifengxia Giant Panda Base in Sichuan Province, where there is open land for pandas to wander.

Map labels

NORTH AMERICA

Arctic Ocean

ARCTIC CIRCLE

R U S S I A

Sea of Okhotsk

MONGOLIA

NORTH KOREA

SOUTH KOREA

JAPAN

East China Sea

C H I N A

NEPAL

BHUTAN

HIMALAYA

BANGLADESH

MYANMAR (BURMA)

LAOS

THAILAND

CAMBODIA

VIETNAM

Taiwan

TROPIC OF CANCER

Pacific Ocean

South China Sea

PHILIPPINES

Gulf of Bengal

BRUNEI

M A L A Y S I A

SINGAPORE

EQUATOR

I N D O N E S I A

TIMOR-LESTE (EAST TIMOR)

OCEANIA

AUSTRALIA

Ocean

LAKE TOBA

Island within a VOLCANIC LAKE

ake Toba in Sumatra, Indonesia, was born from the largest supervolcanic eruption on Earth in the past 2.5 million years. About 74,000 years ago, Mount Toba spewed out 700 cubic miles (2,918 cu km) of magma, or hot, molten rock. Its volcanic ash traveled more than 4,350 miles (7,001 km). Lake Toba, the world's largest volcanic lake, was left behind.

True or False

The Lake Toba region is home to the rare Sumatran tiger. Which of these facts about tigers are true, and which are false? See page 149 for the answers.

A Tigers are endangered because of hunting and destruction of their forest homes by people.

B There are many tigers in zoos and about 15,000 left in the wild.

C An adult tiger can eat up to 100 pounds (45 kg) of meat at one meal.

D A newborn tiger weighs more than a gallon (3.8 l) of its mother milk.

E To help find its way in the dark, a tiger has whiskers on its head, legs, and body.

5 COOL PLACES TO SEE HERE

Lake Toba is so large that an island almost the size of Singapore sits in the middle of it. The lake banks and the island are covered in forest.

Lake Toba
Indonesia

1 KING'S TOMBS
Tomok

The village of Tomok is on Samosir Island. Long ago, highly respected kings ruled over the Sidabutar people. Today, adventurers visit tombs where it is believed the dead kings were placed inside stone sarcophagi.

2 LAKE INSIDE A LAKE
Lake Sidihoni

Samosir Island sits inside Lake Toba. Lake Sidihoni sits inside Samosir Island. The best way to get to Sidihoni is by motorbike on a rocky road. Then you can paraglide over the landscape.

DIGITAL TRAVELER!
The Batak people and their ancestors have lived at Lake Toba for thousands of years. Search the Internet for a sample of their traditional music and for photos of their traditional homes and costumes.

Sibayak
Volcano

Mt. Sibuaten

3 STONE CHAIR VILLAGE
Ambarita

Ambarita is an ancient tribal village on Samosir Island. Adventurers can hike or boat into the village to see a circle of stone chairs where tribal leaders once sat and judged the fate of captured enemies.

4 WATERFALL VIEWING
Tuk-tuk

From the village of Tuk-tuk there are great views of mountain waterfalls. With just a small amount of rain during the dry season, water creeps down the mountain. During the rainy season, waterfalls gush down and provide refreshing pools for swimming.

5 WATER ADVENTURES
Parapat

Adventurers can try all kinds of water activities, from motor boating, skiing, swimming, and canoeing to night fishing. Leisure activities include taking pedal-powered craft along the shoreline.

Singgalang Volcano

Lake Toba

Pasuhbuhit Volcano

R i m

Samosir Island

Sibandang Island

Lake Toba

C a l d e r a

C a l d e r a   R i m

Imun Volcano

Scale varies in this perspective.

ASIA

5 COOL THINGS TO DO HERE

1 ICE TREK
India

As the temperature drops to -13°F (-25°C), brave adventurers set up their tents beside the frozen Zanskar River. They will have a cold night's sleep and continue on their six-day trek along the river from Chilling to Nerak and back.

DID YOU KNOW?

The Bashkaus River in Russia's Siberia is one of the wildest rivers ever. It drops 32 feet each mile (9.8 m each 1.6 km)—four times the drop of the Colorado River in the Grand Canyon. Extreme kayakers must maneuver through jagged rocks, rapids, and traps called siphons.

MAP KEY

🔍 Adventure attraction

NORTH AMERICA

Arctic Ocean

ARCTIC CIRCLE

Sea of Okhotsk

R U S S I A

E U R O P E

Black Sea

TURKEY

GEORGIA
ARMENIA

Mediterranean Sea

LEBANON
SYRIA
ISRAEL
JORDAN
AZERBAIJAN
IRAQ

KAZAKHSTAN

UZBEKISTAN

MONGOLIA

Gobi

Gwangneung Forest

NORTH KOREA
SOUTH KOREA

JAPAN

Fan Mountains

TURKMENISTAN

KYRGYZSTAN

IRAN
KUWAIT
BAHRAIN

SAUDI ARABIA

QATAR
UNITED ARAB EMIRATES

TAJIKISTAN
AFGHANISTAN

K2

P A K I S T A N

H I M A L A Y A

Mt. Everest

NEPAL
BHUTAN

C H I N A

Qiantang River

East China Sea

Pacific Ocean

Himalaya

Annapurna

INDIA

BANGLADESH

Sundarbans N.P.

TROPIC OF CANCER

Taiwan

Red Sea

YEMEN
OMAN

AFRICA

Arabian Sea

Land of monsoons

MYANMAR (BURMA)

LAOS

South China Sea

PHILIPPINES

Western Ghats

THAILAND
VIETNAM

Puerto Princesa

Minneriya N.P.

Gulf of Bengal

CAMBODIA

SRI LANKA

MALDIVES

Taman Negara N.P.

BRUNEI

M A L A Y S I A

Kinabatangan River

EQUATOR

OCEANIA

Indian Ocean

Taba Penanjung Nature Reserve

SINGAPORE

I N D O N E S I A

Java

Komodo N.P.

TIMOR-LESTE (EAST TIMOR)

AUSTRALIA

0   1,000 MILES
0   1,000 KILOMETERS

2 DUNE BASHING
Qatar

What do you get when you try to drive a quadbike on a cruel stretch of desert? Adventurers call it an exciting day of dune bashing! Don't go alone. You may need someone to tow you out if you get stuck.

3 WASHING ELEPHANTS
Nepal

At wildlife sanctuaries, you can get down and dirty with elephants. Volunteers can feed, walk, and wash the animals, while learning about elephant conservation.

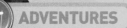

ADVENTURES

BOLD ADVENTURE

Facing down mountains, deserts, and RAPIDS

The world's largest continent offers supersize adventures. Vast deserts, deep gorges, and the highest mountains in the world provide all kinds of extreme activity. While most people may take bus tours or boat rides, extreme adventurers trek across frozen rivers, ride camels in a desert, swim with sharks and barracudas, hike up volcanoes, and more!

5 BASE JUMPING
Malaysia

Each year, 100 daredevils from about 20 countries go to Kuala Lumpur for a BASE jumping competition. In this heart-stopping sport, BASE jumpers leap from a 984-foot (300-m)-high platform with only seconds to release their parachutes.

4 CLIMBING THE TOWERS
Pakistan

Free climbers face 20,000 feet (6,096 m) of vertical rock on Trango Towers in the Himalaya. They use only the tower's natural crevices to help them climb—no ladders allowed. They sleep in hanging tents.

ADVENTURE ATTRACTIONS

ASIA

RING OF FIRE
The island of Java has 42 volcanoes. Climbers hike up these mountains, peer into craters, and soak in hot springs within this Ring of Fire.

SKIING K2
Set between China and Pakistan, K2 is the world's second tallest mountain. Daring skiers face fierce winds and avalanches as they climb to the summit and attempt to ski down.

MYSTERIOUS UNDER-GROUND RIVER
Ride a boat through the world's longest navigable underground river. It is located in Puerto Princesa, Philippines. Wear a raincoat to protect your clothes from bat droppings.

DIGITAL TRAVELER!
Once a year, adventurers drive across northern India in tuk-tuks. These are surprisingly weak vehicles for this expedition. They encounter monsoon rains, jungle tracks, and sand. Search the Internet for details of the Rickshaw Run.

AFRICA

A mighty GIANT

Africa, the second largest continent, stretches 4,600 miles (7,400 km) east to west and 5,000 miles (8,047 km) north to south. The north features the desert countries of Algeria, Libya, Egypt, and Sudan. Central Africa includes Guinea, Ghana, and Nigeria in the west and South Sudan and Ethiopia in the east. Eastern Africa is dominated by the wildlife-rich countries of Kenya, Tanzania, and Uganda. Southern Africa includes Namibia, Zambia, and Botswana. Africa also includes the islands of Cabo Verde (Cape Verde) in the west and Madagascar and the Seychelles in the east.

AUNT BERTHA'S ADVENTURE TRAVEL TIPS

Most of Africa is hot. Wear lightweight clothes. Keep cool by wetting a bandana and wearing it as a scarf.

Go on safari to see the world's greatest concentration of animals. The open savanna is great for wildlife viewing.

Lunch in Africa is often the heaviest meal of the day. Look for dishes made from cassava, yams, and plantains. For dessert, try fermented goat milk or fresh tropical fruits.

In rural areas, tribal people can be seen wearing traditional clothes. These are women of the Hamar tribe in Ethiopia.

ADVENTURE HOT SPOTS

LANDFORMS
The Sahara is home to the Grand Erg Oriental, a large area filled with giant star-shaped dunes.

CLIMATES
The scorching hot ghost town of Dallol, Ethiopia, averages 94°F (34.4°C) during the day.

NGORONGORO CRATER
Explore the rim of one of the world's largest calderas. Keep watch and on guard for leopards and cheetahs.

20°N

HABITATS
Migrating savanna animals graze the grasses in Tanzania's Serengeti National Park and drink from its watering holes.

PLANTS
The Nile River and desert oases, the lifelines of Egypt, are flanked by palm trees, many of them producing dates.

ANIMALS
Go on safari in the Central Kalahari Game Reserve in Botswana. Count how many African lions you see.

MOUNT KILIMANJARO
Scale the Kibo summit. Of the mountain's three volcanoes, Kibo is the only one that is still active.

ADVENTURES
Dive off Zanzibar's Pemba Island. Untouched coral reefs make the island one of the top dive sites in the world.

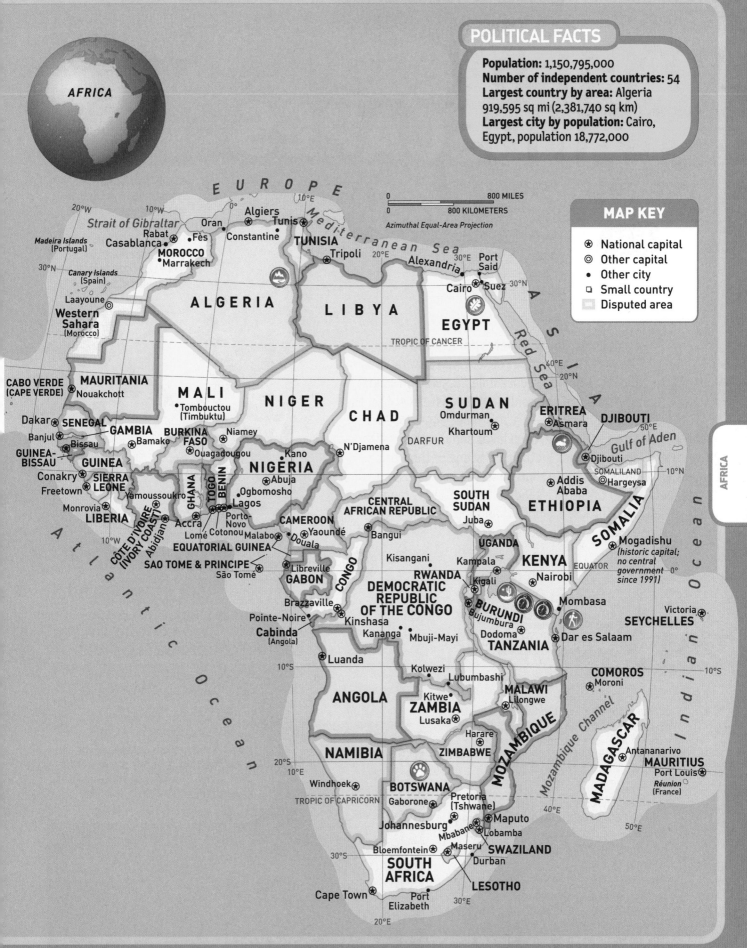

POLITICAL FACTS

Population: 1,150,795,000
Number of independent countries: 54
Largest country by area: Algeria
919,595 sq mi (2,381,740 sq km)
Largest city by population: Cairo,
Egypt, population 18,772,000

MAP KEY

⊛ National capital
◎ Other capital
• Other city
□ Small country
▢ Disputed area

0   800 MILES
0   800 KILOMETERS
Azimuthal Equal-Area Projection

EUROPE

Strait of Gibraltar
Madeira Islands (Portugal)
Algiers
Oran
Rabat
Casablanca
Fès
Constantine
Tunis
TUNISIA
Tripoli
Mediterranean Sea

Canary Islands (Spain)
MOROCCO
Marrakech
Laayoune
Western Sahara (Morocco)

ALGERIA
LIBYA

Alexandria
Port Said
Cairo
Suez
EGYPT
TROPIC OF CANCER

Red Sea
ASIA

CABO VERDE (CAPE VERDE)
MAURITANIA
Nouakchott
MALI
Tombouctou (Timbuktu)
NIGER
CHAD
SUDAN
Omdurman
Khartoum
ERITREA
Asmara
DJIBOUTI
Gulf of Aden
Djibouti

Dakar
SENEGAL
Banjul
GAMBIA
Bissau
GUINEA-BISSAU
GUINEA
Conakry
Freetown
SIERRA LEONE
Monrovia
LIBERIA
Bamako
BURKINA FASO
Niamey
Ouagadougou
Kano
NIGERIA
Abuja
Ogbomosho
Lagos
BENIN
TOGO
GHANA
Yamoussoukro
Accra
Lomé
Porto-Novo
Cotonou
CÔTE D'IVOIRE (IVORY COAST)
Abidjan
N'Djamena
DARFUR
CENTRAL AFRICAN REPUBLIC
SOUTH SUDAN
Juba
Addis Ababa
ETHIOPIA
SOMALILAND
Hargeysa

Atlantic Ocean

CAMEROON
Malabo
Yaoundé
Douala
EQUATORIAL GUINEA
SAO TOME & PRINCIPE
São Tomé
Libreville
GABON
CONGO
Bangui
Kisangani
UGANDA
Kampala
KENYA
Nairobi
Mombasa
SOMALIA
Mogadishu (historic capital; no central government since 1991)
EQUATOR
SEYCHELLES
Victoria

DEMOCRATIC REPUBLIC OF THE CONGO
RWANDA
Kigali
BURUNDI
Bujumbura
Brazzaville
Pointe-Noire
Kinshasa
Cabinda (Angola)
Kananga
Mbuji-Mayi
Dodoma
Dar es Salaam
TANZANIA

Luanda
Kolwezi
Lubumbashi
COMOROS
Moroni

ANGOLA
Kitwe
ZAMBIA
Lusaka
MALAWI
Lilongwe
MOZAMBIQUE
Mozambique Channel
MADAGASCAR
Antananarivo
MAURITIUS
Port Louis
Réunion (France)

Harare
NAMIBIA
Windhoek
ZIMBABWE
BOTSWANA
Gaborone
Pretoria (Tshwane)
Maputo
Johannesburg
Mbabane
Lobamba
SWAZILAND
Bloemfontein
Maseru
LESOTHO
Durban
SOUTH AFRICA
Cape Town
Port Elizabeth
TROPIC OF CAPRICORN

Indian Ocean

LANDFORMS

VARIED LANDSCAPES

Lava lakes to WATERFALLS

5 COOL PLACES TO SEE HERE

1 SPECTACULAR GORGE
Morocco

In the High Atlas Mountains, a hiking trail winds through a narrow gorge. In places, the steep walls measure just 33 feet (10 m) apart but tower more than 500 feet (152 m) tall on either side.

D esert landscape dominates northern Africa. The world's largest hot desert, the Sahara, covers about 3.3 million square miles (8.5 million sq km)—25 percent of the continent. In eastern Africa, the Great Rift Valley—a 3,700-mile (5,955-km)-deep trench—is dotted with large, deep lakes and massive volcanoes. In southern Africa rumbles Victoria Falls, one of the world's largest waterfalls. It is more than 1 mile (1.6 km) across and up to 351 feet (107 m) tall. Africa's Indian Ocean islands range from massive, hilly Madagascar to more than 120 small tropical islands with sandy beaches.

ADVENTURE ATTRACTIONS

STRANGE BUT TRUE

Africa is slowly splitting apart along the Great Rift Valley. As two plates of Earth's crust tear apart, the valley floor sinks lower. The area features hot springs, geysers, and frequent earthquakes.

WINDING RIVER
Africa's longest river, the Nile, flows south to north 4,400 miles (7,081 km). Sail the river in a felucca, a traditional Egyptian wooden sailing boat.

GREAT LAKE
Lake Tanganyika is the longest freshwater lake in the world—420 miles (676 km)—and the second deepest, with a maximum depth of 4,710 feet (1,436 m).

DESERT SCULPTURES
Peer at mushroom-shaped rock formations in the White Desert of Egypt. The limestone has been worn away by blowing winds and blasting sand.

5 VIOLENT VOLCANO
Democratic Republic of Congo

Mount Nyiragongo is a towering volcano 11,382 feet (3,469 m) tall. It is one of the most active volcanoes on the planet and home to the most violent lava lake.

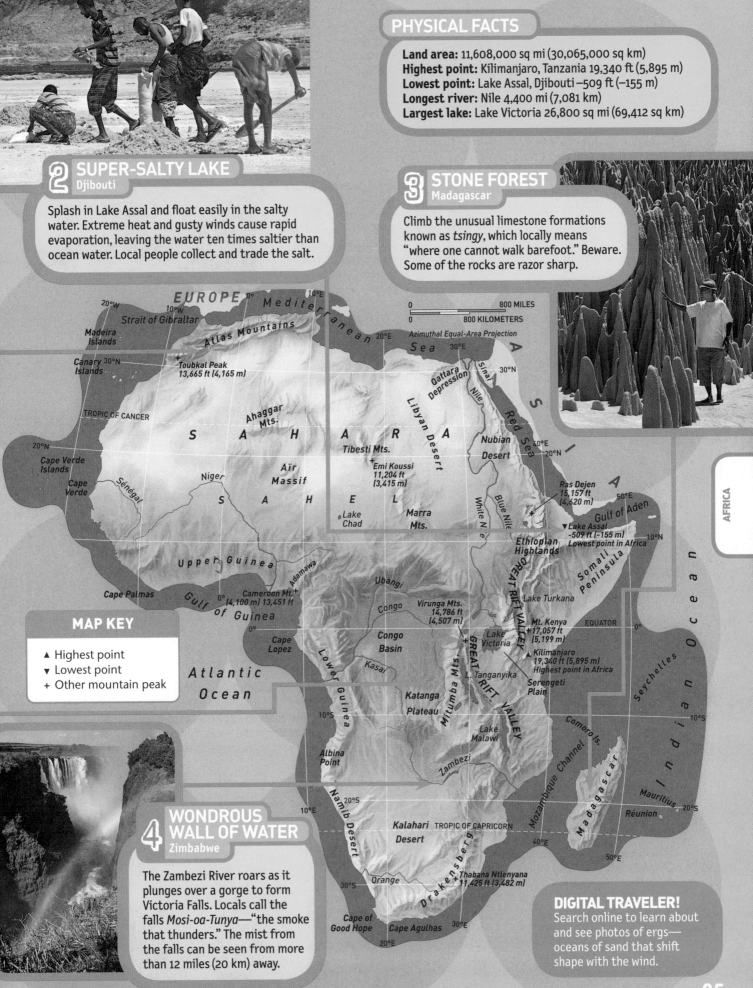

PHYSICAL FACTS

Land area: 11,608,000 sq mi (30,065,000 sq km)
Highest point: Kilimanjaro, Tanzania 19,340 ft (5,895 m)
Lowest point: Lake Assal, Djibouti −509 ft (−155 m)
Longest river: Nile 4,400 mi (7,081 km)
Largest lake: Lake Victoria 26,800 sq mi (69,412 sq km)

2 SUPER-SALTY LAKE
Djibouti

Splash in Lake Assal and float easily in the salty water. Extreme heat and gusty winds cause rapid evaporation, leaving the water ten times saltier than ocean water. Local people collect and trade the salt.

3 STONE FOREST
Madagascar

Climb the unusual limestone formations known as *tsingy*, which locally means "where one cannot walk barefoot." Beware. Some of the rocks are razor sharp.

MAP KEY

▲ Highest point
▼ Lowest point
+ Other mountain peak

4 WONDROUS WALL OF WATER
Zimbabwe

The Zambezi River roars as it plunges over a gorge to form Victoria Falls. Locals call the falls *Mosi-oa-Tunya*—"the smoke that thunders." The mist from the falls can be seen from more than 12 miles (20 km) away.

DIGITAL TRAVELER!
Search online to learn about and see photos of ergs—oceans of sand that shift shape with the wind.

AFRICA

Map labels: EUROPE, Strait of Gibraltar, Madeira Islands, Atlas Mountains, Mediterranean Sea, Toubkal Peak 13,665 ft (4,165 m), Canary Islands, TROPIC OF CANCER, Ahaggar Mts., SAHARA, Libyan Desert, Qattara Depression, Sinai, Nile, Red Sea, Cape Verde Islands, Tibesti Mts., Aïr Massif, Emi Koussi 11,204 ft (3,415 m), Nubian Desert, Ras Dejen 15,157 ft (4,620 m), Cape Verde, Sénégal, Niger, SAHEL, Lake Chad, Marra Mts., White Nile, Blue Nile, Gulf of Aden, Lake Assal −509 ft (−155 m) Lowest point in Africa, Somali Peninsula, Upper Guinea, Ethiopian Highlands, Cape Palmas, Gulf of Guinea, Adamawa, Cameroon Mt. (4,100 m) 13,451 ft, Ubangi, Congo, Virunga Mts. 14,786 ft (4,507 m), Lake Turkana, Mt. Kenya 17,057 ft (5,199 m), EQUATOR, Cape Lopez, Congo Basin, Lake Victoria, Kilimanjaro 19,340 ft (5,895 m) Highest point in Africa, Atlantic Ocean, Lower Guinea, Kasai, Katanga Plateau, Mitumba Mts., GREAT RIFT VALLEY, L. Tanganyika, Serengeti Plain, Albina Point, Lake Malawi, Seychelles, Comoro Is., Namib Desert, Zambezi, Kalahari Desert, TROPIC OF CAPRICORN, Drakensberg, Mozambique Channel, Madagascar, Indian Ocean, Mauritius, Réunion, Orange, Thabana Ntlenyana 11,425 ft (3,482 m), Cape of Good Hope, Cape Agulhas

Scale: 800 MILES / 800 KILOMETERS, Azimuthal Equal-Area Projection

85

5 EXTREME CLIMATES HERE

RECORD BREAKER

In 1922, a temperature of more than 122°F (50°C) was recorded at El Azizia in present-day Libya. It was thought to be the world's hottest weather temperature until experts realized the temperature was inaccurately recorded. Furnace Creek Ranch in California, U.S.A, holds the record at 134°F (56.7°C).

1 DUST DEVIL
Morocco

Whirlwinds can create spinning columns of sand in the Sahara. Grab your camera for a good shot, but keep your distance. The stinging sand is painful.

MAP KEY

Climatic Zones: Based on Köppen System

Tropical
- Tropical wet
- Tropical dry

Mild
- Marine west coast
- Mediterranean
- Humid subtropical

Dry
- Semiarid
- Arid

High Elevations
- Highlands
- Uplands

5 SUN BLOCK
Cameroon

Forest areas around Mount Cameroon typically receive 400 inches (1,016 cm) of rain a year. They are frequently shrouded in mist. The high mountain blocks the clouds from moving on.

ADVENTURE ATTRACTIONS

MOON BOW

At Victoria Falls, for three days around the full moon during the high-water season, a rainbow appears in the night sky. Adventurers trek to the falls to see it.

DUSTY DESERT

Hot, dry winds blow across the Sahara in fall and winter, carrying large amounts of dust. The dust interferes with air travel and settles on the decks of ships at sea.

FIERY GRASSLAND

In the East African savanna, monsoon winds bring rains in the wet season. Then the hot sun comes out and dries the earth quickly.

4 LIGHTNING HOT SPOT
Rwanda

This central African country is a hotspot for lightning. In the town of Kamembe, more lightning strikes the ground each year than anywhere else on Earth.

Map labels: EUROP, 20°W, 10°W, 0°, Strait of Gibraltar, 30°N, MOROCCO, ALGERIA, Western Sahara (Morocco), S A H, TROPIC OF CANCER, MAURITANIA, NI, CAPE VERDE, GAMBIA, 20°W, SENEGAL, M A A, NI, GUINEA-BISSAU, GUINEA, BURKINA FASO, SIERRA LEONE, CÔTE D'IVOIRE (IVORY COAST), GHANA, BENIN, NIGE, LIBERIA, TOGO, Atlantic Ocean, 0°, EQUATORIAL GUINEA, SAO TOME & PRINCIPE

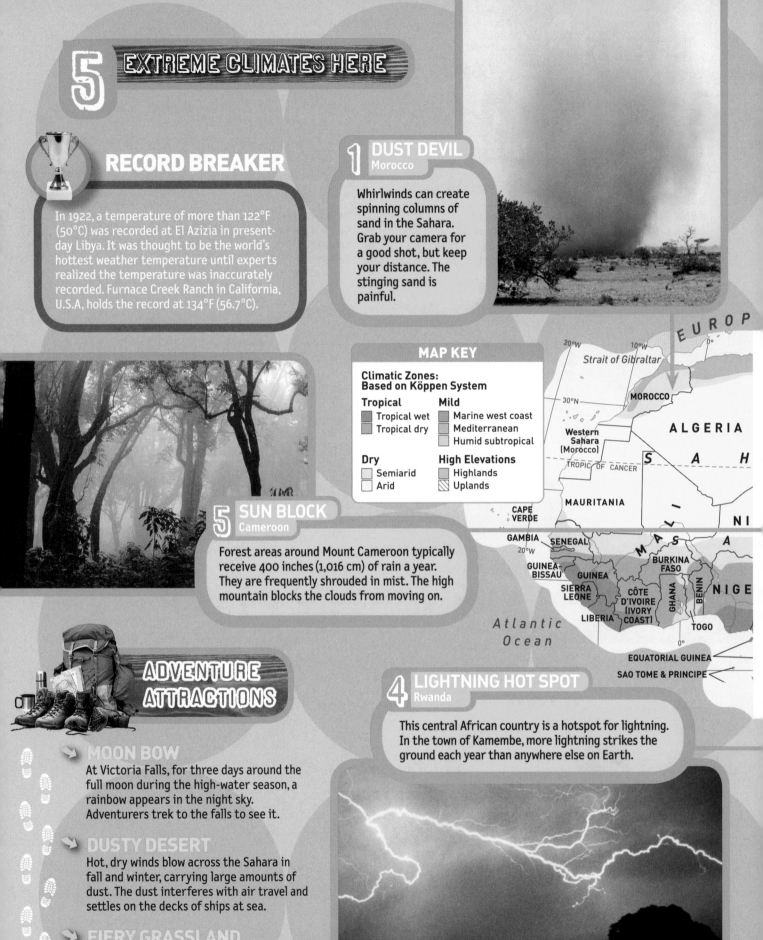

WILD WEATHER

Rain, drought, and MONSOONS

2 SKELETON COAST
Namibia

Wind whips off the ocean and hits desert heat, creating a belt of thick fog. Ships ran aground in the fog and remains of shipwrecks litter the shore.

Adventurers traveling through Africa notice bands of climate spanning the continent. In the north, along the Mediterranean coast, is a band of very warm climate. South of this is a huge band of hot desert conditions. Next is a band of semidry climate, with distinct wet and dry seasons. In the middle, along the Equator, is a hot and wet tropical climate that can receive more than 157 inches (399 cm) of rain each year. South of the Equator, the climate mirrors that to the north. The bands repeat all the way to the continent's southern tip. The island of Madagascar has a climate with two seasons: hot and rainy from November to April and cooler and dry from May to October.

3 ANCIENT DESERT
Namibia

No surface water can be found in the Namib Desert, the oldest desert in the world. The land has been dry for at least 55 million years!

AFRICA

Map Labels

TUNISIA
LIBYA
EGYPT
ARA
GER
HEL
CHAD
SUDAN
ERITREA
DJIBOUTI
RIA
CAMEROON
CENTRAL AFRICAN REPUBLIC
SOUTH SUDAN
ETHIOPIA
SOMALIA
GABON
Congo
Congo Basin
RWANDA
UGANDA
KENYA
DEMOCRATIC REPUBLIC OF THE CONGO
BURUNDI
Cabinda (Angola)
TANZANIA
SEYCHELLES
ANGOLA
COMOROS
MALAWI
ZAMBIA
MOZAMBIQUE
Mozambique Channel
MADAGASCAR
NAMIBIA
ZIMBABWE
MAURITIUS
Namib Desert
BOTSWANA
Kalahari Desert
SWAZILAND
LESOTHO
SOUTH AFRICA

Mediterranean Sea
Red Sea
ASIA
Gulf of Aden
Indian Ocean
EQUATOR
TROPIC OF CAPRICORN

0   800 MILES
0   800 KILOMETERS

10°E 20°E 30°E 40°E 50°E
20°N 10°N 0° 10°S 20°S 30°S

DIGITAL TRAVELER!
The southern part of Bioko Island, Equatorial Guinea, may be the wettest place in Africa. Do an Internet search to see if you can figure out how much rain falls there. How does it compare to rainfall where you live?

NGORONGORO CRATER

Natural WONDER

Welcome to one of the greatest natural wonders on the planet. Ngorongoro is one of the world's largest calderas—craters formed by the explosion and collapse of volcanoes. The jaw-dropping crater is home to more than 25,000 large animals and the world's densest population of lions. Nearby is the famous Olduvai Gorge. The steep-sided, 8.6-mile (13.8-km)-long ravine is an important archaeological site and the source of some of the earliest signs of ancient humans.

Ngorongoro Crater
Tanzania
A F R I C A

5 COOL PLACES TO SEE HERE

Adventurers visiting the crater region often stop at villages of the local Maasai people. There they try milking Maasai cattle, collecting firewood, and learning how to track animals. They can also buy Maasai craftwork.

1 COLOSSAL CRATER
Crater Rim

Drive or climb up the steep slopes of Ngorongoro. Stand on the crater rim and catch the view. The 14-mile (22.5-km)-wide crater formed when a giant volcano exploded and collapsed on itself about 2.5 million years ago.

2 SHIFTING SANDS
Olduvai Gorge

Visit an enormous black sand dune. Thirty feet (9 m) high and 328 feet (100 m) along its curve, the crescent-shaped dune is made of volcanic ash. The dune is slowly being blown westward but always maintains its perfect shape.

Scale varies in this perspective.

3 ACTIVE VOLCANO
Ol Doinyo Lengai

The Maasai name Ol Doinyo Lengai means "Mountain of God." Climb the active volcano as it rises 6,000 feet (1,829 m) above the valley floor. The volcano erupted as recently as 2013.

4 PREHISTORIC GORGE
Olduvai Gorge

See and touch a huge cast of fossilized human footprints at the Olduvai Gorge Museum. The famous footprints, preserved in volcanic rock for 3.6 million years, are some of the earliest signs of ancient humans in the world.

5 PINK, FEATHERED LAKE
Lake Makat

Drive in a four-wheeler to the crater floor and visit the lake in the middle of the crater. Thousands of pink flamingos wade in the water, and wildebeests come to drink. Be sure to keep a lookout for lions.

Ol Doinyo Lengai

Embulbul

Embagai Crater

Olmoti Crater

Ngorongoro Crater

Lake Makat

Oldeani

Olduvai Gorge

N

89

VAST AND VARIED

From sunny grasslands to scorching DESERTS

5 COOL PLACES TO SEE HERE

Africa contains many different habitats. Most habitats are tropical—the result of a warm climate. In the rain forests, vines hang overhead and thick tree canopies filter the sunlight. Adventurers can lose themselves in the lush greenery as they watch for quiet animals in the shadows. On the wide Serengeti, the tropical grassland is dotted with trees, waterholes, and riverbeds. Many large animals live out in the open. Africa's deserts, mountains, coasts, and islands give homes to more amazing plants and animals.

ADVENTURE ATTRACTIONS

WILD GRASSLAND
In the Masai Mara National Reserve in Kenya, millions of hungry wildebeests arrive each year to graze on the nutrient-rich grasses.

MOUNTAIN WILDERNESS
The dry woodlands and scratchy shrublands of the Ahaggar Mountains of Algeria are home to fast cheetahs, leaping gazelles, and woolly Barbary sheep.

RED SEA REEFS
The Red Sea is fringed with coral reefs. Colorful fish, playful dolphins, and graceful turtles swim here.

5 SERENGETI PLAIN
Tanzania

Savanna landscape has a variety of wild habitats, from swamps to grasslands to thick bush. Trees provide homes, shelter, and food for many animals large and small.

CAPE VERDE

4 BAT HAVEN
Zambia

In Kasanka National Park, you'll find a swamp forest filled with wild mangoes. The tasty fruits are food for millions of flapping bats that migrate through the park in November.

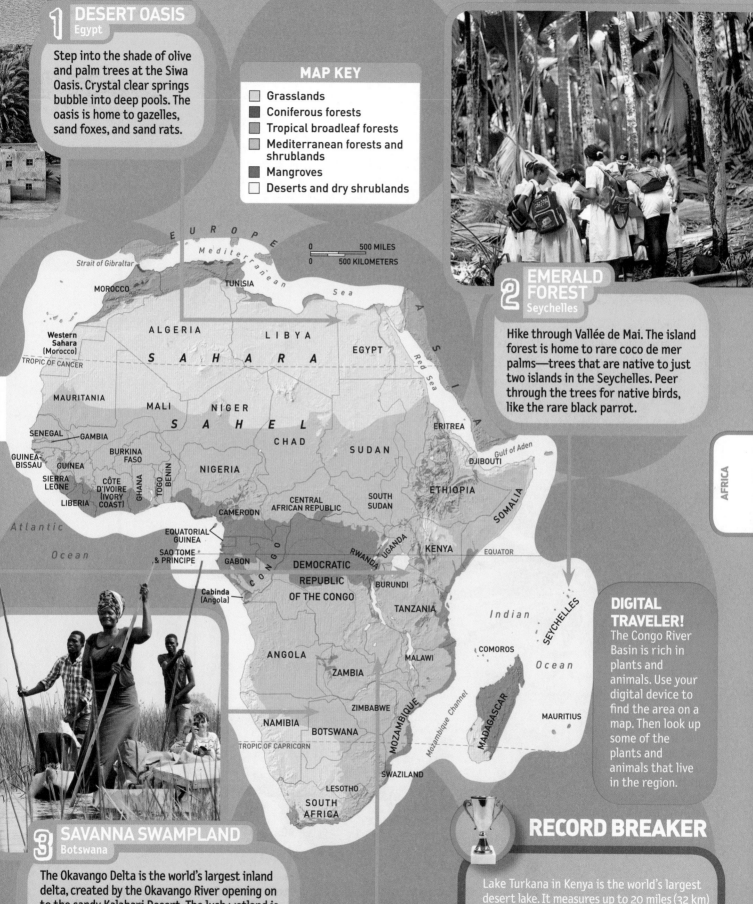

1 DESERT OASIS
Egypt

Step into the shade of olive and palm trees at the Siwa Oasis. Crystal clear springs bubble into deep pools. The oasis is home to gazelles, sand foxes, and sand rats.

MAP KEY

- ☐ Grasslands
- ■ Coniferous forests
- ■ Tropical broadleaf forests
- ☐ Mediterranean forests and shrublands
- ■ Mangroves
- ☐ Deserts and dry shrublands

E U R O P E
Mediterranean Sea

0   500 MILES
0   500 KILOMETERS

Strait of Gibraltar

MOROCCO   TUNISIA

Western Sahara (Morocco)

ALGERIA   LIBYA   EGYPT

TROPIC OF CANCER

S A H A R A

MAURITANIA

MALI   NIGER

S A H E L

SENEGAL   GAMBIA

CHAD

GUINEA-BISSAU   GUINEA   BURKINA FASO

SIERRA LEONE   CÔTE D'IVOIRE (IVORY COAST)   GHANA   TOGO   BENIN

LIBERIA

NIGERIA

CAMEROON   CENTRAL AFRICAN REPUBLIC

SUDAN

SOUTH SUDAN

ERITREA

DJIBOUTI   Gulf of Aden

ETHIOPIA   SOMALIA

Red Sea

EQUATORIAL GUINEA

SAO TOME & PRINCIPE   GABON

Congo

RWANDA   UGANDA

KENYA   EQUATOR

Cabinda (Angola)

DEMOCRATIC REPUBLIC OF THE CONGO

BURUNDI

TANZANIA

Atlantic Ocean

ANGOLA

ZAMBIA

MALAWI

Indian Ocean

SEYCHELLES

COMOROS

MAURITIUS

ZIMBABWE

NAMIBIA   BOTSWANA

MOZAMBIQUE   Mozambique Channel   MADAGASCAR

TROPIC OF CAPRICORN

SWAZILAND

LESOTHO

SOUTH AFRICA

AFRICA

2 EMERALD FOREST
Seychelles

Hike through Vallée de Mai. The island forest is home to rare coco de mer palms—trees that are native to just two islands in the Seychelles. Peer through the trees for native birds, like the rare black parrot.

DIGITAL TRAVELER!

The Congo River Basin is rich in plants and animals. Use your digital device to find the area on a map. Then look up some of the plants and animals that live in the region.

3 SAVANNA SWAMPLAND
Botswana

The Okavango Delta is the world's largest inland delta, created by the Okavango River opening on to the sandy Kalahari Desert. The lush wetland is at odds with the dry climate and attracts thirsty birds, hippos, elephants, and lions.

RECORD BREAKER

Lake Turkana in Kenya is the world's largest desert lake. It measures up to 20 miles (32 km) wide and 180 miles (290 km) long. Hippos and crocodiles live in or near its salty water.

91

ADVENTURE ATTRACTIONS

COOL PLANTS TO SEE HERE

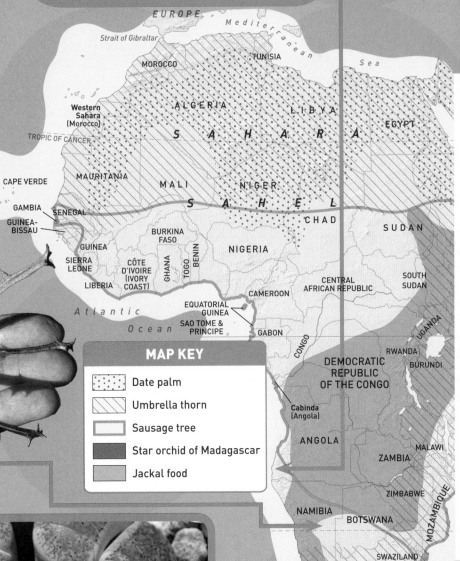

▸ WILDFLOWER WONDERLAND

After the winter rainfall, the dusty valleys of Namaqualand in South Africa are transformed by an explosion of wildflowers that carpet the countryside.

▸ CLOUD FORESTS

The forests in the Mgahinga Gorilla National Park, Uganda, grow thick with bamboo, a key food for mountain gorillas and rare African golden monkeys.

▸ FIRE BUSH

In the dry shrublands of South Africa grows the beautiful sugarbush. Its tough seeds don't sprout until they have been scorched by fire.

1 LONG, LEATHERY LEAVES
Angola

The tree tumbo can live for more than 1,000 years in the desert, drawing moisture from fog and dew. Two ragged leaves grow throughout the plant's life. The leaves can reach more than 20 feet (6 m) long.

MAP KEY

- ⬚ Date palm
- ⧄ Umbrella thorn
- ▭ Sausage tree
- ■ Star orchid of Madagascar
- ▢ Jackal food

5 DEVIL'S CLAW
Namibia

Tread with care near the devil's claw. Its spiny fruits hook on to passing animals and inflict great pain. Yet, devil's claw is also an important medicinal plant.

4 STONE PLANT
South Africa

Stone plants stay alive by trickery. They grow among stones, and the color and shape of the thickened leaves make them look like pebbles. Grazing animals are fooled and overlook them.

FRUITS, SHOOTS, AND FLOWERS

From weird blossoms to prickly THORMS

Africa's plants manage to survive in many harsh environments, from hot and wet jungles to bone-dry deserts. Many plants are adapted to deal with scarce or spotty rainfall. Some draw moisture right out of the air or soak up rainfall like a sponge. Many plants have clever ways of fending off hungry animals. To keep from being somebody's lunch, they camouflage themselves or give shelter to insects that sting the animals.

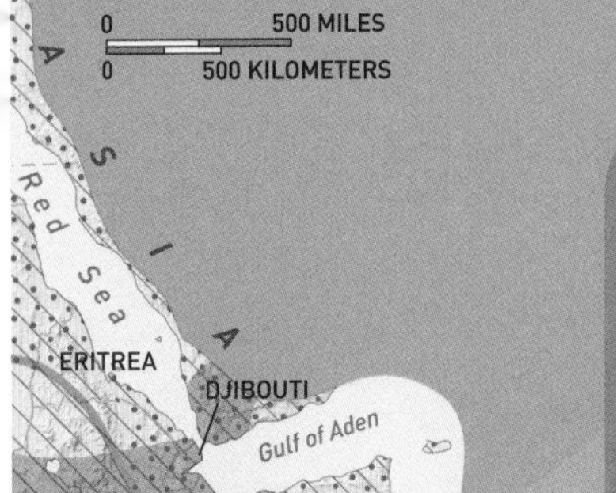

2 WHISTLING TREE
Kenya

Tiny ants make their home inside the soft, bulbous thorns of the whistling acacia. The ants protect the thorny tree. When giraffes and other grazing animals come for lunch, they get a mouthful of stinging ants. Wind blowing over old empty thorns makes a whistling sound, giving the tree its name.

DIGITAL TRAVELER!
The bottle gourd is an African plant that is used for drinking vessels, musical instruments, bottles, and food. Search the Internet to figure out how scientists think the plant made its way from Africa to the Americas.

3 UPSIDE-DOWN TREE
Madagascar

The baobab tree looks like it was planted upside down. The tree stores water in its swollen trunk during the rainy season and produces tasty fruit later during the dry season.

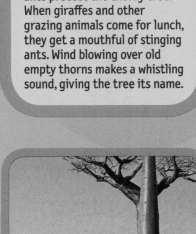

STRANGE BUT TRUE

The flowers of the jackal food plant smell like feces to attract dung beetle pollinators. Other than the flower, the plant grows entirely underground, where it steals nutrients from the roots of other plants.

Map labels: 0 500 MILES / 0 500 KILOMETERS / ASIA / Red Sea / ERITREA / DJIBOUTI / Gulf of Aden / ETHIOPIA / SOMALIA / KENYA / EQUATOR / TANZANIA / SEYCHELLES / COMOROS / Indian Ocean / Mozambique Channel / MADAGASCAR / MAURITIUS / TROPIC OF CAPRICORN

AMAZING ANIMALS

Cheetahs, gorillas, and ZEBRAS

In Africa's many habitats live a magnificent blend of mammals, birds, and reptiles. Adventurers can go on safari in the savanna to see giraffes, zebras, and lions. In Africa's lakes, rivers, and swamps lurk enormous Nile crocodiles. The central mountain forests are home to rare mountain gorillas. On the island of Madagascar scamper 32 different types of lemurs—furry primates found nowhere else in the world.

MIGHTY MIGRATION
Thundering herds of wildebeests migrate across the Serengeti in East Africa. They are hunted by powerful predators, such as lions and hyenas.

HIPPO HAVEN
Wechiau Community Hippo Sanctuary in Ghana is a river refuge for water-loving hippos. Hippos exit the water at night to feed on the shore. They spend the daytime in the water, keeping cool.

ISLAND PRIMATES
Twelve species of tree-hopping lemurs live in Madagascar's Ranomafana National Park, including the endangered golden bamboo lemur.

5 COOL ANIMALS TO SEE HERE

MAP KEY
- Elephant
- Ostrich
- Giraffe
- Mountain gorilla
- Cheetah

POWERFUL PREDATOR
Sudan

The Nile crocodile can grow to be 20 feet (6 m) long and weigh up to 1,650 pounds (748 kg). It will attack almost anything unfortunate enough to cross its path, including zebras, small hippos, porcupines, and birds—even other crocodiles. Take care!

EUROPE

Mediterranean Sea

Strait of Gibraltar

MOROCCO

Western Sahara (Morocco)

ALGERIA

TUNISIA

LIBYA

EGYPT

TROPIC OF CANCER

Red Sea

Gulf of Aden

ERITREA

DJIBOUTI

ETHIOPIA

SOUTH SUDAN

SUDAN

CHAD

NIGER

S A H E L

MALI

NIGERIA

BURKINA FASO

BENIN

TOGO

GHANA

CÔTE D'IVOIRE

GUINEA

SIERRA LEONE

SENEGAL

GUINEA-BISSAU

GAMBIA

MAURITANIA

CAPE VERDE

S A H A R A

A S I A

Atlantic Ocean

0 500 MILES
0 500 KILOMETERS

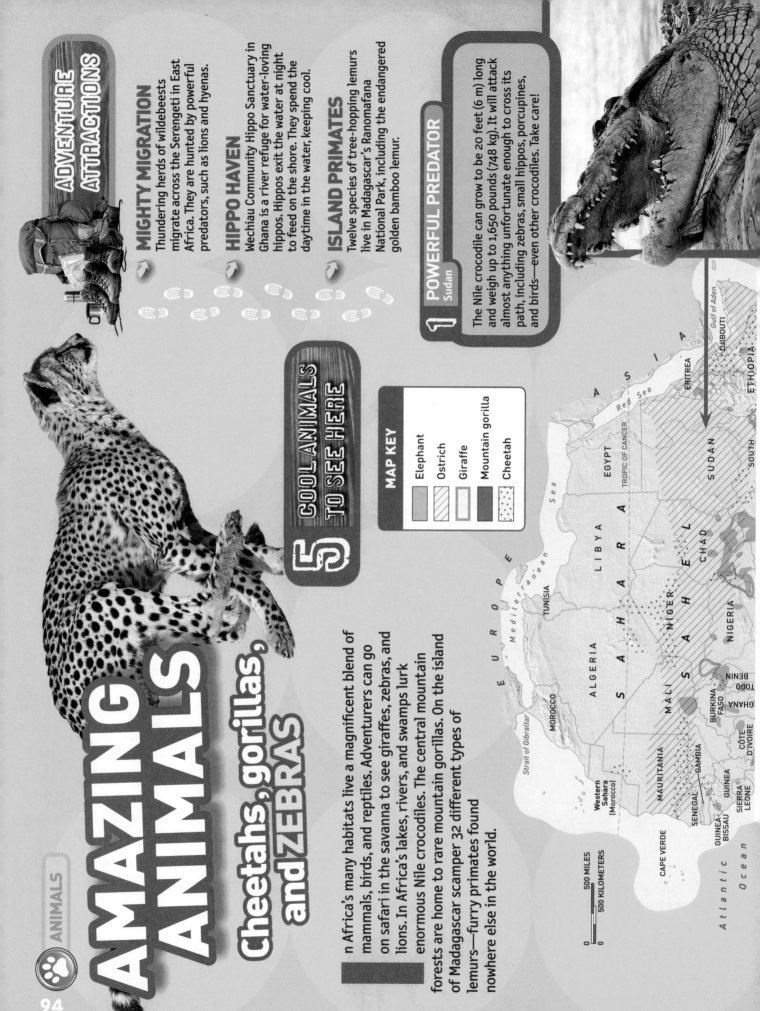

② FIRE-BOMBING BEETLE
Kenya

With an audible pop, the bombardier beetle fires a powerful jet of hot, toxic fluid from its rear end to fight off predators. The beetle itself is not harmed by the liquid.

STRANGE BUT TRUE

Mandrills, the largest of all monkeys, have blue and red faces and brightly colored rumps. The vivid colors grow brighter when the animal is excited.

③ PINK CRITTERS
Ethiopia

The naked mole rat's nearly naked, sausage-shaped body is perfect for underground living. The practically hairless mole rats live in ant-like communities led by the queen rat.

④ DEADLY REPTILE
Swaziland

The black mamba is Africa's deadliest snake. The venomous reptile is among the fastest of all snakes. It can slither at speeds of up to 12.5 miles per hour (20 kph).

⑤ FLOCKS
Uganda

Red-billed queleas are the most numerous wild birds on the planet. They migrate in vast flocks. From a distance, the flocks look like clouds of smoke. Up close, the sound of wingbeats roars like a gusty wind.

DIGITAL TRAVELER!
Search the Internet for more photos of the fennec fox. Can you figure out how the fox's large ears help it survive in the searing heat of the Sahara?

Map labels

SOMALIA
SEYCHELLES
EQUATOR
Indian Ocean
COMOROS
MADAGASCAR
TROPIC OF CAPRICORN
Mozambique Channel
KENYA
SUDAN
UGANDA
RWANDA
BURUNDI
TANZANIA
MALAWI
DEMOCRATIC REPUBLIC OF THE CONGO
ZAMBIA
ZIMBABWE
MOZAMBIQUE
CENTRAL AFRICAN REPUBLIC
ANGOLA
NAMIBIA
BOTSWANA
SWAZILAND
LESOTHO
SOUTH AFRICA
CONGO
EQUATORIAL GUINEA
GABON
CAMEROON
Cabinda (Angola)
SAO TOME & PRINCIPE
LIBERIA
IVORY COAST

AFRICA

MOUNT KILIMANJARO

The icy roof of the CONTINENT

AFRICA

Tanzania   Mount Kilimanjaro

Snow-capped Mount Kilimanjaro is Africa's highest mountain, rising 19,340 feet (5,590 m) above sea level. On their way up the mountain, climbers pass through five distinct vegetation zones, from the hot and sunny base to the icy summit. The mountain is one of the biggest volcanoes on Earth, covering an area of roughly 1,500 sq mi (3,885 sq km). Of its three distinct volcanic peaks, crater-marked Kibo is the one that actually looks like a volcano.

5 COOL PLACES TO SEE HERE

Kilimanjaro's three peaks are Kibo, Mawenzi, and Shira. On Kibo, Uhuru Peak is the highest point and Reusch Crater is volcanically active. Here, one can smell sulfur and feel the heat.

Shira

K i l

5 MOUNTAIN TREK
Kibo

With its gentle slopes, Kilimanjaro is the world's tallest walkable mountain. Routes vary by length and difficulty. Choose carefully. The steep Umbwe Route is the most direct but also the most challenging.

4 HIKE TO THE SUMMIT
Uhuru Peak

Having overcome freezing temperatures, low oxygen, and aching legs, climbers reach a winter wonderland of ice, snow, and awesome views.

eco CONGRATULATIONS YOU ARE NOW AT

UHURU PEAK TANZANIA 5895M. AMSL

AFRICA'S HIG___T PO___
WORLD'S HIG___ FRE___ ___NDING ___UNTAIN
ONE OF WORL___
WELCOME

True or False

In the foothills of Kilimanjaro, leopards lurk in the forests. Which of these facts about leopards are true, and which are false? See page 149 for the answers.

A These amazing athletes can run up to 50 miles per hour (80 kph), leap distances of 30 feet (9 m), and jump 10 feet (3 m) straight up.

B Like many other species of cats, the leopard hates to swim.

C A leopard has no problem climbing 50 feet (15.2 m) up a tree, even while holding large prey in its mouth.

D Leopards eat mainly small, hoofed animals, including gazelles, impalas, deer, and young wildebeests. They will also hunt monkeys, rodents, and birds.

E The leopard is the biggest of the "small cats"—the others include the cheetah, bobcat, lynx, and serval.

F Adult male and female leopards are about the same size, with a head and body length of about 75 inches (191 cm) and weighing 176 pounds (80 kg).

AFRICA

1 LEAP FROM A PEAK
Kibo

Adventurers who want a quick way down paraglide or hang glide from the summit. But the weather here can change quickly, so they take great care.

2 CAMP ABOVE THE CLOUDS
Kibo slopes

A trek to Kilimanjaro should include a few days' acclimatization to the thin air and several days for the ascent and descent. Adventurers rest at base camps before setting off for the summit.

Kibo   The Saddle   Mawenzi

i m a n j a r o

Scale varies in this perspective.

3 HIGH AND DRY
Foothills

There are forest trails to hike low on the mountain. Living in the trees are shy monkeys and noisy bushbabies. Climb higher, and the trees give way to these giant groundsels with swollen tops.

DIGITAL TRAVELER!
Kilimanjaro's snow caps have shrunk by more than 80 percent since 1912. Search online for before and after photos of the mountain's peak. What changes can you see?

ADVENTURES

GO WILD!
Action-packed ADVENTURES

Tropical rain forests, blazing hot deserts, roaring waterfalls, and raging rivers create opportunities for supersize adventures. The huge continent offers thrilling outings for white-water rafters, cross-country cyclists, off-road drivers, hot-air balloonists, and animal lovers alike. Extreme thrill seekers can take an adventure-packed tour of Africa at its wildest. The most daring adventurers can bungee jump off a bridge, cross the desert on a camel, body surf through a river canyon, and tip-toe through a dark jungle at night.

ADVENTURE ATTRACTIONS

HUMPBACK TRAIL
At Erg Chebbi, cross the Sahara on a camel. For salt traders, camels are the main mode of travel across the vast desert.

SUPER CYCLING TOUR
Cycle South Africa from Table Mountain to Addo Elephant National Park. Carry your bike across the Gourits River.

SIZZLING LAVA LAKES
Hover above a lake of molten lava in a helicopter as you view the Danakil Depression, among the hottest places on Earth.

5 COOL PLACES TO SEE HERE

1 GORILLA MOUNTAINS
Uganda
Trek through the cloud forests of Bwindi National Park to see mountain gorillas. Observe a troop of gorillas and experience the spine-tingling gaze of the great silverback male that guards the troop.

MAP KEY
Adventure attraction

ASIA

EUROPE

Mediterranean Sea

Strait of Gibraltar

MOROCCO

Western Sahara (Morocco)

ALGERIA

TUNISIA

LIBYA

EGYPT

TROPIC OF CANCER

Red Sea

Gulf of Aden

SOMALILAND

SOMALIA

DJIBOUTI

ERITREA

ETHIOPIA

SOUTH SUDAN

SUDAN

CHAD

NIGER

NIGERIA

MALI

BURKINA FASO

BENIN

TOGO

GHANA

CÔTE D'IVOIRE (IVORY COAST)

LIBERIA

SIERRA LEONE

GUINEA

GUINEA-BISSAU

SENEGAL

GAMBIA

CAPE VERDE

MAURITANIA

CAMEROON

CENTRAL AFRICAN REPUBLIC

S A H A R A

S A H E L

Atlantic Ocean

Erg Chebbi

Ahaggar Mountains

Sahara

White Desert N.P.

Nile River

Danakil Depression

Savanna

Red Sea

Wechiau Community Hippo Sanctuary

0   500 MILES
0   500 KILOMETERS

98

DIGITAL TRAVELER!

The town of Chã Das Caldeiras sits inside a volcano's crater on Fogo Island in the island country of Cape Verde. Search online to see photos of the volcano. What crops do villagers grow in the rich volcanic soil?

2 MOUNTAIN BACKDROP
South Africa

Step up to the heart-pumping thrill of the Bloukrans Bridge, the highest bridge bungee in the world. Make your way along the caged-in walkway to the jump point. Take one last look at the mountains and the distant sea before you plunge.

5 PITCH BLACK RAIN FOREST
Ghana

Hike through a rain forest at night in Kakum National Park. Feel your way in the dark along paths carved by elephants, buffalo, and leopards. Watch for snakes at your feet. Sense the wildlife lurking in the forest around you. By day, explore treetop walkways.

4 GIANT SAND DUNE
Namibia

Climb the giant sand pile known as Dune 7 in the Namib Desert. At 1,256 feet (383 m) it is the tallest dune in the world. Bring plenty of water. There is not a spot of shade along the way.

3 WHITE-WATER RIVER
Zimbabwe

Raft the Zambezi River as it thunders 75 miles (121 km) through Batoka Gorge. Get soaked on rapids with names like "Washing Machine" and "Oblivion." If you've got the nerve, you can charge the rapids on a bodyboard.

AFRICA

Bwindi N.P.
Mgahinga Gorilla N.P.
UGANDA
GUINEA
EQUATORIAL
GUINEA
SAO TOME &
PRINCIPE
GABON
CONGO
DEMOCRATIC
REPUBLIC
OF THE CONGO
Cabinda
(Angola)
RWANDA
BURUNDI
KENYA
Masai Mara National Reserve
Serengeti Plain
Lake Tanganyika
TANZANIA
MALAWI
ANGOLA
ZAMBIA
Victoria Falls
ZIMBABWE
MOZAMBIQUE
Mozambique Channel
MADAGASCAR
Ranomafana N.P.
COMOROS
SEYCHELLES
Indian Ocean
MAURITIUS
TROPIC OF CAPRICORN
BOTSWANA
NAMIBIA
SOUTH AFRICA
SWAZILAND
LESOTHO
Namaqualand
Cycling Tour
Sugarbush

AUSTRALIA AND OCEANIA

World of WONDER

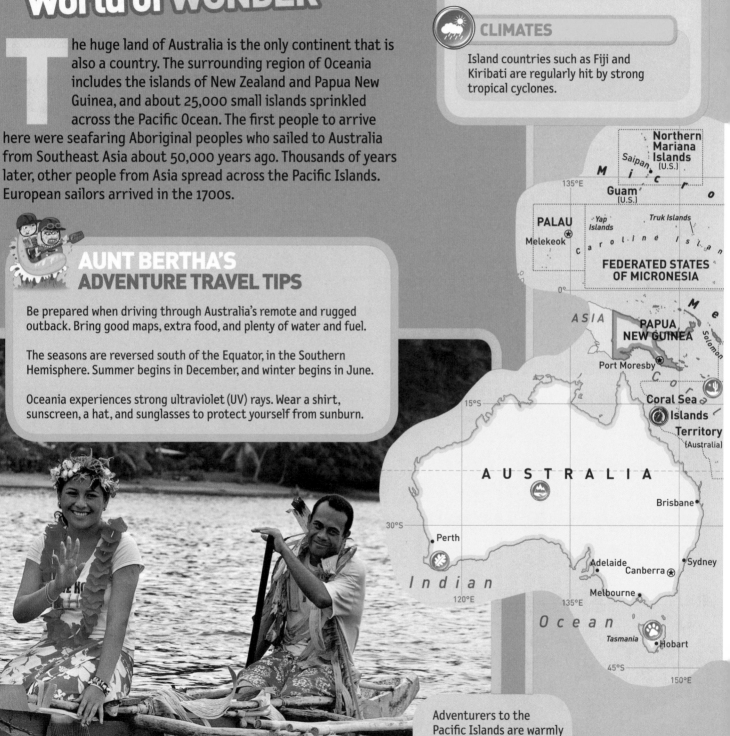

The huge land of Australia is the only continent that is also a country. The surrounding region of Oceania includes the islands of New Zealand and Papua New Guinea, and about 25,000 small islands sprinkled across the Pacific Ocean. The first people to arrive here were seafaring Aboriginal peoples who sailed to Australia from Southeast Asia about 50,000 years ago. Thousands of years later, other people from Asia spread across the Pacific Islands. European sailors arrived in the 1700s.

AUNT BERTHA'S ADVENTURE TRAVEL TIPS

Be prepared when driving through Australia's remote and rugged outback. Bring good maps, extra food, and plenty of water and fuel.

The seasons are reversed south of the Equator, in the Southern Hemisphere. Summer begins in December, and winter begins in June.

Oceania experiences strong ultraviolet (UV) rays. Wear a shirt, sunscreen, a hat, and sunglasses to protect yourself from sunburn.

ADVENTURE HOT SPOTS

LANDFORMS

The world's biggest rock, Australia's Uluru, or Ayers Rock, rises 1,142 feet (348 m) above the ground.

CLIMATES

Island countries such as Fiji and Kiribati are regularly hit by strong tropical cyclones.

Northern Mariana Islands (U.S.)
Saipan
135°E
Guam (U.S.)
M i c r o
PALAU
Yap Islands
Truk Islands
Melekeok
C a r o l i n e I s l a n
FEDERATED STATES OF MICRONESIA
0°
ASIA
PAPUA NEW GUINEA
Port Moresby
Solomon
Coral Sea Islands Territory (Australia)
15°S
AUSTRALIA
Brisbane
30°S
Perth
Adelaide
Canberra
Sydney
Indian
Melbourne
120°E
135°E
Ocean
Tasmania
Hobart
45°S
150°E

Adventurers to the Pacific Islands are warmly welcomed by local people and encouraged to join in traditional events.

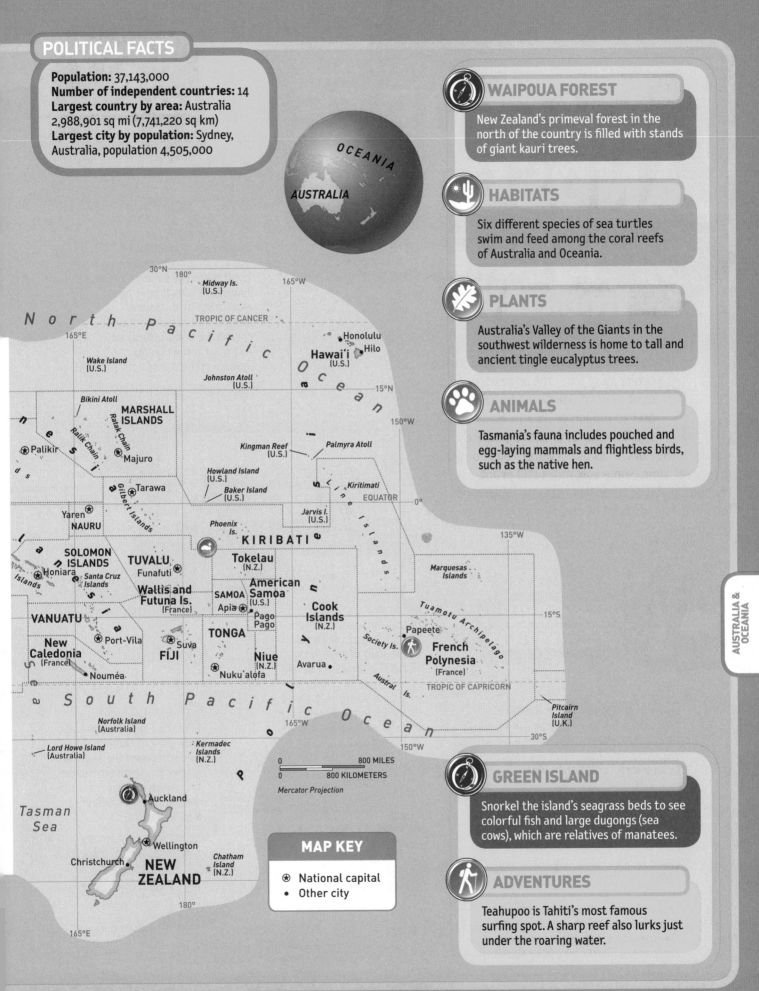

POLITICAL FACTS

Population: 37,143,000
Number of independent countries: 14
Largest country by area: Australia
2,988,901 sq mi (7,741,220 sq km)
Largest city by population: Sydney,
Australia, population 4,505,000

OCEANIA

AUSTRALIA

WAIPOUA FOREST

New Zealand's primeval forest in the north of the country is filled with stands of giant kauri trees.

HABITATS

Six different species of sea turtles swim and feed among the coral reefs of Australia and Oceania.

PLANTS

Australia's Valley of the Giants in the southwest wilderness is home to tall and ancient tingle eucalyptus trees.

ANIMALS

Tasmania's fauna includes pouched and egg-laying mammals and flightless birds, such as the native hen.

GREEN ISLAND

Snorkel the island's seagrass beds to see colorful fish and large dugongs (sea cows), which are relatives of manatees.

ADVENTURES

Teahupoo is Tahiti's most famous surfing spot. A sharp reef also lurks just under the roaring water.

North Pacific Ocean

South Pacific Ocean

30°N · 180°
Midway Is. (U.S.)
165°W
TROPIC OF CANCER
165°E
Wake Island (U.S.)
Honolulu
Hilo
Hawai'i (U.S.)
Johnston Atoll (U.S.)
15°N
Bikini Atoll
150°W
MARSHALL ISLANDS
Ralik Chain
Ratak Chain
Palikir
Majuro
Kingman Reef (U.S.)
Palmyra Atoll
Tarawa
Gilbert Islands
Howland Island (U.S.)
Baker Island (U.S.)
Kiritimati
Line Islands
EQUATOR
0°
Yaren
NAURU
Jarvis I. (U.S.)
Phoenix Is.
KIRIBATI
135°W
SOLOMON ISLANDS
TUVALU
Tokelau (N.Z.)
Marquesas Islands
Honiara
Santa Cruz Islands
Funafuti
Wallis and Futuna Is. (France)
SAMOA
American Samoa (U.S.)
Tuamotu Archipelago
15°S
VANUATU
Apia
Pago Pago
Cook Islands (N.Z.)
Society Is.
Papeete
Port-Vila
Suva
TONGA
French Polynesia (France)
New Caledonia (France)
FIJI
Niue (N.Z.)
Avarua
Nouméa
Nuku'alofa
Austral Is.
TROPIC OF CAPRICORN
Pitcairn Island (U.K.)
Norfolk Island (Australia)
165°W
Ocean
150°W
30°S
Lord Howe Island (Australia)
Kermadec Islands (N.Z.)

0   800 MILES
0   800 KILOMETERS
Mercator Projection

Auckland
Tasman Sea
Wellington
Christchurch
Chatham Island (N.Z.)
NEW ZEALAND
180°
165°E

MAP KEY

⊛ National capital
• Other city

ASSORTED LANDSCAPES

Icy glaciers to tropical VOLCANOES

Australia, New Guinea, and New Zealand broke away from the ancient, huge continent of Gondwana between 85 and 30 million years ago. Many of the smaller islands of the region are volcanic. They began as underwater volcanoes that grew over time. Some volcanoes still erupt, reminding you of their fiery origins. Coral atolls are low-lying islands built of coral on top of underwater volcanoes.

ADVENTURE ATTRACTIONS

ACTIVE VOLCANO
Living in an active volcano is always dangerous! The town of Rabaul in Papua New Guinea, sits entirely inside a volcano. Most of the town was destroyed by a powerful eruption in 1994.

STRING OF ISLANDS
Many of Tonga's 169 islands are extinct or dormant volcanoes, including northernmost Niuafo'ou, home to a large crater lake and steaming hot springs.

BEEHIVE ROCKS
Explore beehive-shaped towers and cones in Australia's Bungle Bungle Range. The odd shapes formed over millions of years as the quartz sandstone was worn away by wind and rain.

1 SCULPTED ISLANDS
Palau

Snorkel or kayak the mushroom-shaped Rock Islands. Originally ancient coral reefs, the bases of these limestone islands have been worn away into strange shapes. The islands contain 52 marine lakes. Divers can explore coral walls and underwater caverns.

2 GIANT ROCK SLAB
Australia

Uluru, also known as Ayers Rock, is one of the largest single slabs of rock in the world. It is a mass of limestone with a circumference of almost six miles (9.7 km). Uluru lies in the dry, remote interior of Australia known as the outback.

3 STEEP GLACIER
New Zealand

Hike the Franz Josef Glacier as it plunges through rain forests toward the sea. The glacier is a remnant from a time when massive ice sheets covered much of New Zealand.

Arafura

Timor Sea

15°S Kimberley Plateau

Great Sandy Desert Macdonnell Ranges

A U S T R

Great Victoria Desert

30°S

I n d i a n

120°E

O c e a n

5 COOL PLACES TO SEE HERE

PHYSICAL FACTS

Land area: 3,278,000 sq mi (8,490,000 sq km)
Highest point: Mount Wilhelm, Papua New Guinea 14,793 ft (4,509 m)
Lowest point: Lake Eyre, Australia -49 ft (-15 m)
Longest river: Murray–Darling, Australia 2,282 mi (3,672 km)
Largest lake: Lake Eyre, Australia 3,741 sq mi (9,690 sq km)

MAP KEY

▲ Highest point
▼ Lowest point
+ Other mountain peak

Map labels

30°N · 180° · 165°W
Midway Is. · Hawaiian Islands
TROPIC OF CANCER
150°E · 165°E · Wake Island · Johnston Atoll · Hawai'i
North Pacific Ocean
15°N · 135°E · MICRONESIA · Bikini Atoll · 15°S · 150°W
Mariana Islands · Marshall Is. · Ratak Chain · Kingman Reef · Palmyra Atoll
Yap Islands · Truk Islands · Ralik Chain · Kiritimati
Caroline Islands · Gilbert Islands · Howland Island · Baker Island · Line Islands
EQUATOR · 0°
Bismarck Archipelago · Phoenix Is. · Jarvis Island
New Guinea · MELANESIA · Santa Cruz Islands · Tuvalu · Tokelau · Marquesas Is.
Mount Wilhelm 14,793 ft (4,509 m) · Highest point in Oceania
Solomon Islands · Samoa Is. · Tahiti · Tuamotu Archipelago · 15°S
Sea · Coral Sea · Vanuatu · Fiji Is. · Tonga Is. · Cook Islands · Society Is. · Austral Is.
Great Artesian Basin · New Caledonia · TROPIC OF CAPRICORN · Pitcairn Island
AUSTRALIA · ▼ Lake Eyre -49 ft (-15 m) Lowest point in Oceania
Great Dividing Range · South Pacific Ocean · 30°S
Murray · Darling · Norfolk Island · Kermadec Islands · 165°W · 150°W · 135°W
+ Mt. Kosciuszko 7,310 ft (2,228 m) · Lord Howe Island
Tasman Sea · North Island · 800 MILES / 800 KILOMETERS · Mercator Projection
Tasmania · Mt. Ruapehu 9,177 ft (2,797 m) · Chatham Island
Mt. Cook (Aoraki) 12,218 ft (3,724 m) · New Zealand · 45°S
Southern Alps · South Island · 180°
150°E · 165°E

DIGITAL TRAVELER!

At the Tessellated Pavement in Tasmania, rocks have fractured into polygonal blocks. Use the Internet to look up a photo of this rare geological feature.

5 SPOUTING CAVE
Samoa

The Alofaaga Blowholes are generated by wave power. The incoming tide rockets through a cave, shooting a roaring jet of water high into the air. Watch as locals toss coconuts into the holes and the coconuts are blasted sky-high.

4 STINKING HOT SPRINGS
New Zealand

Wander among steaming hot springs, bubbling mud pools, and spurting geysers in Rotorua. The sulfur gases make it one of the stinkiest places on Earth. Lakes fill craters left by huge volcanic eruptions.

INTENSE WEATHER

From downpours to WILDFIRES

5 **CYCLONE ISLAND** Solomon Islands

Rennell Island, the southernmost island in the Solomons, is hit by frequent cyclones. Scientists use the island as a natural laboratory for studying the effects of these strong storms.

Explorers will find a mix of extreme weather across Oceania. Australia's large size gives it a diverse climate, from the well-watered coasts to its parched outback interior. New Guinea receives heavy rainfall, as do many Pacific Islands. New Zealand's weather is mild but can change unexpectedly several times a day—"all four seasons in one day," as the locals say. Tropical hurricanes—known as cyclones in this part of the world—regularly pay a visit to islands large and small.

Map labels:
150°E
Northern Mariana Islands (U.S.)
15°N
135°E
Guam (U.S.)
PALAU
FEDERATED STATES OF MICRONESIA
0°
ASIA
PAPUA NEW GUINEA
15°S
Coral Sea Islands Territory (Australia)
Coral Sea
AUSTRALIA
30°S
120°E
135°E
Indian Ocean
Tasman Sea
Tasmania
45°S
150°E

4 WINDY ISLE
Australia

During Tropical Cyclone Olivia, in 1996, wind gusts reached 253.5 miles per hour (408 kph) on Barrow Island. This set a new world record for the highest surface wind speed ever recorded.

3 DUSTY BASIN
Australia

Droughts regularly hit the Murray-Darling Basin. In drought years, bushfires scorch the land. The Murray River turns into a string of waterholes along the drying waterway.

DIGITAL TRAVELER!
Samoa and Tonga lie just west of the International Date Line and are some of the first countries to see the sunrise. Which of these two countries leaped ahead a day in 2011 by moving this line? Search the Internet to find out.

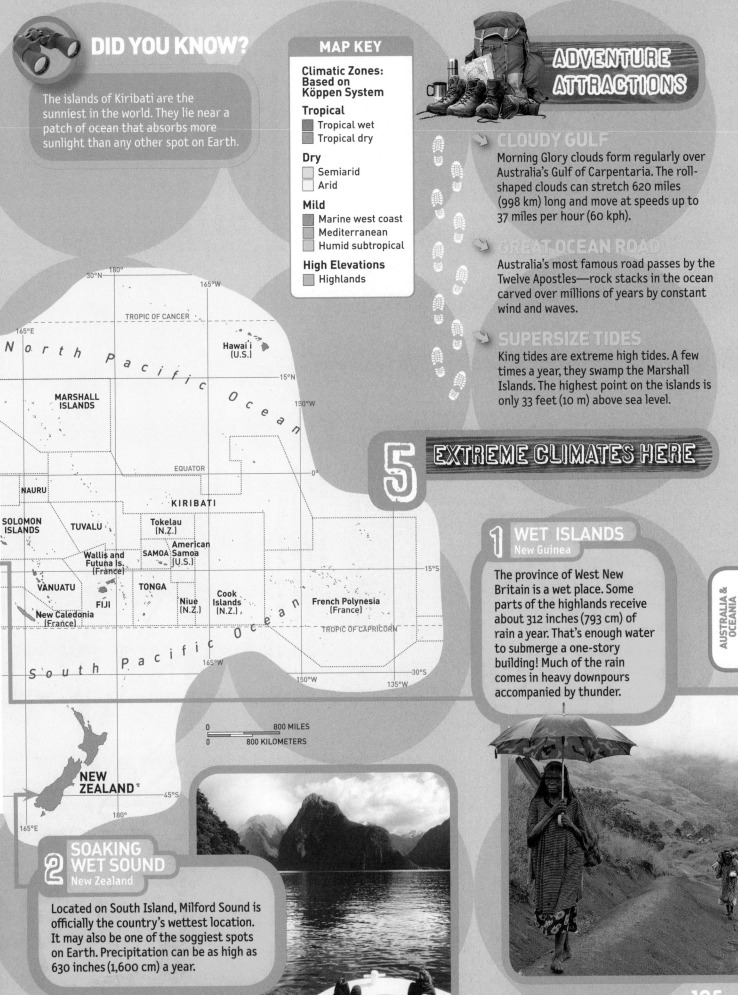

DID YOU KNOW?

The islands of Kiribati are the sunniest in the world. They lie near a patch of ocean that absorbs more sunlight than any other spot on Earth.

MAP KEY

Climatic Zones: Based on Köppen System

Tropical
- Tropical wet
- Tropical dry

Dry
- Semiarid
- Arid

Mild
- Marine west coast
- Mediterranean
- Humid subtropical

High Elevations
- Highlands

ADVENTURE ATTRACTIONS

CLOUDY GULF

Morning Glory clouds form regularly over Australia's Gulf of Carpentaria. The roll-shaped clouds can stretch 620 miles (998 km) long and move at speeds up to 37 miles per hour (60 kph).

GREAT OCEAN ROAD

Australia's most famous road passes by the Twelve Apostles—rock stacks in the ocean carved over millions of years by constant wind and waves.

SUPERSIZE TIDES

King tides are extreme high tides. A few times a year, they swamp the Marshall Islands. The highest point on the islands is only 33 feet (10 m) above sea level.

5 EXTREME CLIMATES HERE

1 WET ISLANDS
New Guinea

The province of West New Britain is a wet place. Some parts of the highlands receive about 312 inches (793 cm) of rain a year. That's enough water to submerge a one-story building! Much of the rain comes in heavy downpours accompanied by thunder.

2 SOAKING WET SOUND
New Zealand

Located on South Island, Milford Sound is officially the country's wettest location. It may also be one of the soggiest spots on Earth. Precipitation can be as high as 630 inches (1,600 cm) a year.

Map labels: North Pacific Ocean, South Pacific Ocean, TROPIC OF CANCER, EQUATOR, TROPIC OF CAPRICORN, Hawai'i (U.S.), MARSHALL ISLANDS, NAURU, KIRIBATI, SOLOMON ISLANDS, TUVALU, Tokelau (N.Z.), Wallis and Futuna Is. (France), SAMOA, American Samoa (U.S.), VANUATU, TONGA, FIJI, New Caledonia (France), Niue (N.Z.), Cook Islands (N.Z.), French Polynesia (France), NEW ZEALAND

0 — 800 MILES
0 — 800 KILOMETERS

30°N, 180°, 165°W, 15°N, 150°W, 165°E, 0°, 15°S, 165°W, 150°W, 135°W, 30°S, 45°S, 180°, 165°E

GREEN ISLAND

Rain forest, coral, and WILDLIFE

Green Island is a beautiful coral cay—a sandy island—that sits on top of Australia's Great Barrier Reef. This island jewel is uniquely cloaked with lush rain forests surrounded by sandy, white beaches. In the water, magnificent coral reefs teem with colorful marine life. Green Island is a nature lover's paradise and a fun place for adventure lovers.

5 COOL PLACES TO SEE HERE

Green Island has formed over about 6,000 years. You can get there from Cairns on the Australian mainland by a 45-minute catamaran journey across the Coral Sea.

OCEANIA

Green Island

Australia

Reef

1 UNDERWATER CRUISE
Coral Reef

Cruise through the reef on a glass-bottom boat and watch marine life under your feet. Or move under water on an aquatic scooter—no swimming required! Your head sits inside a roomy air bubble while you steer through the water.

Scale varies in this perspective.

Green Island

Helipad

Jetty

Marineland

Green Island

Pacific Ocean

N

5 REEF ISLAND
Helipad

Take to the sky for a bird's-eye view of the island. Fly above the clear water in a parasail or ride over the reef in a helicopter.

4 FOREST WALK
Boardwalk

Take a guided hike through the only rain forest–covered coral cay on the Great Barrier Reef. Walk along the boardwalk deep into the forest. See colorful birds, such as the male frigate bird, with its red pouch that it puffs up to attract females.

2 MARINELAND WILDLIFE
North beach

Visit a collection of aquaria to see coral reef life that includes puffer fish and sharks. Green Island is also home to a group of Australia and New Guinea crocodiles. You can watch them being fed.

DIGITAL TRAVELER!
Coral cays are islands made of reef debris—coral rubble, broken mollusk shells, and sand—cemented together with seabird droppings. Search the Internet to find out how many coral cays are found in the Great Barrier Reef. How old are they?

3 SEAGRASS MEADOW
Western reef

Grab your snorkeling gear and head to the water. Say "hi" to sea turtles swimming in the shallow seagrass close to the shore. Or take a short boat trip to snorkel farther offshore to see more marine life.

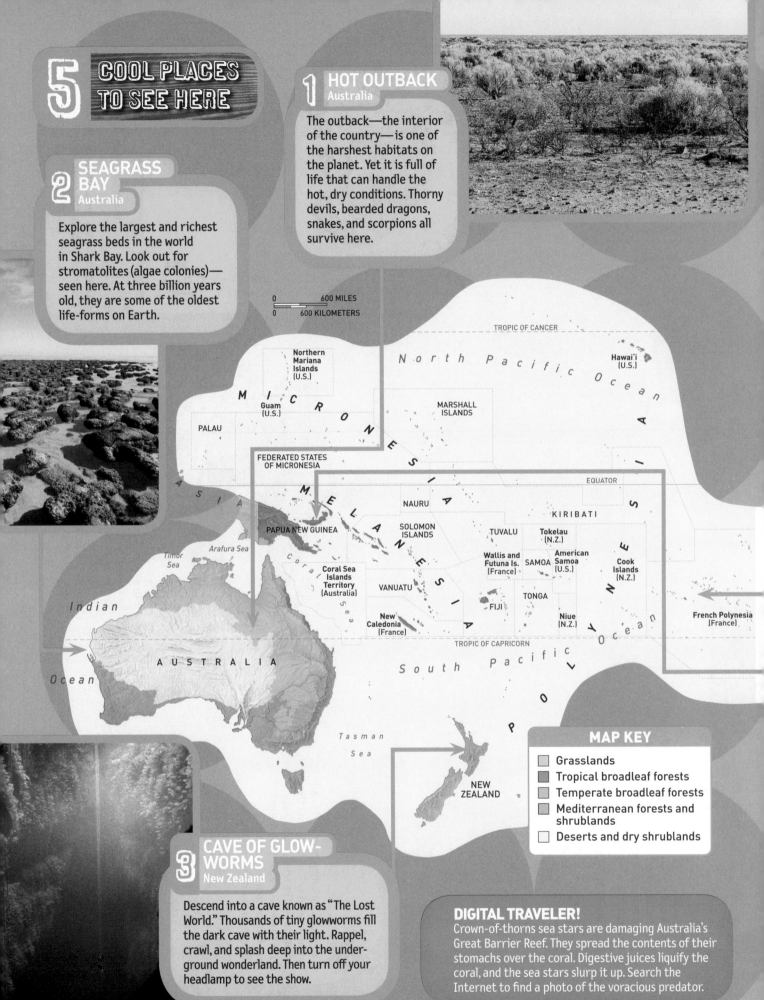

5 COOL PLACES TO SEE HERE

1 HOT OUTBACK
Australia

The outback—the interior of the country—is one of the harshest habitats on the planet. Yet it is full of life that can handle the hot, dry conditions. Thorny devils, bearded dragons, snakes, and scorpions all survive here.

2 SEAGRASS BAY
Australia

Explore the largest and richest seagrass beds in the world in Shark Bay. Look out for stromatolites (algae colonies)—seen here. At three billion years old, they are some of the oldest life-forms on Earth.

3 CAVE OF GLOW-WORMS
New Zealand

Descend into a cave known as "The Lost World." Thousands of tiny glowworms fill the dark cave with their light. Rappel, crawl, and splash deep into the underground wonderland. Then turn off your headlamp to see the show.

DIGITAL TRAVELER!
Crown-of-thorns sea stars are damaging Australia's Great Barrier Reef. They spread the contents of their stomachs over the coral. Digestive juices liquify the coral, and the sea stars slurp it up. Search the Internet to find a photo of the voracious predator.

MAP KEY
- Grasslands
- Tropical broadleaf forests
- Temperate broadleaf forests
- Mediterranean forests and shrublands
- Deserts and dry shrublands

0   600 MILES
0   600 KILOMETERS

TROPIC OF CANCER

North Pacific Ocean

Northern Mariana Islands (U.S.)

Hawai'i (U.S.)

M I C R O N E S I A

Guam (U.S.)

MARSHALL ISLANDS

PALAU

FEDERATED STATES OF MICRONESIA

EQUATOR

A S I A

M E L A N E S I A

NAURU

KIRIBATI

PAPUA NEW GUINEA

SOLOMON ISLANDS

TUVALU

Tokelau (N.Z.)

Arafura Sea

Coral Sea Islands Territory (Australia)

Wallis and Futuna Is. (France)

SAMOA

American Samoa (U.S.)

Cook Islands (N.Z.)

Timor Sea

VANUATU

FIJI

TONGA

P O L Y N E S I A

Coral Sea

New Caledonia (France)

Niue (N.Z.)

French Polynesia (France)

Indian

TROPIC OF CAPRICORN

South Pacific Ocean

A U S T R A L I A

Ocean

Tasman Sea

NEW ZEALAND

FORESTS, CAVES, AND CORALS

Birds, fish, and glowing WORMS

Australia and Oceania are packed with many kinds of habitats. On the region's many islands, habitats vary from lush forests and mangroves to tropical beaches and rugged mountains. The Great Barrier Reef is a maze of colorful reefs that stretches 1,430 miles (2,300 km)—a living thing so large it can be seen from space. The hot, dry outback of Australia is home to plants and animals that are adapted to handle the harsh conditions.

MUDDY MANGROVES

The coastal forests of Gunung Lorentz National Park in Papua New Guinea support the world's highest diversity of mangroves. Their roots protect the coastline and provide a home for coastal fish.

RARE BIRD FOREST

Te Wahipounamu in New Zealand is packed with beech and conifer trees, some more than 800 years old. The forest is home to the rare takahe, a large, flightless bird.

GREAT BARRIER REEF

The world's largest string of coral reefs contains at least 400 types of coral, 1,500 species of fish, and 4,000 types of mollusks.

STRANGE BUT TRUE

Scientists have found gold in the leaves and bark of trees in the Australian outback. How is this possible? In the desert, many trees have roots that push deep into the soil to find water. Some trees dig so deep that they strike gold!

AUSTRALIA & OCEANIA

4 COLORFUL CORAL
Papua New Guinea

Dive in Kimbe Bay, home to more than half of the world's coral species. More than 820 species of coral reef fish swim through the bay. See if you can spot the pygmy seahorse, the world's smallest seahorse.

5 PARADISE ISLANDS
French Polynesia

In this isolated island group, volcanic peaks soar into the clouds. Lush plants fill habitats ranging from beaches to mountains. More than 78 different species of snails live here.

ANCIENT PLANTS
Weird and WONDERFUL

Many of this region's plants are one-of-a-kind. They are adapted to its varied habitats that range from deserts and eucalyptus tree forests to tropical beaches. The palm-like cycads are a group of plants with a long history on Earth. Their ancient relatives date back to before the time of the dinosaurs. On many Pacific islands are unusual plant species found nowhere else in the world.

ADVENTURE ATTRACTIONS

FORESTED ISLANDS
Many of Fiji's 333 volcanic islands are cloaked with rain forest habitat and fields of sugarcane.

FLOWER OF HADES
On New Zealand's North Island, this parasitic plant lives underground, wrapped around the roots of trees. Only the flowers appear above ground.

SHIMMERING MOUNTAINS
The Blue Mountains of Australia get their name from the blue shimmer that rises into the air from the oil of the area's many eucalyptus trees.

DID YOU KNOW?

The fleshy, egg-shaped cheesefruit is edible—if you can take the rotten cheese smell and taste! The stinky fruit is high in vitamin C. Pacific Islanders regard it as a powerful cure for a range of ailments.

5 COOL PLANTS TO SEE HERE

1 STAPLE FOOD
New Guinea

Breadfruit has long been an important food in the South Pacific. Baked or roasted on a fire, the starchy fruit tastes like fresh-baked bread. Milky sap from the tree can be rubbed into the skin to treat skin problems.

MAP KEY
- Cycads
- Cabbage tree
- Soft spinifex
- Norfolk tree fern
- Mountain ash

North Pacific Ocean

TROPIC OF CANCER

Hawai'i (U.S.)

EQUATOR

Northern Mariana Islands (U.S.)

Guam (U.S.)

MARSHALL ISLANDS

MICRONESIA

FEDERATED STATES OF MICRONESIA

PALAU

0   600 MILES
0   600 KILOMETERS

DIGITAL TRAVELER!

The South Pacific's unique plants are the result of isolation. The lands that make up Australia, New Guinea, and New Zealand began to break off from the ancient supercontinent Gondwana about 85 million years ago. Search online to see what the Gondwana supercontinent looked like.

2 STINGING TREE
Australia

The gympie gympie tree delivers an agonizing sting with the gentlest touch. Stinging hairs cover the whole plant and contain a potent neurotoxin. The sting can remain painful for months.

3 GIANT PINE CONES
Australia

The Bunya tree makes pineapple-size cones that can weigh up to 15 pounds (6.8 kg). As the cones ripen and fall to the ground, they clatter through the branches, giving advance notice to any person standing below.

4 TREES WITHOUT TRUNKS
New Zealand

Growing within temperate forests of many Pacific islands are giant ferns that have crowns of fanlike leaves atop a trunk. The trunk is not woody like those of true trees but is made of a mass of upright stems and overground roots.

5 PLUMERIA FLOWERS
Tahiti

Pacific islanders use native white, pink, and yellow flowers to make floral tiaras, garlands, and necklaces. It is traditional to give this floral jewelry to visitors as a welcome to the islands.

AUSTRALIA & OCEANIA

111

AWESOME ANIMALS
Extreme and EXOTIC

A ustralia and Oceania are packed with unusual animals. Red kangaroos—the world's largest marsupials (pouched mammals)—use their powerful legs to hop through Australia's deserts and grasslands. The giant weta—the world's heaviest insect—inhabits New Zealand, as do flightless birds such as the rare kakapo and the shy kiwi. Beautiful birds of paradise can be found on tropical islands and on the Australian mainland. Poisonous snakes and spiders are widespread.

Map labels:
0 — 600 MILES
0 — 600 KILOMETERS
MICRONE
Nort
Northern Mariana Islands (U.S.)
Guam (U.S.)
PALAU
FEDERATED STATES OF MICRONESIA
MELAN
ASIA
PAPUA NEW GUINEA
SOLOMON ISLANDS
Arafura Sea
Coral Sea Islands Territory (Australia)
New Caledonia (France)
Timor Sea
Indian
Coral Sea
TROPIC
AUSTRALIA
Ocean
So
Tasman Sea

5 PATCHWORK PLATYPUS
Australia

The egg-laying platypus looks like it was patched together from other animals. It has a bill and webbed feet like a duck, a body like an otter, and a tail like a beaver. Males have poisonous stingers on their back legs.

ADVENTURE ATTRACTIONS

SALTY DESERT POOLS
The Simpson Desert is Australia's harshest and hottest desert. Seasonal salt lakes teem with fish and are a breeding ground for large numbers of waterbirds.

JELLYFISH LAKE
This saltwater lake in Palau is packed with golden jellyfish. The animal's sting is so mild that people can swim among them without getting hurt.

MEGAPODE FIELDS
On the beach at night in the Solomon Islands, female megapodes (flightless birds) dig about three feet (1 m) into the sand to bury their eggs. The volcanic soil is warmed from below, providing an ideal temperature for the eggs to incubate.

DID YOU KNOW?

The box jellyfish is the most venomous marine animal known. Its powerful sting stuns or kills prey instantly. Each tentacle can reach ten feet (3 m) in length and is covered with about 5,000 stinging cells.

5 COOL ANIMALS TO SEE HERE

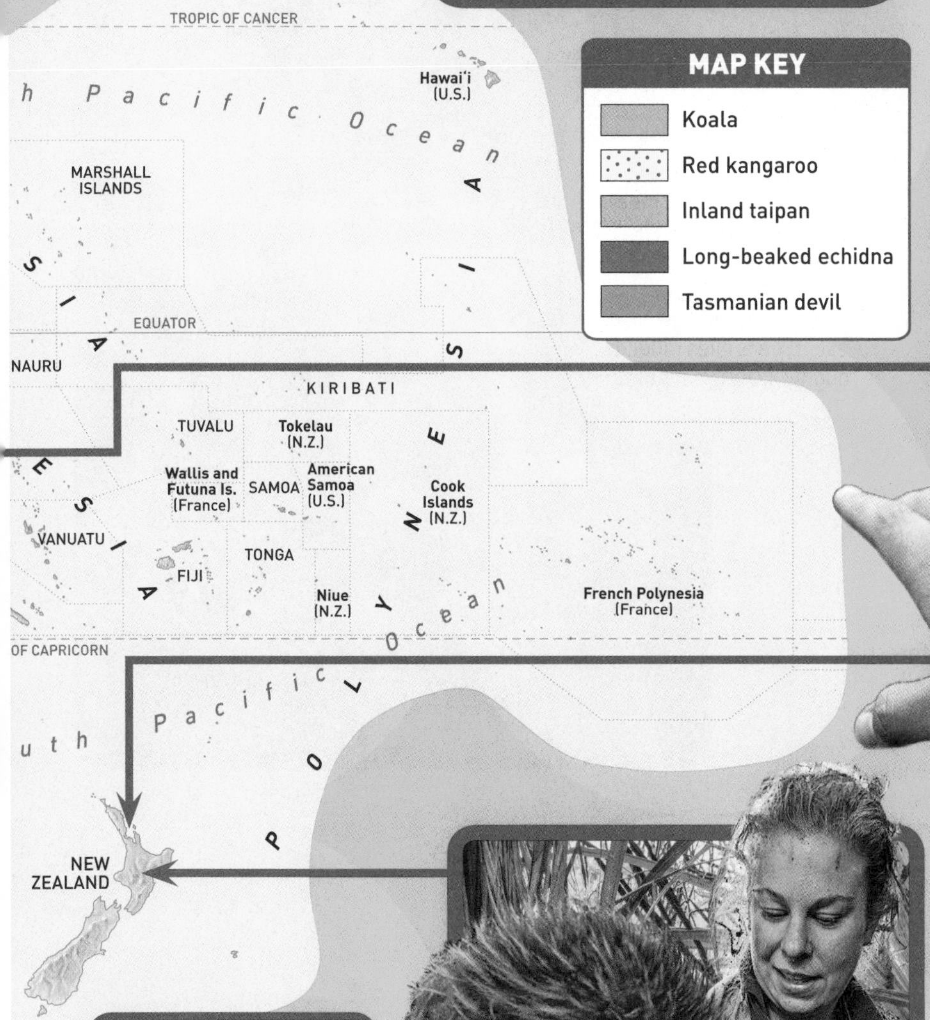

MAP KEY

- Koala
- Red kangaroo
- Inland taipan
- Long-beaked echidna
- Tasmanian devil

Map labels: Pacific Ocean, TROPIC OF CANCER, Hawai'i (U.S.), MARSHALL ISLANDS, EQUATOR, NAURU, KIRIBATI, TUVALU, Tokelau (N.Z.), Wallis and Futuna Is. (France), SAMOA, American Samoa (U.S.), Cook Islands (N.Z.), VANUATU, TONGA, FIJI, Niue (N.Z.), French Polynesia (France), OF CAPRICORN, NEW ZEALAND, MICRONESIA, POLYNESIA

1 GIANT CRAB
Solomon Islands

Coconut crabs are the biggest shelled, jointed-legged animals on land. They can grow up to three feet (1 m) across and weigh nine pounds (4.1 kg). The crab's favorite food is coconuts. It breaks open the tough husks with its massive claws.

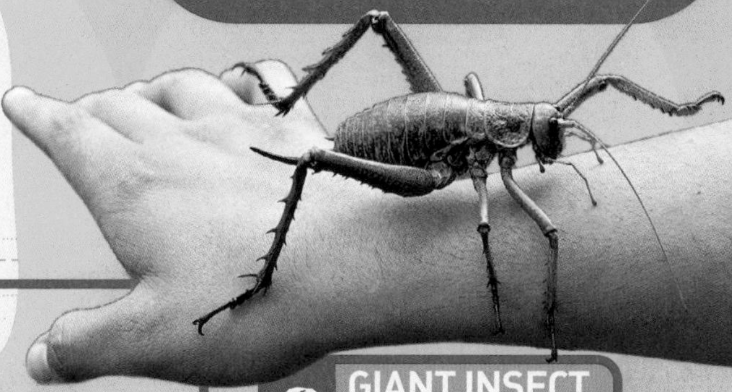

2 GIANT INSECT
Little Barrier Island, New Zealand

The enormous cricket-like weta qualifies as the world's heaviest insect. When fully grown, the giant weta can weigh up to 1.2 pounds (0.5 kg). That's heavier than a mouse or sparrow.

4 VENOMOUS SPIDER
Australia

The Sydney funnel-web spider is the most dangerous spider in the world. Large fangs and highly toxic venom give it a deadly bite. The spider's main food is insects, but it sometimes eats frogs and lizards.

3 FUZZY, FLIGHTLESS BIRD
New Zealand

The kiwi is covered with fuzzy feathers that look like fur. This chicken-size bird has short legs, a round body, a long beak, and no tail. Despite its awkward shape, the kiwi can easily outrun a person.

DIGITAL TRAVELER!

The shingleback lizard has a tail that resembles its head to confuse potential predators. If that doesn't work, the lizard sticks out its bright blue tongue. Search the Internet for photos of this cool lizard. Then find out where it lives.

AUSTRALIA & OCEANIA

5 COOL PLACES TO SEE HERE

Waipoua Forest lies near the northern tip of New Zealand's North Island. Until 1952, the forest was largely unexplored. Now trails have been built so people can discover its beauty.

OCEANIA

Waipoua Forest

New Zealand

1 MIGHTY KAURI
Kauri Walk

The largest kauri tree in the forest is called "the Lord of the Forest." It measures 168 feet (51 m) tall and 46 feet (14 m) around, and is about 1,500 years old. The "Father of the Forest" tree is even older. It is roughly 3,000 years old!

2 BIRD'S-EYE VIEW
Lookout Trail

The ancient forest stretches in all directions for miles. For an unending view of the lush canopy, walk along the boardwalk trail and climb to the top of the lookout tower.

Hokianga Harbour

Tasman Sea

3 HELPING HANDS
Waipoua Sanctuary

You can help forest rangers restore parts of the kauri forests that have been logged. Tasks include growing new trees from seeds and getting rid of pests such as rats and possums.

DIGITAL TRAVELER!
The kokako is a New Zealand bird known for its loud, clear song, which travels far across the forest. Do an Internet search to hear the extraordinary song of this unique bird.

WAIPOUA FOREST

Kauri is KING

An ancient world of huge trees and rare birds awaits adventurers on New Zealand's North Island. Waipoua Forest, and the neighboring Mataraua and Waima Forests, together make up a large tract of primeval land. The dark woodland is the perfect place to see kauri—giant conifer trees that have changed little from the Jurassic period about 190 million years ago, when dinosaurs ruled the world. Birds fill the forest, including the endangered brown kiwi and gray kokako.

True or False

The kiwi is the national bird of New Zealand. Which of the following facts about kiwis are true, and which are false? See page 149 for the answers.

- (A) There are five species of kiwi and all live only in New Zealand.
- (B) It is known as a flightless bird but adult kiwis can fly short distances.
- (C) A female kiwi can lay no more than about ten eggs in her lifetime.
- (D) Kiwis eat worms, insects, seeds, and berries.
- (E) Kiwis fight and fend off enemies with their sharp beaks.

Waipoua Forest

Scale varies in this perspective.

AUSTRALIA & OCEANIA

5 TIMEKEEPING CREATURES
Tane Mahuta Trail

Dawn and dusk are great times to see the forest's animals. Some awake from sleep at daybreak and become active. Others are active at night. Spot the kingfisher in its natural habitat. Look for mouse-size insects known as wetas and the giant carnivorous kauri snail.

4 PRIMEVAL JUNGLE
Mataraua Forest

Venture deep into the heart of the kauri forest. Listen for the amazing song of the endangered kokako as it sings at dawn. Rainfall is high and the brush is thick here. Bring rain gear and a handheld GPS to find your way.

EPIC ADVENTURES

A thrill seeker's PARADISE

MAP KEY

🔍 Adventure attraction

Bold adventurers can find big opportunities in the region. New Zealand's adventurous national spirit and rugged landscape have made it a daredevil's playground. This is, after all, the country that invented bungee jumping. Surfers can head to Australia for some of the best surf beaches on the planet. Scuba divers can slip into warm waters off the region's many sun-drenched Pacific Islands and find their thrills under the sea.

Map labels:
MICRO... Northern Mariana Islands (U.S.), Guam (U.S.), Jellyfish Lake, PALAU, FEDERATED STATES OF MICRONESIA, ASIA, Gunung Lorentz N.P., PAPUA NEW GUINEA, Rabaul, Coral Sea, Timor Sea, Arafura Sea, Gulf of Carpentaria, Coral Sea Islands Territory (Australia), Great Barrier Reef, Bungle Bungle Range, Indian Ocean, Simpson Desert, AUSTRALIA, Blue Mountains, Three Sisters, Great Ocean Road

600 MILES
600 KILOMETERS

RECORD BREAKER

New Zealand's tallest bungee jump is also the world's scariest. Jumpers ride an open-air cable car to a pod suspended high above the stony Nevis gorge. Adventurers who take the plunge experience eight terrifying seconds of freefall.

4 BREEZY BEACH
New Zealand

On a windy day, sail Muriwai Beach in a "blokart," a go-cart powered by wind. As a gust hits your sail, you'll zip across the sand. Don't forget to steer!

5 SURF BREAKS
Australia

Head to Sydney, where 70 surf beaches offer first-class waves for all abilities. Beginners can learn to surf at Bondi. Experienced surfers can try the breaks at Shark Island. Beware of the sharp reef just under the churning waves.

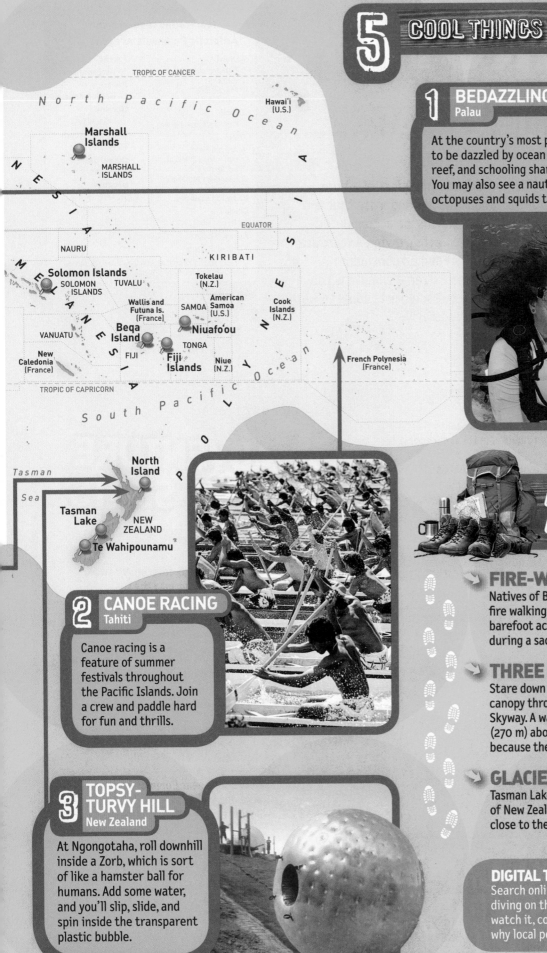

North Pacific Ocean

TROPIC OF CANCER

Hawai'i (U.S.)

Marshall Islands

MARSHALL ISLANDS

MICRONESIA

EQUATOR

NAURU

KIRIBATI

MICRONESIA

Solomon Islands

SOLOMON ISLANDS

TUVALU

Tokelau (N.Z.)

MELANESIA

Wallis and Futuna Is. (France)

SAMOA

American Samoa (U.S.)

Cook Islands (N.Z.)

Beqa Island

Niuafo'ou

VANUATU

TONGA

POLYNESIA

New Caledonia (France)

FIJI

Fiji Islands

Niue (N.Z.)

French Polynesia (France)

TROPIC OF CAPRICORN

South Pacific Ocean

POLYNESIA

Tasman Sea

North Island

Tasman Lake

NEW ZEALAND

Te Wahipounamu

1 BEDAZZLING BLUE CORNER
Palau

At the country's most popular dive spot, expect to be dazzled by ocean life. Remain still in the reef, and schooling sharks will cruise past you. You may also see a nautilus—a relative of octopuses and squids that has a fantastic shell.

ADVENTURE ATTRACTIONS

FIRE-WALKING ISLAND
Natives of Beqa, an island in Fiji, practice fire walking. Watch participants trek barefoot across white-hot stones during a sacred ceremony.

THREE SISTERS PEAKS
Stare down at an Australian rain forest canopy through a glass-bottomed Scenic Skyway. A walkway is suspended 885 feet (270 m) above ancient ravines. Hold on tight, because the walkway sways over the treetops.

GLACIER LAKE
Tasman Lake is filled with icebergs, once part of New Zealand's longest glacier. Kayak up close to the floating chunks of ice.

2 CANOE RACING
Tahiti

Canoe racing is a feature of summer festivals throughout the Pacific Islands. Join a crew and paddle hard for fun and thrills.

3 TOPSY-TURVY HILL
New Zealand

At Ngongotaha, roll downhill inside a Zorb, which is sort of like a hamster ball for humans. Add some water, and you'll slip, slide, and spin inside the transparent plastic bubble.

DIGITAL TRAVELER!
Search online for a photo or video of land diving on the Vanuatu islands. After you watch it, continue your search to find out why local people take the plunge.

AUSTRALIA & OCEANIA

117

ANTARCTICA

An enormous ICE CAP

MAP KEY

• Year-round research station*
Antarctic Peninsula Area Stations

Argentina
1 Esperanza
2 Jubany
3 Marambio
4 San Martín

Brazil
5 Comandante Ferraz

Chile
6 Arturo Prat
7 Bernardo O'Higgins
8 Eduardo Frei
9 Estación Maritima
   Antártica
10 Julio Escudero

China
11 Great Wall

Korea, South
12 King Sejong

Poland
13 Arctowski

Russia
14 Bellingshausen

Ukraine
15 Vernadsky

United Kingdom
16 Rothera

United States
17 Palmer

Uruguay
18 Artigas

*Year-round research stations north of the 60°
south line of latitude are not shown on this map.

Antarctica is the coldest, windiest, and iciest of all the continents. Most of the land is buried under ice that is nearly three miles (4.8 km) thick. This ice accumulated over millions of years through snowfall, giving Antarctica the highest average elevation among all continents (though not the highest point on Earth). The extreme climate is too harsh for people to live there permanently, but scientists come to work for long periods of time, and tourists visit regularly.

SOUTH
AMERICA

75°W

AUNT BERTHA'S ADVENTURE TRAVEL TIPS

Winter occurs during the months of June, July, and August. During this time the continent is in total darkness.

Look out for a Fata Morgana illusion. Light reflected off ice and snow creates the appearance of solid mountains in the distance. It is similar to a mirage in a hot desert.

If you fly to Antarctica, prepare for a slippery landing. With no paved runways, planes must land on ice or snow.

ADVENTURE HOT SPOTS

90°W

105°W

LANDFORMS

The snow- and ice-covered Antarctic Peninsula juts out into the sea. Penguins and seals live here.

CLIMATES

A desert is land that receives only tiny amounts of water. Antarctica is the world's largest desert, with little snowfall.

ADVENTURES

Sail the seas near Commonwealth Bay, where downhill-blowing katabatic winds whip off the ice-covered interior.

Take an airboat tour to walk among and stand practically toe-to-tail with penguins on Antarctica's coasts.

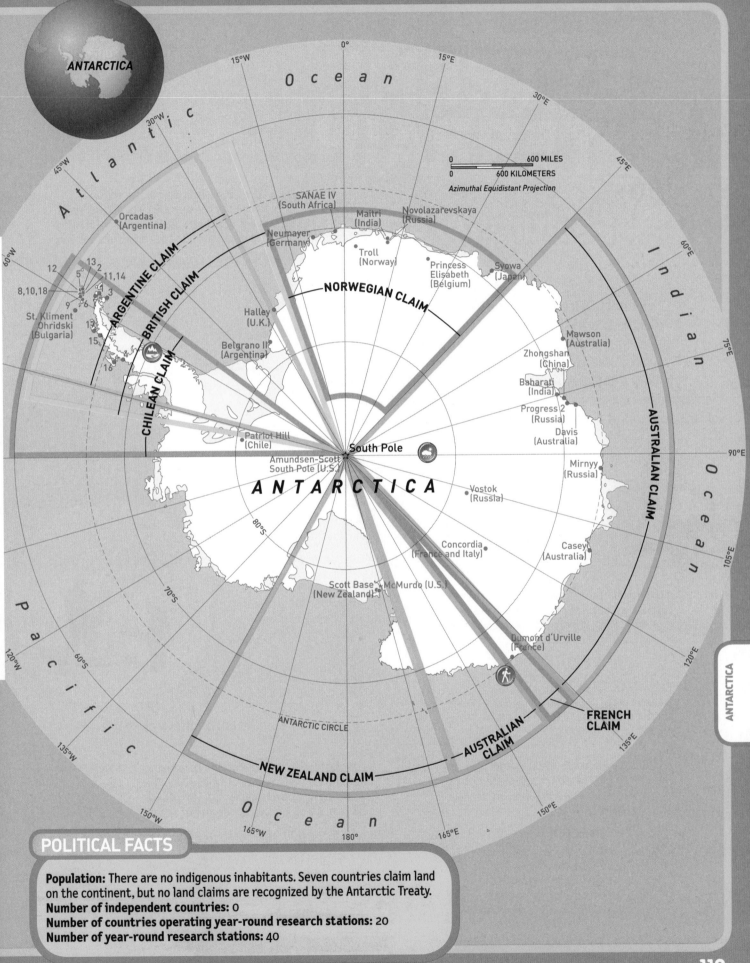

ANTARCTICA

Ocean

15°W 0° 15°E

30°E

Atlantic

45°E

30°W

0   600 MILES
0   600 KILOMETERS
Azimuthal Equidistant Projection

Indian

45°W

SANAE IV
(South Africa)

Maitri
(India)

Novolazarevskaya
(Russia)

60°E

60°W

Orcadas
(Argentina)

Neumayer
(Germany)

Troll
(Norway)

Princess
Elisabeth
(Belgium)

Syowa
(Japan)

ARGENTINE CLAIM

BRITISH CLAIM

NORWEGIAN CLAIM

75°E

12

13 2

5   11,14

8,10,18   3

9   6

St. Kliment
Ohridski
(Bulgaria)

17

15

16

Halley
(U.K.)

Belgrano II
(Argentina)

CHILEAN CLAIM

Mawson
(Australia)

Zhongshan
(China)

Bharati
(India)

Progress 2
(Russia)

Davis
(Australia)

AUSTRALIAN CLAIM

Patriot Hill
(Chile)

South Pole

90°E

Amundsen-Scott
South Pole (U.S.)

ANTARCTICA

Mirnyy
(Russia)

Vostok
(Russia)

80°S

70°S

Concordia
(France and Italy)

Casey
(Australia)

105°E

Scott Base
(New Zealand)

McMurdo (U.S.)

Dumont d'Urville
(France)

FRENCH
CLAIM

120°W

60°S

120°E

ANTARCTIC CIRCLE

AUSTRALIAN
CLAIM

135°E

135°W

Pacific

NEW ZEALAND CLAIM

150°W

150°E

Ocean

165°W 180° 165°E

ANTARCTICA

POLITICAL FACTS

Population: There are no indigenous inhabitants. Seven countries claim land
on the continent, but no land claims are recognized by the Antarctic Treaty.
Number of independent countries: 0
Number of countries operating year-round research stations: 20
Number of year-round research stations: 40

 **LANDFORMS**

EXTREME TERRAIN
Features of a frigid CONTINENT

The Antarctic Ice Sheet is the largest single piece of ice on Earth. Its area is greater than that of the United States and Mexico combined! Dividing the continent are the towering Transantarctic Mountains that stretch from the Weddell Sea to the Ross Sea. Along Antarctica's frozen coasts are mountains, islands, and volcanoes, including Mount Erebus, the continent's most active volcano. Icebergs of all shapes and sizes float just off the shore.

ADVENTURE ATTRACTIONS

CONTINENTAL ICE SHEET
A large part of the massive ice sheet that covers West Antarctica is a sight to see, but it is melting. Most scientists believe that this is a result of global climate change.

MASSIVE MOUNTAIN CHAIN
The 2,200-mile (3,541-km)-long Transantarctic Mountain range is one of the longest mountain chains on the planet.

THICK ICE
Lambert Glacier is the world's largest glacier. This ice river is more than 249 miles (401 km) long and 1.5 miles (2.4 km) thick.

DIGITAL TRAVELER!
Go online to find pictures of animals you may find around the Antarctic Peninsula. Then make a photo album of your picture collection. The peninsula waters are home to concentrations of various penguins, seals, and whales.

5 COOL PLACES TO SEE HERE

1 RING-SHAPED ISLAND
West Antarctica Islands

Deception Island is an active volcano flooded by the sea. The ring-shaped island is one of the only places in the world where a ship can sail into the center of a volcano.

DID YOU KNOW?

Scientists extract huge ice cores from ice sheets and study them to learn about climates from the past. Ice sheets contain a history of Earth's climate, written in the layers of snow and ice that have collected over millions of years.

2 ICY PLATFORM
Ross Ice Shelf

The largest ice shelf in the world has formed where the ice sheet reaches the Ross Sea. The floating ice measures roughly 182,000 square miles (471,378 sq km), about the size of Spain.

120

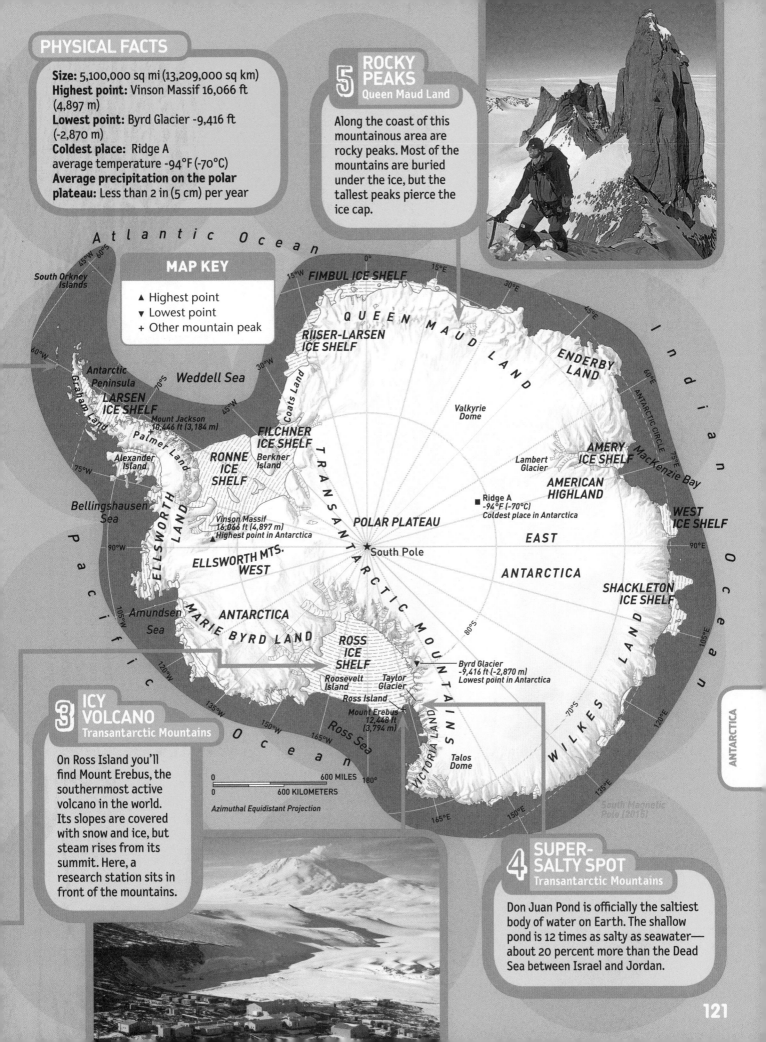

PHYSICAL FACTS

Size: 5,100,000 sq mi (13,209,000 sq km)
Highest point: Vinson Massif 16,066 ft (4,897 m)
Lowest point: Byrd Glacier -9,416 ft (-2,870 m)
Coldest place: Ridge A average temperature -94°F (-70°C)
Average precipitation on the polar plateau: Less than 2 in (5 cm) per year

5 ROCKY PEAKS
Queen Maud Land

Along the coast of this mountainous area are rocky peaks. Most of the mountains are buried under the ice, but the tallest peaks pierce the ice cap.

MAP KEY

▲ Highest point
▼ Lowest point
+ Other mountain peak

Atlantic Ocean

South Orkney Islands

FIMBUL ICE SHELF

QUEEN MAUD LAND

RIISER-LARSEN ICE SHELF

ENDERBY LAND

Antarctic Peninsula

Weddell Sea

Graham Land

LARSEN ICE SHELF

Coats Land

Valkyrie Dome

ANTARCTIC CIRCLE

Mount Jackson 10,446 ft (3,184 m)

FILCHNER ICE SHELF

Palmer Land

AMERY ICE SHELF

Lambert Glacier

Alexander Island

RONNE ICE SHELF

Berkner Island

AMERICAN HIGHLAND

Mackenzie Bay

Bellingshausen Sea

ELLSWORTH LAND

Ridge A -94°F (-70°C) Coldest place in Antarctica

WEST ICE SHELF

Vinson Massif 16,066 ft (4,897 m) Highest point in Antarctica

EAST ANTARCTICA

ELLSWORTH MTS. WEST

★ South Pole

Amundsen Sea

MARIE BYRD LAND

ANTARCTICA

SHACKLETON ICE SHELF

ROSS ICE SHELF

Byrd Glacier -9,416 ft (-2,870 m) Lowest point in Antarctica

Pacific Ocean

Roosevelt Island

Taylor Glacier

Ross Island

Ross Sea

Mount Erebus 12,448 ft (3,794 m)

VICTORIA LAND

WILKES LAND

Talos Dome

South Magnetic Pole (2015)

ANTARCTICA

Indian Ocean

TRANSANTARCTIC MOUNTAINS

POLAR PLATEAU

3 ICY VOLCANO
Transantarctic Mountains

On Ross Island you'll find Mount Erebus, the southernmost active volcano in the world. Its slopes are covered with snow and ice, but steam rises from its summit. Here, a research station sits in front of the mountains.

0 — 600 MILES
0 — 600 KILOMETERS

Azimuthal Equidistant Projection

4 SUPER-SALTY SPOT
Transantarctic Mountains

Don Juan Pond is officially the saltiest body of water on Earth. The shallow pond is 12 times as salty as seawater—about 20 percent more than the Dead Sea between Israel and Jordan.

ICE-COLD WEATHER

Coldest, windiest, and DRIEST

No matter what kinds of adventures you face in Antarctica, there is one thing that you can be sure of: It will be cold. In winter, temperatures regularly drop below -76°F (-60°C). Summer temperatures along the coast hover around 32°F (0°C). Fierce winds blow up unexpectedly, causing stormy seas, blizzards, and whiteouts. Despite the continent's ice-covered surface, Antarctica is also very dry. The interior gets two to four inches (5 to 10 cm) of snow a year, about the same amount of precipitation as the Sahara.

SOLAR HALO
The South Pole is a great place to see halos, created when light passes through ice crystals in the air.

WHITE SKY
Whiteouts are common on the Ekström Ice Shelf. It can be impossible to tell where the sky ends and the snow-covered ground begins.

BLINDING BLIZZARD
In a West Antarctic snowstorm, snow is picked up from the surface and blown sideways. Objects just a few feet away may be invisible.

DID YOU KNOW?

Among all of the habitats on Earth, the Dry Valleys are the closest equivalent to the planet Mars. Scientists come to the valleys for clues into what life may possibly be like on Mars.

5 EXTREME CLIMATES HERE

1 POLAR SUN
Polar Plateau

The South Pole experiences only one sunrise and one sunset each year. The sun rises on September 21 and remains in the sky. The sun finally sets on March 21 and stays below the horizon for the next six months.

2 DRY VALLEYS
Transantarctic Mountains

Most of the continent is buried under a thick layer of ice, but the frozen valleys are mostly silt and rocks. The valleys are so dry that ice quickly turns from solid into vapor.

3 CLOUD BANK
Antarctic Peninsula

A *föhn* wind is a warm, ground-hugging wind that blows over contours of the land. It causes snow and ice to turn from a solid into a gas, creating a thick cloud layer that blankets the ground.

MAP KEY

Ice shelf

Climatic Zones: Based on Köppen System

Polar

Ice cap

ANTARCTIC CONVERGENCE
Atlantic Ocean
Indian Ocean
Pacific Ocean
SOUTH AMERICA
AUSTRALIA
ANTARCTICA
LARSEN ICE SHELF
Weddell Sea
RIISER-LARSEN ICE SHELF
FIMBUL ICE SHELF
QUEEN MAUD LAND
ENDERBY LAND
FILCHNER ICE SHELF
RONNE ICE SHELF
Ellsworth Mts.
ELLSWORTH LAND
TRANSANTARCTIC MOUNTAINS
POLAR PLATEAU
AMERICAN HIGHLAND
AMERY ICE SHELF
WEST ICE SHELF
SHACKLETON ICE SHELF
WILKES LAND
VICTORIA LAND
ROSS ICE SHELF
Ross Sea
MARIE BYRD LAND
Amundsen Sea
ANTARCTIC CIRCLE
70°S
60°S
50°S
0°
15°E
30°E
45°E
60°E
75°E
90°E
105°E
120°E
135°E
150°E
165°E
180°
165°W
150°W
135°W
120°W
105°W
90°W
75°W
60°W
45°W
30°W
15°W
0
1,000 MILES
0
1,000 KILOMETERS

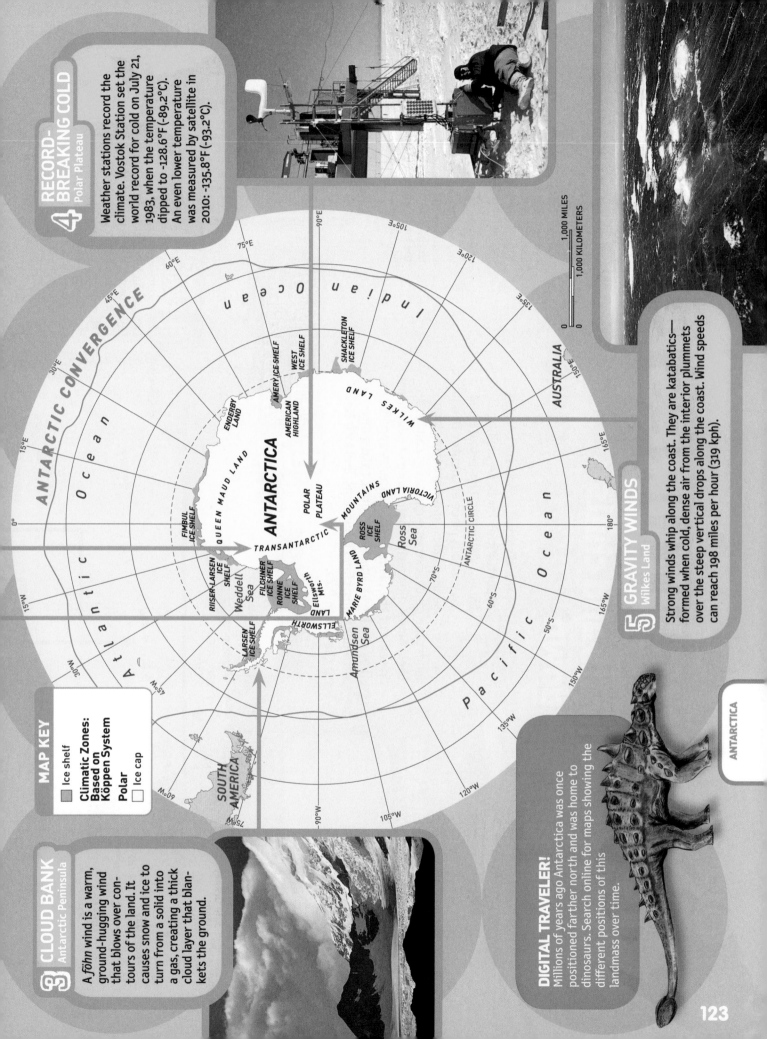

4 RECORD-BREAKING COLD
Polar Plateau

Weather stations record the climate. Vostok Station set the world record for cold on July 21, 1983, when the temperature dipped to -128.6°F (-89.2°C). An even lower temperature was measured by satellite in 2010: -135.8°F (-93.2°C).

DIGITAL TRAVELER!
Millions of years ago Antarctica was once positioned farther north and was home to dinosaurs. Search online for maps showing the different positions of this landmass over time.

5 GRAVITY WINDS
Wilkes Land

Strong winds whip along the coast. They are katabatics—formed when cold, dense air from the interior plummets over the steep vertical drops along the coast. Wind speeds can reach 198 miles per hour (319 kph).

ICY ADVENTURES
Thrills and chills down SOUTH

The world's iciest continent creates opportunities for bone-chilling thrills. Visitors to this remote and mysterious place encounter penguins, seals, whales, and a breathtaking landscape of ice. Extreme explorers can test their limits, along with their sense of adventure, in some of the planet's most intense conditions. They can kayak among icebergs, take a dip with penguins, climb mountains, and kite ski to the South Pole.

ADVENTURE ATTRACTIONS

WILDLIFE BEACH
Take a plunge in Whalers Bay, where the seawater is heated by geothermal activity and penguins roam the beach.

SEAL HEAVEN
Cruise the South Orkney Islands aboard a sturdy Zodiac landing craft. Look for huge leopard seals lazing on the ice and playful fur seals frolicking in the water.

SOUTH POLE TRIP
You can fly by ski plane to 89 degrees south and ski the final 68 miles (109 km) to the Pole. If you're feeling bold, take the longer route: Start at the continent's edge and ski 727 miles (1,170 km).

RECORD BREAKER
Felicity Aston became the first woman to ski solo across Antarctica without the help of machines or kites. She skied 1,084 miles (1,745 km) over 59 days in temperatures as low as -22°F (-30°C).

5 COOL THINGS TO DO HERE

1 PENGUIN PENINSULA
Antarctic Peninsula

Explore the Antarctic coast by boat. Weave past icebergs to reach the wildlife-filled Antarctic Peninsula. See penguins and seals up close. Walk on shore amid thousands of quirky penguins, including gentoo, Adélie, and chinstrap.

MAP KEY
🔴 Adventure attraction

South Orkney Islands
Whalers Bay
Weddell Sea
Atlantic Ocean
LARSEN ICE SHELF
RONNE ICE SHELF
FILCHNER ICE SHELF
RIISER-LARSEN ICE SHELF
Ekström Ice Shelf
FIMBUL ICE SHELF
QUEEN MAUD LAND
ENDERBY LAND
ANTARCTIC CIRCLE
Lambert Glacier
MacKenzie Bay
AMERY ICE SHELF
AMERICAN
Indian
TRAN
Pac

600 MILES
600 KILOMETERS

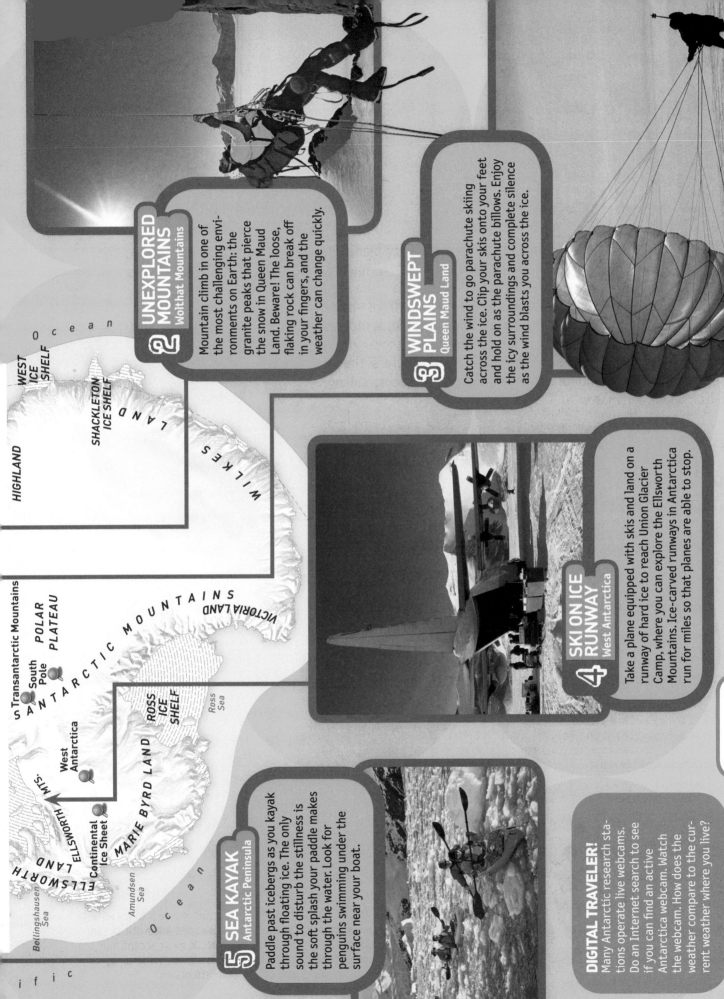

2 UNEXPLORED MOUNTAINS
Wolthat Mountains

Mountain climb in one of the most challenging environments on Earth: the granite peaks that pierce the snow in Queen Maud Land. Beware! The loose, flaking rock can break off in your fingers, and the weather can change quickly.

3 WINDSWEPT PLAINS
Queen Maud Land

Catch the wind to go parachute skiing across the ice. Clip your skis onto your feet and hold on as the parachute billows. Enjoy the icy surroundings and complete silence as the wind blasts you across the ice.

4 SKI ON ICE RUNWAY
West Antarctica

Take a plane equipped with skis and land on a runway of hard ice to reach Union Glacier Camp, where you can explore the Ellsworth Mountains. Ice-carved runways in Antarctica run for miles so that planes are able to stop.

5 SEA KAYAK
Antarctic Peninsula

Paddle past icebergs as you kayak through floating ice. The only sound to disturb the stillness is the soft splash your paddle makes through the water. Look for penguins swimming under the surface near your boat.

DIGITAL TRAVELER!

Many Antarctic research stations operate live webcams. Do an Internet search to see if you can find an active Antarctica webcam. Watch the webcam. How does the weather compare to the current weather where you live?

Map labels:
HIGHLAND
WEST ICE SHELF
SHACKLETON ICE SHELF
LAND
WILKES LAND
VICTORIA LAND
ANTARCTIC MOUNTAINS
Transantarctic Mountains
South Pole
POLAR PLATEAU
ROSS ICE SHELF
Ross Sea
West Antarctica
MARIE BYRD LAND
ELLSWORTH MTS.
Continental Ice Sheet
ELLSWORTH LAND
Amundsen Sea
Bellingshausen Sea
Ocean
ific

ANTARCTICA

125

OCEANS
The surging SEA

LANDFORMS

Most of the world's volcanoes are located in "The Ring of Fire" along the edge of the Pacific Ocean.

The oceans cover more than 70 percent of the planet's surface and make all life on Earth possible. The major oceans of the world—Pacific, Atlantic, Indian, and Arctic—harbor amazing creatures in their waters, from whales, sea turtles, and leopard seals to giant squid, octopuses, and stinging jellyfish. Deep-ocean submersibles are discovering and exploring new areas of ocean all the time. For adventurers, the oceans are a playground for swimming, diving, boat racing, sailing, water skiing, and more.

AUNT BERTHA'S ADVENTURE TRAVEL TIPS

The open ocean is a great place to spot whales. Keep your binoculars handy to see one breach, or leap into the air, and shoot air and water from its blowhole.

While getting used to being at sea, watch the horizon and stay on deck. These will help with sea sickness.

Swimming in the ocean is different from swimming in a pool. Look out for currents and waves.

Get wet and go wild in a Jet Ski race. Jet Skis can reach a speed of 80 miles per hour (129 kph). You can experience a ride at resorts around the world.

Map labels

Barents Sea
Kara
ARCTIC CIRCLE
EUROPE
ASIA
Black Sea
Caspian Sea
Mediterranean Sea
Persian Gulf
TROPIC OF CANCER
East China Sea
Red Sea
Gulf of Aden
Arabian Sea
Laccadive Sea
Bay of Bengal
Andaman Sea
South China Sea
Sulu Sea
AFRICA
EQUATOR
Celebes Sea
Java Sea
Banda Sea
Timor Sea
(-7,125 m) -23,376 ft
Indian Ocean's deepest point
INDIAN
TROPIC OF CAPRICORN
OCEAN
AUST
ANTARCTIC CIRCLE

OCEAN AREAS

The Atlantic, Indian, and Pacific Oceans merge into icy waters around Antarctica. Some define this as the Antarctic Ocean, Austral Ocean, or Southern Ocean. While most accept four oceans, including the Arctic, there is no international agreement on the name and extent of a fifth ocean.

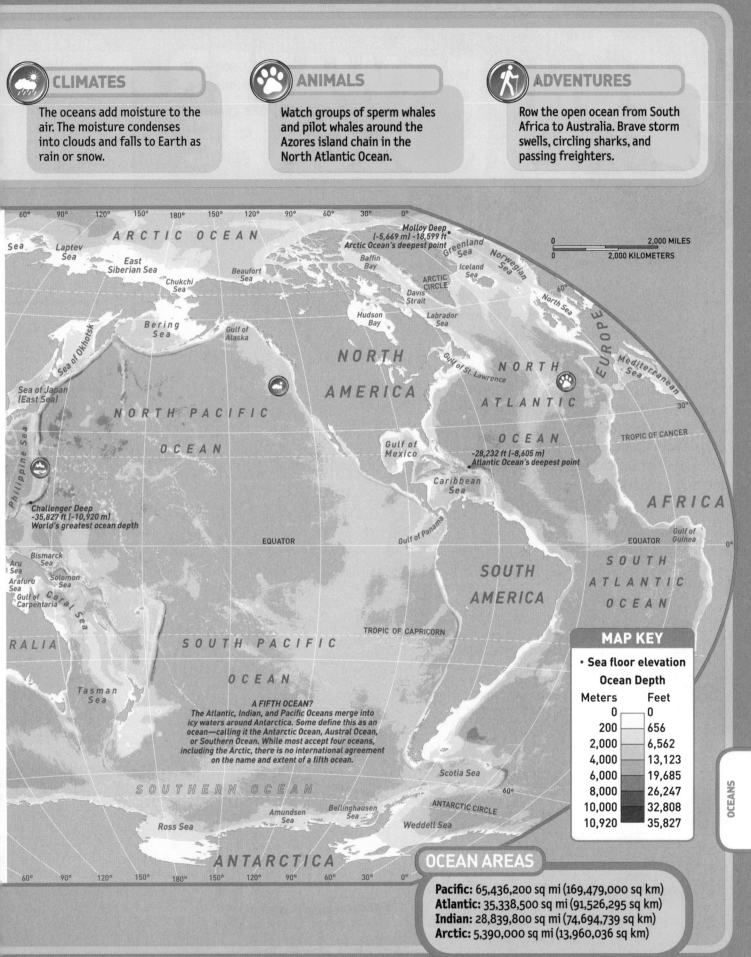

CLIMATES

The oceans add moisture to the air. The moisture condenses into clouds and falls to Earth as rain or snow.

ANIMALS

Watch groups of sperm whales and pilot whales around the Azores island chain in the North Atlantic Ocean.

ADVENTURES

Row the open ocean from South Africa to Australia. Brave storm swells, circling sharks, and passing freighters.

60° 90° 120° 150° 180° 150° 120° 90° 60° 30° 0°

ARCTIC OCEAN

Sea

Laptev Sea

East Siberian Sea

Chukchi Sea

Beaufort Sea

Molloy Deep
(-5,669 m) -18,599 ft
Arctic Ocean's deepest point

Greenland Sea

Baffin Bay

Iceland Sea

Norwegian Sea

ARCTIC CIRCLE

Davis Strait

North Sea

Hudson Bay

Labrador Sea

0 2,000 MILES
0 2,000 KILOMETERS

Sea of Okhotsk

Bering Sea

Gulf of Alaska

NORTH AMERICA

Gulf of St. Lawrence

NORTH

ATLANTIC

EUROPE

Mediterranean Sea

Sea of Japan (East Sea)

NORTH PACIFIC

OCEAN

Gulf of Mexico

OCEAN

-28,232 ft (-8,605 m)
Atlantic Ocean's deepest point

TROPIC OF CANCER

30°

Philippine Sea

Challenger Deep
-35,827 ft (-10,920 m)
World's greatest ocean depth

Caribbean Sea

AFRICA

Aru Sea

Bismarck Sea

Solomon Sea

EQUATOR

Gulf of Panama

EQUATOR

Gulf of Guinea

0°

Arafuru Sea

Gulf of Carpentaria

Coral Sea

SOUTH

AMERICA

SOUTH

ATLANTIC

OCEAN

RALIA

Tasman Sea

SOUTH PACIFIC

OCEAN

TROPIC OF CAPRICORN

MAP KEY

• **Sea floor elevation**

Ocean Depth

A FIFTH OCEAN?
The Atlantic, Indian, and Pacific Oceans merge into icy waters around Antarctica. Some define this as an ocean—calling it the Antarctic Ocean, Austral Ocean, or Southern Ocean. While most accept four oceans, including the Arctic, there is no international agreement on the name and extent of a fifth ocean.

Scotia Sea

Meters	Feet
0	0
200	656
2,000	6,562
4,000	13,123
6,000	19,685
8,000	26,247
10,000	32,808
10,920	35,827

SOUTHERN OCEAN

60°

Amundsen Sea

Bellinghausen Sea

ANTARCTIC CIRCLE

Weddell Sea

Ross Sea

ANTARCTICA

60° 90° 120° 150° 180° 150° 120° 90° 60° 30° 0°

OCEANS

OCEAN AREAS

Pacific: 65,436,200 sq mi (169,479,000 sq km)
Atlantic: 35,338,500 sq mi (91,526,295 sq km)
Indian: 28,839,800 sq mi (74,694,739 sq km)
Arctic: 5,390,000 sq mi (13,960,036 sq km)

UNDERWATER LANDSCAPE

Hidden mountains, active VOLCANOES

The world's flattest place is found in the deep ocean and is called the abyssal plain. Rising from the plain is the Mid-Oceanic Ridge, an immense chain of mostly underwater mountains. The chain circles the globe, stretching more than 40,000 miles (64,374 km) and marking the seams where Earth's tectonic plates—giant sections of the crust—are moving apart. The ocean also has amazing underwater hot springs, called hydrothermal vents, and pitch-black trenches that are the deepest spots on Earth.

5 UNDERWATER RESOURCES
Arabian Sea

Massive pools of natural gas and crude oil, or petroleum, lie underground close to the edge of the continent. These fossil fuels are extracted at offshore wells, then shipped across the Indian Ocean all over the world.

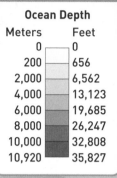

Map labels: EURASIA BASIN, Nansen Basin, ARCTIC, ARCTIC CIRCLE, EUROPE, ASIA, Aleutian Basin, ALEUTIAN, Kuril-Kamchatka Trench, Emperor Seamounts, NORTHWEST PACIFIC BASIN, TROPIC OF CANCER, AFRICA, ARABIAN BASIN, Kyushu-Palau Ridge, Mariana Trench, PHILIPPINE BASIN, South China Basin, Mid-Pacific Mountains, CENTRAL PACIFIC BASIN, EQUATOR, Somali Basin, Chagos-Laccadive Ridge, MID-INDIAN RIDGE, MID-INDIAN BASIN, Cocos Basin, Ninety-East Ridge, Caroline Basin, Melanesian Basin, Ontong-Java Rise, Mascarene Ridge, Mascarene Plateau, JAVA TRENCH, WHARTON BASIN, INDIAN OCEAN, Coral Sea Basin, North Fiji Basin, Kermadec Trench, Tonga Trench, TROPIC OF CAPRICORN, Madagascar Basin, Perth Basin, AUSTRALIA, Lord Howe Rise, South Fiji Basin, Mozambique Basin, SOUTHWEST INDIAN RIDGE, CROZET BASIN, SOUTHEAST INDIAN RIDGE, SOUTH AUSTRALIAN BASIN, TASMAN BASIN, Campbell Plateau, Kerguelen Plateau, AUSTRALIAN-ANTARCTIC BASIN, INDIAN-ANTARCTIC RIDGE, ANTARCTIC CIRCLE, SOU

0   2,000 MILES
0   2,000 KILOMETERS

DID YOU KNOW?

The largest volcano in the world is underwater. Roughly the size of New Mexico, Tamu Massif sits in the Pacific Ocean about 1,000 miles (1,609 km) east of Japan. The giant volcano has been inactive for at least 100 million years.

DIGITAL TRAVELER!

Some low-lying countries, such as the Netherlands, are known for floating homes or homes built on stilts. These offer protection from floods and rising sea levels. Search the Internet for photos of floating homes.

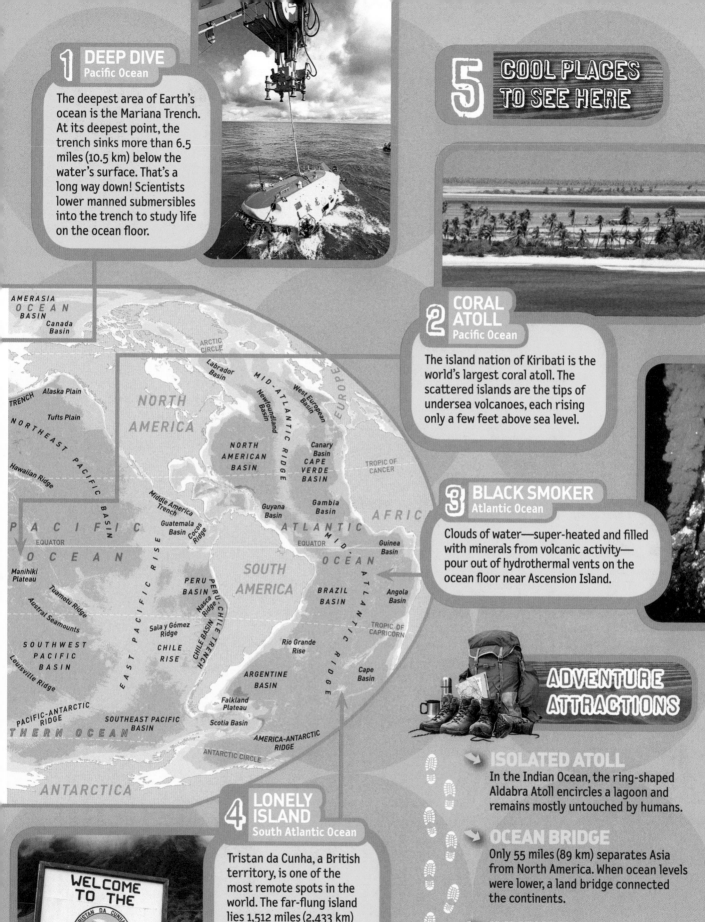

1 DEEP DIVE
Pacific Ocean

The deepest area of Earth's ocean is the Mariana Trench. At its deepest point, the trench sinks more than 6.5 miles (10.5 km) below the water's surface. That's a long way down! Scientists lower manned submersibles into the trench to study life on the ocean floor.

5 COOL PLACES TO SEE HERE

2 CORAL ATOLL
Pacific Ocean

The island nation of Kiribati is the world's largest coral atoll. The scattered islands are the tips of undersea volcanoes, each rising only a few feet above sea level.

3 BLACK SMOKER
Atlantic Ocean

Clouds of water—super-heated and filled with minerals from volcanic activity—pour out of hydrothermal vents on the ocean floor near Ascension Island.

ADVENTURE ATTRACTIONS

ISOLATED ATOLL
In the Indian Ocean, the ring-shaped Aldabra Atoll encircles a lagoon and remains mostly untouched by humans.

OCEAN BRIDGE
Only 55 miles (89 km) separates Asia from North America. When ocean levels were lower, a land bridge connected the continents.

IMMENSE MOUNTAIN CHAIN
The Mid-Atlantic Ridge stretches for about 10,000 miles (16,093 km) at the bottom of the Atlantic Ocean. This mountain chain runs along a boundary of tectonic plates.

4 LONELY ISLAND
South Atlantic Ocean

Tristan da Cunha, a British territory, is one of the most remote spots in the world. The far-flung island lies 1,512 miles (2,433 km) from the nearest inhabited island and 1,750 miles (2,816 km) from Africa, the nearest continent.

WELCOME TO THE
TRISTAN DA CUNHA
SOUTH ATLANTIC
REMOTEST ISLAND

WATERY EXTREMES

Ocean rivers and STORMY SEAS

Ocean water is always moving, with a powerful pull on weather around the world. Fast-moving surface currents carry warm water north from the tropics toward the North Pole. As the water cools, it sinks and flows south again like a deep-sea river. The water flows through the ocean around Antarctica before heading north again. It takes about 500 years for this giant conveyor to move water through the ocean and make one complete trip around Earth.

ADVENTURE ATTRACTIONS

FOGGY OUTLOOK
Southeast of Newfoundland, the cold Labrador Current meets the warm Gulf Stream, producing frequent heavy fogs.

SUPPORTING WILDLIFE
The plankton-rich Peru Current that flows along the coast of Peru and Chile supports marine birds, fish, and mammals.

A MIX OF BLUES
The Kuroshio Current flows off Japan's coast. Its warm, salty water is a deeper blue than the surrounding ocean.

EXTREME CLIMATES HERE

1 MIGHTY RIVER
North Pacific Ocean

The North Pacific Current flows like a fast-moving river. It moves water from the tropics up the east coast of Asia and across the Pacific Ocean. Ships use the current to carry them to North America.

2 HURRICANE ALLEY
Mid-Atlantic Ocean

Hurricane Alley stretches from northern Africa to Central America and the Gulf Coast of the United States. The warm water is a hotbed for hurricanes. The West Indies are usually the first landmass to be hit.

3 WIDE AND WEEDY SEA
West Atlantic Ocean

The Sargasso Sea is the world's only sea bordered only by ocean currents. The spiraling currents sweep vast mats of floating, golden seaweed into the weedy water. The weather in the sea is calm, humid, and very hot.

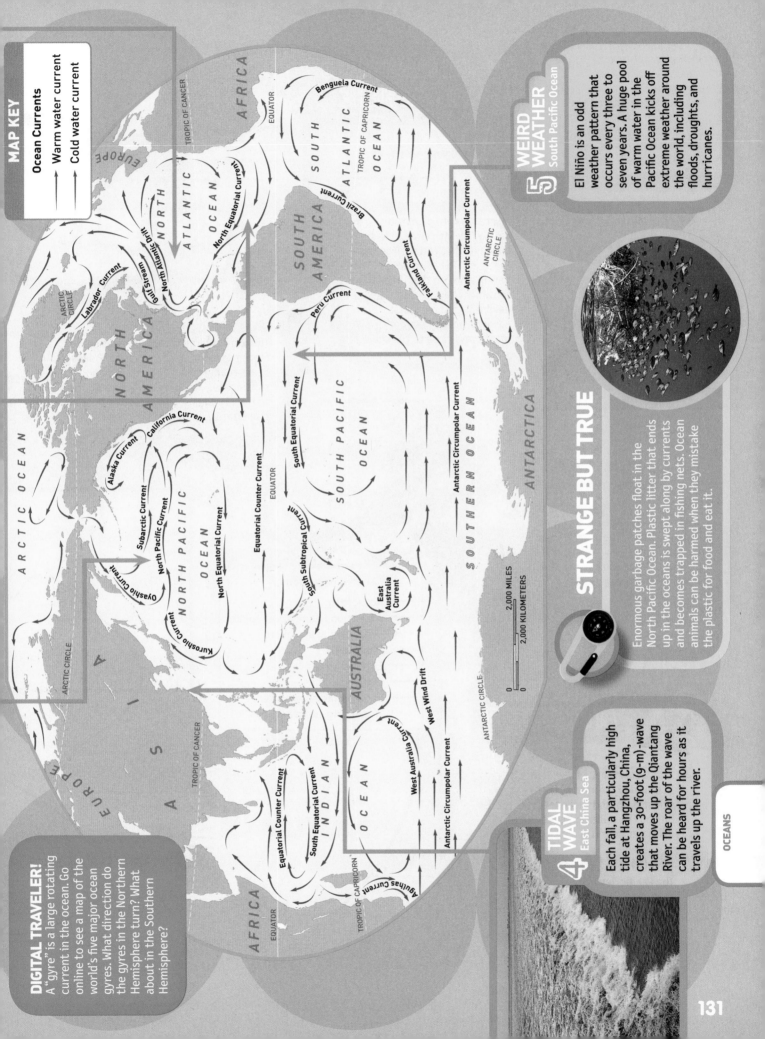

MAP KEY

Ocean Currents
→ Warm water current
→ Cold water current

DIGITAL TRAVELER!

A "gyre" is a large rotating current in the ocean. Go online to see a map of the world's five major ocean gyres. What direction do the gyres in the Northern Hemisphere turn? What about in the Southern Hemisphere?

WEIRD WEATHER
South Pacific Ocean

5

El Niño is an odd weather pattern that occurs every three to seven years. A huge pool of warm water in the Pacific Ocean kicks off extreme weather around the world, including floods, droughts, and hurricanes.

STRANGE BUT TRUE

Enormous garbage patches float in the North Pacific Ocean. Plastic litter that ends up in the oceans is swept along by currents and becomes trapped in fishing nets. Ocean animals can be harmed when they mistake the plastic for food and eat it.

TIDAL WAVE
East China Sea

4

Each fall, a particularly high tide at Hangzhou, China, creates a 30-foot (9-m)-wave that moves up the Qiantang River. The roar of the wave can be heard for hours as it travels up the river.

2,000 MILES
2,000 KILOMETERS

DIGITAL TRAVELER!
Some ocean animals hide in plain sight with bodies that are as clear as glass. Search the Internet to find a photo of a transparent sea creature. Then write a caption to describe this animal in 25 words or less.

5 COOL ANIMALS TO SEE HERE

1 GIANT WATER WINGS
West Pacific Ocean

Manta rays are plankton-eating fish with large, triangular wings that can span seven feet (2 m). They also have hornlike fins on their heads, for which they are also called devilfish. At Kona, Hawaii, adventurers can swim with manta rays close to the shore.

2 POLAR BEARS
Arctic Ocean

The world's largest bear depends on frozen seas for most of its food. Polar bears roam the Arctic by walking on shifting ice. They prey on seals that come to the surface to breathe. Polar bears also hunt by swimming beneath the ice.

3 OCEAN WANDERERS
Southern Ocean

Albatrosses have the largest wingspan of any bird—up to 11 feet (3.4 m). Adults spend most of their lives—up to 60 years—at sea. They feed on fish.

ADVENTURE ATTRACTIONS

SEABIRD CITY
In crowded colonies in the North Atlantic, northern gannets dive for fish, hitting the water at speeds up to 70 miles per hour (113 kph).

MARINE PARK
The Pacific Remote Islands National Monument is filled with manta rays, silky sharks, and beaked whales.

TURTLE ISLANDS
The isolated Chagos Archipelago in the center of the Indian Ocean is a nesting site for green and hawksbill sea turtles.

MAP KEY

Animal Migrations
→ Arctic tern
→ Ascension Island green turtle
→ Australian spiny lobster
→ Blue whale
→ European eel
→ Gentoo penguin
→ Short-tailed shearwater
→ Wandering albatross

ARCTIC

ASIA

NORTH PACIFIC OCEAN

EQUATOR

AFRICA

INDIAN OCEAN

TROPIC OF CAPRICORN

AUSTRALIA

SOUTH

0   2,000 MILES
0   2,000 KILOMETERS

 **ANIMALS**

UNIQUE CREATURES
From the surface to the ABYSS

RECORD BREAKER

A Pacific deep-sea octopus protects her eggs for 53 months—nearly 4.5 years! That's the longest period that any animal is known to brood its eggs.

The world's biggest and weirdest creatures inhabit the oceans. They live near the shore, in the wide-open ocean, or on the frozen sea. A great variety of animals live around coral reefs, including fish, sea urchins, and sea turtles. In the deep ocean, animals survive conditions of crushing pressure, ice-cold temperatures, and total darkness. The deep sea has barely been explored, which means many amazing ocean animals have yet to be discovered.

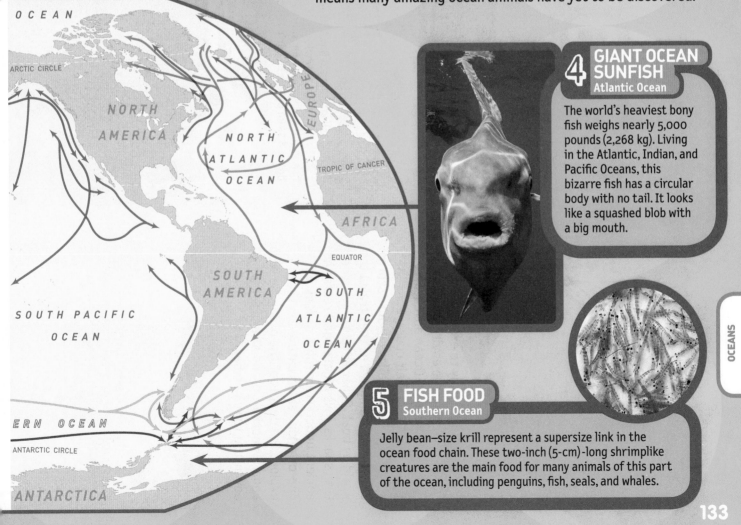

4 GIANT OCEAN SUNFISH
Atlantic Ocean

The world's heaviest bony fish weighs nearly 5,000 pounds (2,268 kg). Living in the Atlantic, Indian, and Pacific Oceans, this bizarre fish has a circular body with no tail. It looks like a squashed blob with a big mouth.

5 FISH FOOD
Southern Ocean

Jelly bean–size krill represent a supersize link in the ocean food chain. These two-inch (5-cm)-long shrimplike creatures are the main food for many animals of this part of the ocean, including penguins, fish, seals, and whales.

(Map labels) OCEAN · ARCTIC CIRCLE · NORTH AMERICA · NORTH ATLANTIC OCEAN · EUROPE · TROPIC OF CANCER · AFRICA · EQUATOR · SOUTH AMERICA · SOUTH ATLANTIC OCEAN · SOUTH PACIFIC OCEAN · ...ERN OCEAN · ANTARCTIC CIRCLE · ANTARCTICA

OCEANS

133

MARINE ACTION

Wet and WILD

G et ready to explore the most extreme environment on the planet. Ocean adventurers can test their courage in different ways. Sailors endure storms and the pounding sea as they travel the world by boat. Other adventurers swim with sharks, investigate coral reefs and ancient underwater ruins, or look for one-of-a-kind sea creatures as they explore the depths of the ocean. So step aboard, snorkel up, and dive in for an adventure to remember.

DID YOU KNOW?

Only three people have reached Challenger Deep, the deepest point in the ocean: Jacques Piccard and Don Walsh aboard *Bathyscaphe Trieste* in 1960 and James Cameron aboard *DEEPSEA CHALLENGER* in 2012.

5 COOL THINGS TO DO HERE

1 SWIM WITH SHARKS
Pacific Ocean

Ride a boat into Donsol Bay. You are likely to see a school of supersize whale sharks, the largest fish in the sea. Put on your snorkel mask and fins and swim beside them, if you dare.

2 ROUND-THE-WORLD SAIL
Atlantic Ocean

Daring sailors travel around the world on yachts or catamarans. They face huge waves and lurking marine creatures in the world's most challenging waters.

ADVENTURE ATTRACTIONS

SUNKEN CITY
Deep-sea divers explore strange carved rocks on the ocean floor near Yonaguni, Japan. Some experts think they are the sunken ruins of a 5,000-year-old city.

NORTH POLE
In the middle of the frozen Arctic Ocean, explorers can stand at the one spot on Earth where every direction is south.

EXTREME SAILING
Between Africa's Cape of Good Hope and South America's Cape Horn blow fierce winds known as the Roaring Forties and Furious Fifties.

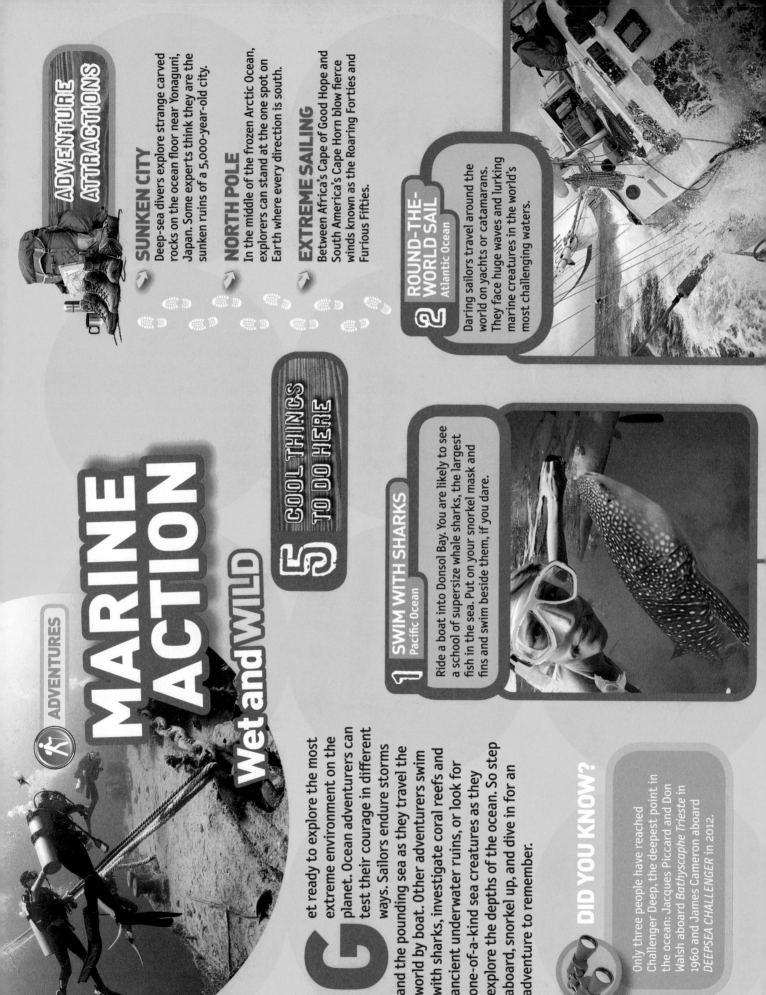

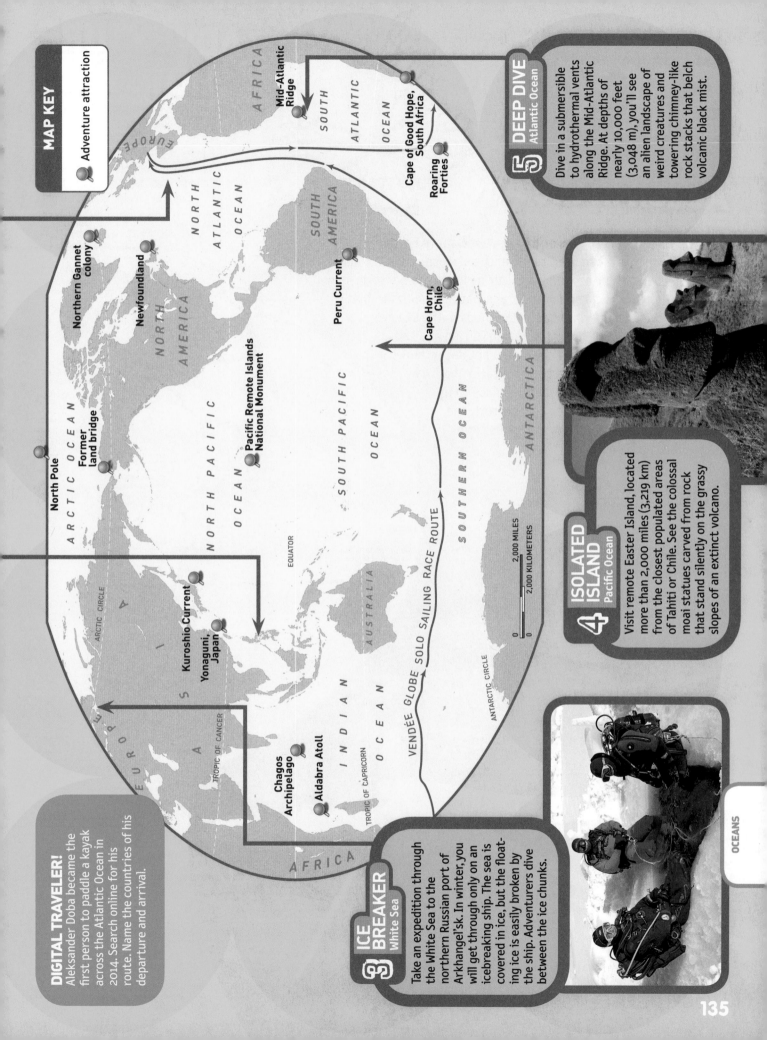

MAP KEY

🔘 Adventure attraction

DIGITAL TRAVELER!

Aleksander Doba became the first person to paddle a kayak across the Atlantic Ocean in 2014. Search online for his route. Name the countries of his departure and arrival.

North Pole

Former land bridge

ARCTIC OCEAN

ARCTIC CIRCLE

Northern Gannet colony

Newfoundland

NORTH AMERICA

NORTH ATLANTIC OCEAN

Kuroshio Current

Yonaguni, Japan

TROPIC OF CANCER

Chagos Archipelago

Aldabra Atoll

INDIAN OCEAN

TROPIC OF CAPRICORN

NORTH PACIFIC OCEAN

EQUATOR

Pacific Remote Islands National Monument

SOUTH PACIFIC OCEAN

AUSTRALIA

VENDÉE GLOBE SOLO SAILING RACE ROUTE

SOUTHERN OCEAN

ANTARCTIC CIRCLE

ANTARCTICA

AFRICA

EUROPE

AFRICA

Mid-Atlantic Ridge

SOUTH ATLANTIC OCEAN

Cape of Good Hope, South Africa

Roaring Forties

SOUTH AMERICA

Peru Current

Cape Horn, Chile

0   2,000 MILES
0   2,000 KILOMETERS

③ ICE BREAKER
White Sea

Take an expedition through the White Sea to the northern Russian port of Arkhangel'sk. In winter, you will get through only on an icebreaking ship. The sea is covered in ice, but the floating ice is easily broken by the ship. Adventurers dive between the ice chunks.

④ ISOLATED ISLAND
Pacific Ocean

Visit remote Easter Island, located more than 2,000 miles (3,219 km) from the closest populated areas of Tahiti or Chile. See the colossal moai statues carved from rock that stand silently on the grassy slopes of an extinct volcano.

⑤ DEEP DIVE
Atlantic Ocean

Dive in a submersible to hydrothermal vents along the Mid-Atlantic Ridge. At depths of nearly 10,000 feet (3,048 m), you'll see an alien landscape of weird creatures and towering chimney-like rock stacks that belch volcanic black mist.

OCEANS

135

SKY

Action in the AIR

The sky is really everything we see above Earth, but the term is often used to mean the atmosphere—a thick band of air around Earth. Air includes the gases oxygen, nitrogen, carbon dioxide, and water vapor, as well as dust, smoke, and bacteria. Clouds in the sky are dense masses of water vapor that bring us rain and snow. The wind can be a force that cools off a hot day or blows away rain clouds. The sky is a transportation highway for birds, bats, and insects—and the place to fly kites, planes, and rockets. For adventurers, the sky is a playground for daring activities from hang gliding to free falling.

For sky-high thrills, some adventurers take to gliding—with no engine, glider pilots use the air currents to fly.

See pp. 46–47 for the countries of Europe

See p. 11 for the countries of North America

See pp. 100–101 for the countries of Oceania

See p. 29 for the countries of South America

ADVENTURE HOT SPOTS

CLIMATES

People at the Mont-Mégantic Dark Sky Observatory near Sherbrooke, Canada, study light pollution that stops us from seeing stars at night.

0   2,000 MILES
0   2,000 KILOMETERS

Winkel Tripel Projection

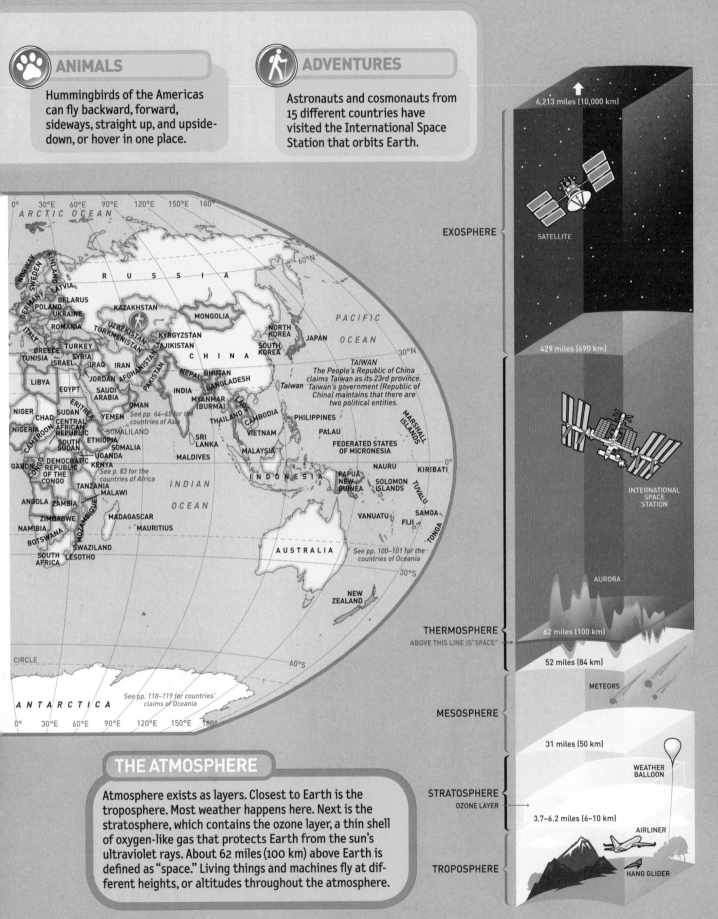

ANIMALS

Hummingbirds of the Americas can fly backward, forward, sideways, straight up, and upside-down, or hover in one place.

ADVENTURES

Astronauts and cosmonauts from 15 different countries have visited the International Space Station that orbits Earth.

ARCTIC OCEAN

NORWAY
SWEDEN
FINLAND
GERMANY
LATVIA
BELARUS
POLAND
UKRAINE
ROMANIA
ITALY
GREECE
TUNISIA
TURKEY
SYRIA
ISRAEL
LIBYA
JORDAN
IRAQ
IRAN
EGYPT
SAUDI ARABIA
NIGER
CHAD
SUDAN
ERITREA
YEMEN
OMAN
NIGERIA
CAMEROON
CENTRAL AFRICAN REPUBLIC
SOUTH SUDAN
ETHIOPIA
SOMALILAND
SOMALIA
GABON
CONGO
DEMOCRATIC REPUBLIC OF THE CONGO
UGANDA
KENYA
TANZANIA
ANGOLA
ZAMBIA
MALAWI
ZIMBABWE
MOZAMBIQUE
NAMIBIA
BOTSWANA
MADAGASCAR
MAURITIUS
SWAZILAND
SOUTH AFRICA
LESOTHO

RUSSIA
KAZAKHSTAN
MONGOLIA
UZBEKISTAN
TURKMENISTAN
KYRGYZSTAN
TAJIKISTAN
AFGHANISTAN
PAKISTAN
NEPAL
BHUTAN
INDIA
BANGLADESH
MYANMAR (BURMA)
CHINA
NORTH KOREA
SOUTH KOREA
JAPAN

TAIWAN
The People's Republic of China claims Taiwan as its 23rd province. Taiwan's government (Republic of China) maintains that there are two political entities.

LAOS
THAILAND
CAMBODIA
VIETNAM
SRI LANKA
MALDIVES
MALAYSIA
PHILIPPINES
PALAU
FEDERATED STATES OF MICRONESIA
INDONESIA
PAPUA NEW GUINEA
NAURU
KIRIBATI
SOLOMON ISLANDS
TUVALU
MARSHALL ISLANDS
VANUATU
FIJI
SAMOA
TONGA

AUSTRALIA

NEW ZEALAND

PACIFIC OCEAN
INDIAN OCEAN

ANTARCTICA

See pp. 64–65 for the countries of Asia

See p. 83 for the countries of Africa

See pp. 100–101 for the countries of Oceania

See pp. 118–119 for countries' claims of Oceania

60°N
30°N
0°
30°S
60°S
CIRCLE

0° 30°E 60°E 90°E 120°E 150°E 180°

EXOSPHERE
6,213 miles (10,000 km)
SATELLITE

429 miles (690 km)
INTERNATIONAL SPACE STATION

AURORA
THERMOSPHERE
62 miles (100 km)
ABOVE THIS LINE IS "SPACE"
52 miles (84 km)

METEORS
MESOSPHERE
31 miles (50 km)

WEATHER BALLOON
STRATOSPHERE
OZONE LAYER
3.7–6.2 miles (6–10 km)

AIRLINER
TROPOSPHERE
HANG GLIDER

THE ATMOSPHERE

Atmosphere exists as layers. Closest to Earth is the troposphere. Most weather happens here. Next is the stratosphere, which contains the ozone layer, a thin shell of oxygen-like gas that protects Earth from the sun's ultraviolet rays. About 62 miles (100 km) above Earth is defined as "space." Living things and machines fly at different heights, or altitudes throughout the atmosphere.

CLOUDS AND SUNLIGHT

Thunder, lightning, and falling STARS

The pattern of climate across the world—as shown on the map below—depends on sunlight and changes in the atmosphere. Winds and ocean currents move clouds in the sky, affecting the fall of rain, snow, sleet, and hail. Here are five specific climate stories, but similar cloud formations, storms, changes, and eclipses are found all over the world at various times.

DIGITAL TRAVELER!
Go online to see photos taken from space of aurora Australis (the southern lights) and aurora borealis (the northern lights).

EXTREME CLIMATES HERE

5

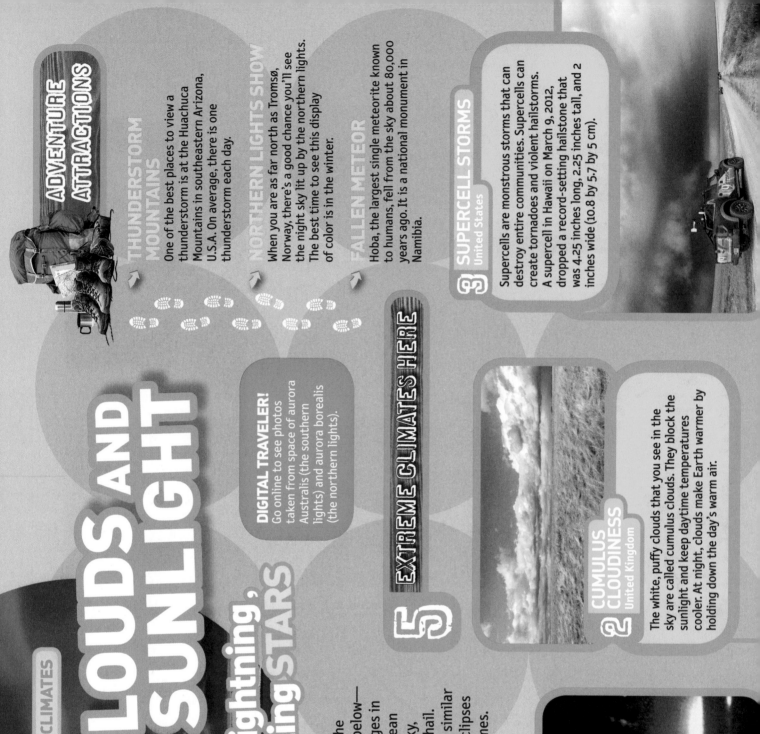

ADVENTURE ATTRACTIONS

THUNDERSTORM MOUNTAINS
One of the best places to view a thunderstorm is at the Huachuca Mountains in southeastern Arizona, U.S.A. On average, there is one thunderstorm each day.

NORTHERN LIGHTS SHOW
When you are as far north as Tromsø, Norway, there's a good chance you'll see the night sky lit up by the northern lights. The best time to see this display of color is in the winter.

FALLEN METEOR
Hoba, the largest single meteorite known to humans, fell from the sky about 80,000 years ago. It is a national monument in Namibia.

3 SUPERCELL STORMS
United States
Supercells are monstrous storms that can destroy entire communities. Supercells can create tornadoes and violent hailstorms. A supercell in Hawaii on March 9, 2012, dropped a record-setting hailstone that was 4.25 inches long, 2.25 inches tall, and 2 inches wide (10.8 by 5.7 by 5 cm).

2 CUMULUS CLOUDINESS
United Kingdom
The white, puffy clouds that you see in the sky are called cumulus clouds. They block the sunlight and keep daytime temperatures cooler. At night, clouds make Earth warmer by holding down the day's warm air.

1 SPRITES OF LIGHT
Argentina
Sprites are bright reddish flashes of light high above thunder clouds. They may occur during thunderstorms, but they flash so quickly that it takes a high-speed camera to help us know what they look like.

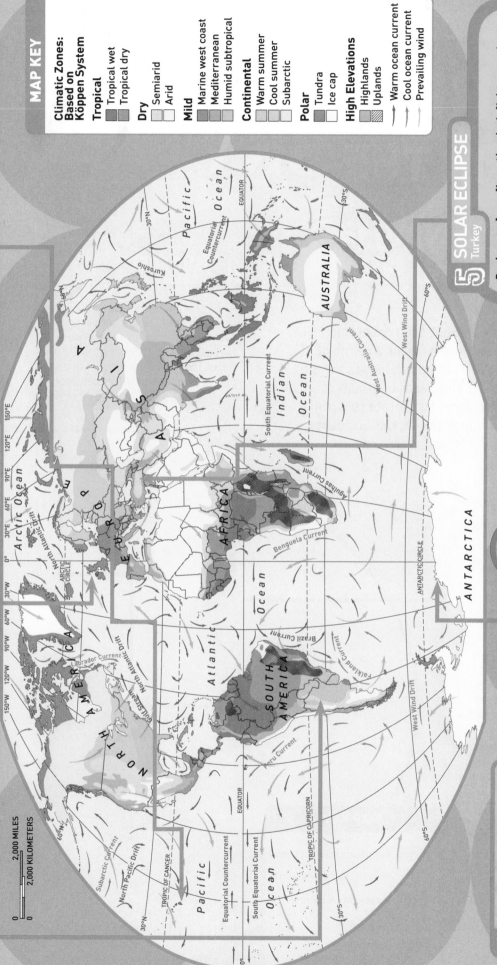

MAP KEY

Climatic Zones:
Based on
Köppen System

Tropical
- Tropical wet
- Tropical dry

Dry
- Semiarid
- Arid

Mild
- Marine west coast
- Mediterranean
- Humid subtropical

Continental
- Warm summer
- Cool summer
- Subarctic

Polar
- Tundra
- Ice cap

High Elevations
- Highlands
- Uplands

→ Warm ocean current
→ Cool ocean current
→ Prevailing wind

---

5 SOLAR ECLIPSE
Turkey

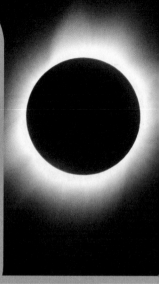

During a solar eclipse, the sky is light one minute and then is dark for a few minutes. Then it's light again. A solar eclipse happens when the moon blocks our view of the sun by getting between Earth and the sun. Solar eclipses are visible somewhere in the world about twice a year.

DID YOU KNOW?

During a thunderstorm, thunder and lightning happen at the same time. But you will probably see the lightning before you hear the thunder because light travels through air faster than sound.

---

4 GLOBAL WARMING
Antarctica

Weather satellites tell us that Earth is getting warmer and warmer. Melting glaciers in Antarctica and other polar regions create problems for humans as well as animals. If glaciers continue to melt, the oceans will rise so high that cities along the coasts will be underwater.

SKY

139

CRITTERS IN THE SKY

Flying far and HIGH

The largest animal to ever fly through the sky became extinct millions of years ago. The pterosaur, a cousin of dinosaurs, was twice as big as a jet fighter. Today's sky is a highway for smaller creatures. Thousands of groups of birds and bats fly across the planet to migrate to warm winter places. Some insects migrate through the air, too. Scientists have even tracked microscopic bacteria catching a ride on dust.

4 BLUE FEET
Galápagos Islands

When blue-footed boobies are hungry, they soar over the sea. With keen eyesight, they can spot tasty fish 80 feet (24 m) below the surface of the water. They fold their long wings and plunge into the water for their food.

3 PARACHUTING SPIDERS
United States

Some tiny spiders release a thin line of silk that gets caught by the wind. As if traveling by hot-air balloon, they sail on the wind for hundreds of miles. Scientists think this may explain why these spiders are often the first to colonize new volcanic islands. They can survive on the wind without food for up to three weeks.

DID YOU KNOW?

A group of tiny eight-legged creatures called tardigrades traveled into outer space in 2007. When they returned from their ten-day orbit, they became the only animals native to Earth that are known to have survived extraterrestrial conditions without help from humans.

Arctic

ARCTIC CIRCLE

NORTH AMERICA

TROPIC OF CANCER

Pacific Ocean

Atlantic Ocean

EQUATOR

SOUTH AMERICA

TROPIC OF CAPRICORN

ANTARCTIC CIRCLE

MAP KEY

	American golden plover
	Short-tailed shearwater
	Wandering albatross
	Arctic tern
	Bobolink

Some of the highest-flying birds are bar-headed geese. They fly over the highest mountains in the world—the Himalaya. They must do this each spring when they migrate from India to Mongolia. The trip covers 5,000 miles (8,047 km) and can take two months. The geese fly over the mountains in about eight hours.

5 COOL ANIMALS TO SEE HERE

1 LOCUST SWARMS
Madagascar

Locusts invade and destroy massive amounts of crops. A single swarm can include 80 million insects packed into less than a half-mile (0.8-km) square. On Madagascar in 2013, locusts demolished food for more than 13 million people.

2 FLYING FOX
Australia

One of the largest bats on the planet is the pteropus. Its wingspan can be almost five feet (1.5 m). It is nicknamed "the flying fox" because of its foxlike face. Keen eyesight helps it spot food from the air. When it sees appealing fruit on a tree, it dives down to grab it.

ADVENTURE ATTRACTIONS

MIGRATION STOPOVER
Each spring, snow geese fly from California to Alaska. After flying about 1,000 miles (1,609 km), they stop to rest at Freezeout Lake in Montana, U.S.A.

BUTTERFLIGHTS
In late October, about 30 million monarch butterflies arrive in Monarch Butterfly Biosphere Reserve, near Chincua, Mexico. They cover the treetops and spend the winter there.

BIG BIRD PLACE
The kori bustard is the world's heaviest flying bird. The martial eagle is Africa's biggest eagle. Both birds—and more species—can be found in Kruger National Park in South Africa.

Ocean

EUROPE

ASIA

AFRICA

Pacific Ocean

EQUATOR

Indian Ocean

TROPIC OF CAPRICORN

AUSTRALIA

ANTARCTICA

0   2,000 MILES
0   2,000 KILOMETERS

SKY

141

EXTREME FLYING

The sky's the LIMIT

Ever since people began watching birds soar through the sky, they too have tried to take flight. Around the world, adventurers try to go higher, faster, to reach for the stars—and to find new ways to get back to ground!

A company has designed money to be used by space travelers. It is called Quid, which stands for Quasi Universal Intergalactic Denomination. The rounded "coins" have no sharp edges to injure astronauts and no magnetic strips that can be damaged by cosmic radiation.

5 COOL THINGS TO DO HERE

1 JUMP WITH A WINGSUIT
Palau

Jump from a helicopter and fly—actually fly! These jumpers wear "bat suits" that have fabric between the legs and under the arms that act like wings. After flying, the jumper pulls a chord, and a parachute provides a soft landing.

2 ZERO GRAVITY!
Russia

When astronauts fly into space in rockets, they become weightless: There is no gravity pulling on them. A few countries have a jet that can create zero-gravity conditions without going into orbit. Russia's jet flies from Star City near Moscow.

DIGITAL TRAVELER!

The spacecraft Juno is more than 416 million miles (670 million km) from Earth on a mission to gather information about the planet Jupiter. Can Juno help us unlock the mysteries of our solar system? Visit the Juno mission website at missionjuno.swri.edu.

ADVENTURE ATTRACTIONS

MOUNT EVEREST SKYDIVE
Skydivers jump from helicopters beside Mount Everest. They free fall past the world's highest peaks.

HANG GLIDING OVER FJORDS
During Norway's summer, the sun never sets. So hang gliding adventurers soar over breathtaking waterways all hours of the day and night.

SKY FULL OF KITES
At Ahmadabad Police Stadium in India, thousands of people lie down and gaze up at a sky filled with kites during the International Kite Festival.

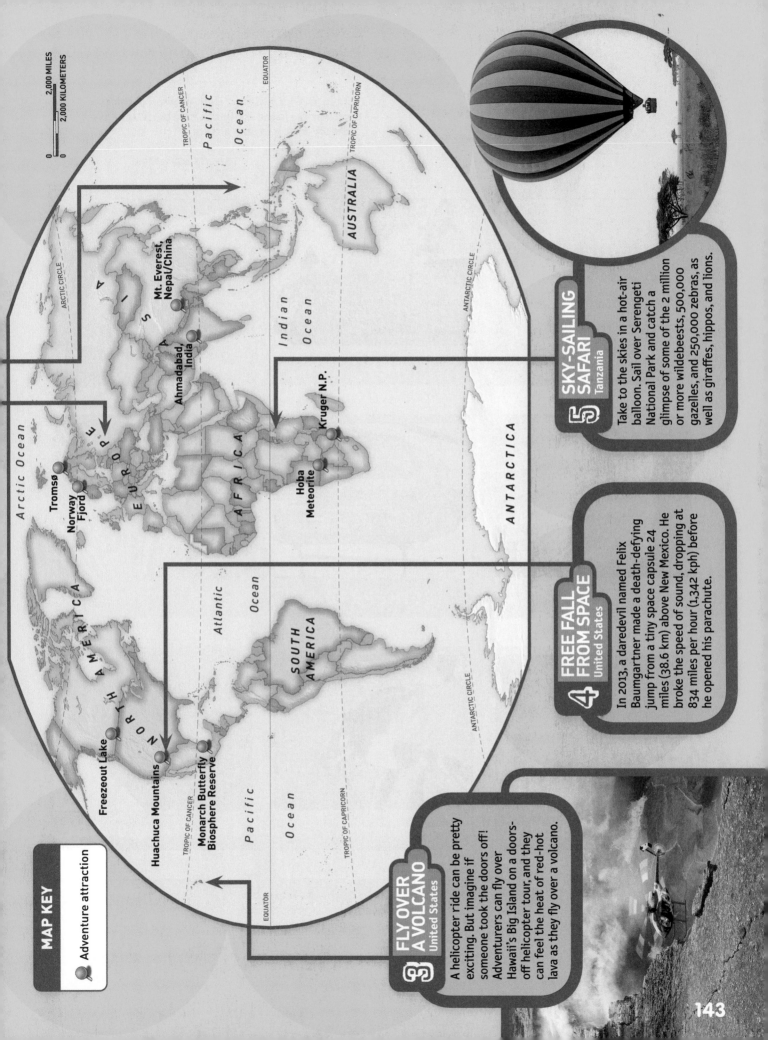

MAP KEY

🔴 Adventure attraction

2,000 MILES
2,000 KILOMETERS

Arctic Ocean

ARCTIC CIRCLE

Pacific Ocean

TROPIC OF CANCER

EQUATOR

TROPIC OF CAPRICORN

Indian Ocean

ANTARCTIC CIRCLE

AUSTRALIA

Mt. Everest, Nepal/China

Ahmadabad, India

A S I A

E U R O P E

A F R I C A

Kruger N.P.

Hoba Meteorite

Tromsø

Norway Fjord

ANTARCTICA

NORTH AMERICA

Freezeout Lake

Huachuca Mountains

Monarch Butterfly Biosphere Reserve

Atlantic Ocean

SOUTH AMERICA

Pacific Ocean

TROPIC OF CANCER

EQUATOR

TROPIC OF CAPRICORN

ANTARCTIC CIRCLE

5 SKY-SAILING SAFARI
Tanzania

Take to the skies in a hot-air balloon. Sail over Serengeti National Park and catch a glimpse of some of the 2 million or more wildebeests, 500,000 gazelles, and 250,000 zebras, as well as giraffes, hippos, and lions.

4 FREE FALL FROM SPACE
United States

In 2013, a daredevil named Felix Baumgartner made a death-defying jump from a tiny space capsule 24 miles (38.6 km) above New Mexico. He broke the speed of sound, dropping at 834 miles per hour (1,342 kph) before he opened his parachute.

3 FLY OVER A VOLCANO
United States

A helicopter ride can be pretty exciting. But imagine if someone took the doors off! Adventurers can fly over Hawaii's Big Island on a doors-off helicopter tour, and they can feel the heat of red-hot lava as they fly over a volcano.

What in the World?

UP IN THE AIR

These photographs show close-up views of things you may see in the sky. Unscramble the letters to identify what is in each picture.
Bonus: Use the highlighted letters to solve the puzzle below. ANSWERS ON PAGE 149.

EKIT

_____

IFTUR ATB

_____

GHAN LEDIRG

_____

AROTPR

_____

ECIHEPRTOL

_____

FRIKOSWRE

_____

RONTREHN HGTLSI

_____

AGLYDBU

_____

OTH-RIA ALOBNOL

_____

HINT: What goes up when rain comes down?

ANSWER: ___ ___   ___ M ___ ___ ___ ___ ___ ___

144

What in the World?

MAKING FACES

These photos show close-up views of animal faces. Unscramble the letters to identify what is in each picture.

Bonus: Use the highlighted letters to solve the puzzle below. ANSWERS ON PAGE 149.

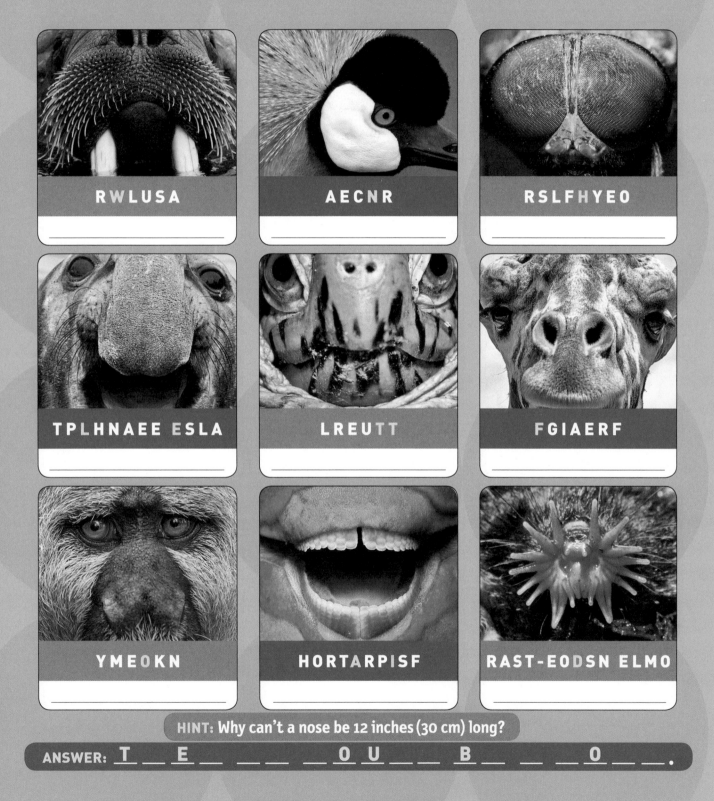

RWLUSA

_____

AECNR

_____

RSLFHYEO

_____

TPLHNAEE ESLA

_____

LREUTT

_____

FGIAERF

_____

YMEOKN

_____

HORTARPISF

_____

RAST-EODSN ELMO

_____

HINT: Why can't a nose be 12 inches (30 cm) long?

ANSWER: __T__ __E__ ___ __O__U____ __B__ ___ __O____ .

145

RAIN FOREST ROUNDUP

These photographs show close-up views of animals that live in the rain forest. Unscramble the letters to identify what is in each picture.

Bonus: Use the highlighted letters to solve the puzzle below. **ANSWERS ON PAGE 149.**

GRFO

_____

ABT

_____

OTSHL

_____

RGAAUJ

_____

PREVI

_____

ARPHNIA

_____

SPAGSREHROP

_____

IRAPT

_____

OATNCU

_____

HINT: Where would you go to buy bananas from a loud primate?

ANSWER: ___ ___ H ___ W ___ R ___ M ___ ___ K ___ Y
___ ___ ___ S ___ E ___ ___

PURPLE ADVENTURE PIZZAZZ

These photos show close-up views of adventure things that are purple. Unscramble the letters to identify what is in each picture.

Bonus: Use the highlighted letters to solve the puzzle below. ANSWERS ON PAGE 149.

ISAYD

_____

MULSP

_____

ANRY

_____

TGRETIL

_____

ESA RAST

_____

RSMOMOUH

_____

EILHYJSLF

_____

LOTLAUCCRA

_____

HAMTTYES

_____

HINT: Why did the grape stop in the middle of the road?

ANSWER: ___ ___ N ___ U ___ O ___ ___ I ___ ___.

What in the World?

GREEN ADVENTURE SCENE
These photographs show close-up views of adventure things that are green. Unscramble the letters to identify what is in each picture.
Bonus: Use the highlighted letters to solve the puzzle below. **ANSWERS ON PAGE 149.**

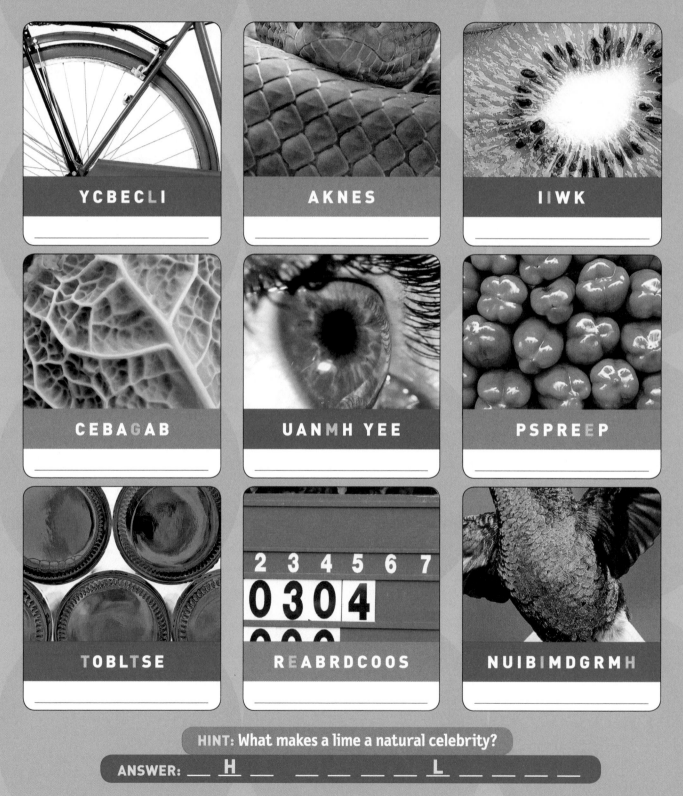

YCBECLI

AKNES

IIWK

CEBAGAB

UANMH YEE

PSPREEP

TOBLTSE

2 3 4 5 6 7

0 3 0 4

REABRDCOOS

NUIBIMDGRMH

HINT: What makes a lime a natural celebrity?

ANSWER: __ **H** __ __ __ __ **L** __ __ __ __

ANSWERS

TRUE OR FALSE Statements

25: Yellowstone National Park
A. True

B. False. Coyotes weigh between 15 and 44 pounds (6.8 and 20 kg)

C. False. Unlike wolves, coyotes don't howl. They communicate with woofs, growls, and barks.

D. True

E. False. A coyote's paw print is about 2.5 inches (6.4 cm) long and 2.1 inches (5.3 cm) wide.

43: Manú National Park
A. True

B. False. Males are bright orange, whereas females are a drab olive gray or brown.

C. True.

D. False. It is about 12 inches (30.5 cm) long.

E. True

60: The Lake District
A. False. It is limited to quiet areas around ponds, streams, rivers, and lakes.

B. True

C. True

D. True

E. True

78: Lake Toba
A. True

B. False. There are only hundreds of tigers in zoos and about 3,200 tigers left in the wild.

C. False. Tigers can eat up to 60 pounds (27.2 kg) at one meal.

E. False. It would take about four cubs to weigh as much as a gallon of milk.

F. True.

97: True or False
Mount Kilimanjaro

A. False. A leopard can run at only 36 miles per hour (58 kph) and leap 20 feet (6.1 m). It can jump 10 feet (3 m) straight up.

B. False. It likes swimming.

C. True

D. True

E. False. It is the smallest of the big cats, after the tiger and lion.

F. False. This is size for males: Females are much smaller.

115: True or False
Waipoua Forest

A. True

B. False. Kiwis cannot fly.

C. False. She can lay up to 100 eggs.

D. True

E. False. They use their powerful legs and sharp claws as weapons.

WHAT IN THE WORLD? Puzzles

144: Up in the Air
Top row: kite, fruit bat, hang glider

Middle row: parrot, helicopter, fireworks

Bottom row: Northern lights, ladybug, hot-air balloon

Bonus: an umbrella

145: Making Faces
Top row: walrus, crane, horse fly

Middle row: elephant seal, turtle, giraffe

Bottom row: monkey, parrot fish, star-nosed mole

Bonus: Then it would be a foot.

146: Rain Forest Roundup
Top Row: frog, bat, sloth

Middle row: jaguar, viper, piranha

Bottom row: grasshopper, tapir, toucan

Bonus: a howler monkey business

147: Purple Adventure Pizzazz
Top Row: daisy, plums, yarn

Middle row: glitter, sea star, mushroom

Bottom row: jellyfish, calculator, amethyst

Bonus: It ran out of juice.

148: Green Adventure Scene
Top row: bicycle, snake, kiwi

Middle row: cabbage, human eye, peppers

Bottom row: bottles, scoreboard, hummingbird

Bonus: the limelight

GLOSSARY

bay a body of water, usually smaller than a gulf, that is partially surrounded by land

border the area on either side of a boundary

boundary most commonly, a line that has been established by people to mark the limit of one political unit, such as a country or state, and the beginning of another. Geographical features such as mountains sometimes act as boundaries.

bush in Australia, any area with little or no human settlement. It may have very little plant growth or be wooded and forested.

canal a human-made waterway that is used by ships or to carry water for irrigation

canyon a deep, narrow valley that has steep sides

cape a point of land that extends into an ocean, a lake, or a river

capital in a country, the city where the government headquarters are. The capital is often the largest and most important city.

cliff a very steep rock face, usually along a coast but also on the side of a mountain

climate the average weather conditions over many years

continent one of the seven main landmasses on Earth's surface

country a territory whose government is the highest legal authority over the land and people within its boundaries

delta a lowland formed by silt, sand, and gravel deposited by a river at its mouth

desert a hot or cold region that receives ten inches (25 cm) or less of rain or other kinds of precipitation a year

divide an elevated area drained by different river systems flowing in different directions

dune a mound or ridge of wind-blown sand

Eastern Hemisphere the half of the globe that lies east of the prime meridian. It includes most of Africa, most of Europe, all of Asia, all of Australia and Oceania, and about half of Antarctica.

elevation the distance above sea level, usually measured in feet or meters

environment the conditions surrounding and affecting any living thing, including the climate and landscape

Equator an imaginary line circling the broadest part of Earth and representing 0° latitude. It divides the globe into the Northern and Southern Hemispheres.

fault a break in Earth's crust along which movement up, down, or sideways occurs

fjord a narrow sea inlet enclosed by high cliffs. Fjords are found in Norway and New Zealand and in Scotland in the United Kingdom.

fork in a river, the place where two streams come together

geographic pole 90°N, 90°S latitude; the location of the ends of Earth's axis

geomagnetic pole the point where the axis of Earth's magnetic field intersects Earth's surface. Compass needles align with Earth's magnetic field so that one end points to the magnetic north pole, the other to the magnetic south pole.

geyser a spout of hot water and steam shooting from the ground

glacier a large, slow-moving mass of ice. As a glacier moves, it scours the land and, near its end, dumps rock debris.

globe a scale model of Earth with accurate relative sizes and locations of continents

gorge a deep channel between two masses of rock

gulf a portion of the ocean that cuts into the land; usually larger than a bay

harbor a body of water, sheltered by natural or artificial barriers, that is deep enough for ships

hemisphere literally half a sphere. Earth has four hemispheres: Northern, Southern, Eastern, and Western.

highlands an elevated area or the more mountainous region of a country

iceberg a large, floating mass of ice

inlet a narrow opening in the land that is filled with water flowing from an ocean, a lake, or a river

island a landmass, smaller than a continent, that is completely surrounded by water

isthmus a narrow strip of land that connects two larger landmasses and has water on two sides

lagoon a shallow body of water that is open to the sea but also protected from it by a reef or sandbar

lake a body of water surrounded by land. Large lakes are sometimes called seas.

landform a physical feature that is shaped by tectonic activity, weathering, and erosion. The four major kinds on Earth are plains, mountains, plateaus, and hills.

landmass a large area of Earth's crust that lies above sea level, such as a continent

Latin America a cultural region generally considered to include Mexico, Central America, South America, and the West Indies. Portuguese and Spanish are the principal languages.

latitude the distance north and south of the Equator, which is 0° latitude

leeward the side away from, or sheltered from, the wind

longitude the distance east and west of the prime meridian, which is 0° longitude

lowland an area of land lower than the surrounding countryside that is usually flat and without hills and mountains

mangrove swamp a wetland area along tropical coasts thick with mangrove trees that have special breathing roots leading down from branches

Middle East a term commonly used for the countries of Southwest Asia, but it can also include northern Africa from Morocco to Somalia

molten liquefied by heat; melted

monsoon a seasonal change in the direction of the normal winds, which causes very wet and dry seasons in some tropical areas

mountain a landform, higher than a hill, that rises at least 1,000 feet (305 m) above the surrounding land and is wider at its base than at its top, or peak. A series of mountains is called a range.

national park an area of a country set aside to protect the landscape or wildlife from human interference

navigable deep or wide enough to allow boats, ships, barges, and other vessels to pass

Northern Hemisphere the half of the globe that lies north of the Equator. It includes all of North America, a small part of South America, all of Europe, about 65 percent of Africa, and almost all of Asia.

oasis a part of a desert or other dry region where water is near the surface and plants grow well

ocean the large body of salt water that surrounds the continents and covers more than two-thirds of Earth's surface

Pampas a flat, treeless part of southern South America between the Atlantic Coast and the Andes Mountains. It contains large cattle ranches.

peninsula a piece of land that is almost completely surrounded by water

permafrost a permanently frozen subsurface soil in frigid regions

plain a large area of relatively flat land that is often covered with grasses

plateau a relatively flat area, larger than a mesa, that rises above the surrounding landscape

point a narrow piece of land smaller than a cape that extends into a body of water

polar climates climates that occur near the North and South Poles—the Arctic and Antarctic regions—that are generally too cold for plants to grow

population density in a country, the average number of people living on each square mile or square kilometer of land (calculated by dividing total population by land area)

prime meridian an imaginary line that runs through Greenwich, England, and is accepted as the line of 0° longitude

primeval belonging to the first or oldest period or era of living things

rain forest a dense forest found on or near the Equator, where the climate is hot and wet

reef an offshore ridge made of coral, rocks, or sand.

renewable resources resources that are replenished naturally, but the supply of which can be endangered by overuse and pollution

Sahel a semiarid grassland in Africa along the Sahara's southern border

savanna a tropical grassland with scattered trees

scale on a map, a means of explaining the relationship between distances on the map and actual distances on Earth's surface

sea the ocean or a partially enclosed body of salt water that is connected to the ocean. Completely enclosed bodies of salt water, such as the Dead Sea, are really lakes.

sound a long, broad inlet of the ocean that lies parallel to the coast and often separates an island from the mainland

Southern Hemisphere the half of the globe that lies south of the Equator. It includes most of South America, a third of Africa, all of Australia and Oceania, all of Antarctica, and a small part of Asia.

species a unique type of living thing, usually considered as a group of individuals that can breed, or mate, with one another. For example, lion, tiger, cheetah, leopard, and civet are different cat species.

spit a long, narrow strip of land, often of sand or silt, extending into a body of water from the land

staple a chief component of a people's diet

steppe a Slavic word referring to relatively flat, mostly treeless temperate grasslands that stretch across much of central Europe and central Asia

strait a narrow passage of water that connects two larger bodies of water

temperate broadleaf forest a region with distinct seasons and dependable rainfall where deciduous trees such as oak, maple, and beech trees grow

temperate coniferous forest a region with mild winters and heavy rainfall where needleleaf trees such as pines and confers grow

territory land that is under the jurisdiction of a country but that is not a state or a province

tributary a stream that flows into a larger river

tropics the region lying within 23.5° north and south of the Equator that experiences warm temperatures year-round

upwelling the process by which nutrient-rich water rises from ocean depths to the surface

valley a long depression, usually created by a river, that is bordered by higher land

volcano an opening in Earth's crust through which molten rock erupts

weather the day-to-day variation in sunshine, rainfall, wind, cloud cover, and other effects of Earth's atmosphere

Western Hemisphere the half of the globe that lies west of the prime meridian. It includes North America, South America, a part of Europe and Africa, and about half of Antarctica.

windward the unsheltered side toward which the wind blows

Plant and Animal Species

The Plant and Animal maps used in this book show the distribution of a range of "extreme" species. Brief descriptions and scientific names (in Latin) of these species are given below.

NORTH AMERICAN PLANTS

Giant hogweed (*Heracleum mantegazzianum*), a flowering plant that grows in southern Canada and northern United States. Grows to 18 ft (5.5 m) high. Touching the plant can cause skin blisters.

Poison sumac (*Toxicodendron vernix*), a plant that grows in the eastern United States and Canada. Grows to 30 ft (9.1 m), with leaves and stems that can turn red. It makes a sticky oil that can cause a serious itchy rash.

Giant redwood (*Sequoiadendron giganteum*), the largest and tallest tree in the world. It grows on the Pacific coast of California and Oregon, U.S.A. It can grow to be 275 ft (83.8 m) tall and thousands of years old. In California, there are a few giant sequoia with tunnels cut through the trunk for cars to drive through.

Skunk cabbage (*Symplocarpus foetidus*), a low-growing plant with large leaves that can be 20 in (50.8 cm) long and 15 in (38 cm) wide. Found in eastern Canada, northeastern U.S., and westward to Minnesota and Tennessee. The plant smells horrible, like rotting meat.

Jones' pitcher plant (*Sarracenia jonesii*), a tube-shaped plant that grows in the mountain bogs of North and South Carolina, U.S.A. Grows to a height of 29 in (73.7 cm). Insects are drawn inside by its sweet smell and color. The slippery sides make it impossible for the flies to escape. The insects are trapped and digested by the plant.

NORTH AMERICAN ANIMALS

Kodiak bear (*Ursus arctos middendorffi*), one of the largest bears in the world. A male can be eight ft (2.4 m) long and five ft high (1.5 m) on all fours—ten ft (3 m) when standing up on its hind legs. Can weigh 1,656 lb (751 kg). Females are smaller. About 3,400 of these bears live on the islands of the Kodiak Peninsula, Alaska, U.S.A.

Star-nosed mole (*Condylura cristata*), lives in Canada and eastern U.S including the Appalachian Mountains. Adults are about six in (15.2 cm) long and weigh about two oz (57 g). The 22 tentacles on its snout help it quickly find and devour insects and worms for its meals.

California condor (*Gymnogyps californianus*), the largest bird in North America. Lives in southwestern U.S. and northern Mexico. Has a wingspan of 9.5 ft (2.9 m). Between 1988 and 1991, there were none in the wild. Humans saved the condor from extinction by breeding them and returning them to the wild. Can fly 15,000 ft (4,572 m) high and at 55 mph (88.5 kph).

Texas horned lizard (*Phrynosoma cornutum*), an endangered species that lives in deserts and grasslands of south-central U.S. and northern Mexico. Average length is 2.7 in (6.9 cm). When under attack, it can puff up its spiny scales and be nearly impossible to swallow. Also squirts blood from its eyes to startle its enemy.

Horseshoe crab

Horseshoe crab (*Limulus polyphemus*), more closely related to spiders and scorpions than to crabs. Can grow to 24 in (61 cm) long. Lives along the Atlantic and Gulf of Mexico seashores. The world's largest horseshoe crab population lives in southern New Jersey, U.S.A., in the Delaware Bay. The crab's sharp tail looks harmful, but it is not. The crab uses its tail to flip itself if accidentally overturned.

SOUTH AMERICAN PLANTS

Monkey puzzle tree (*Araucaria araucana*), an evergreen tree in Chile and Argentina that grows 130 ft (39.6 m) tall with a huge 7-ft-(2.1-m)-thick trunk. Its sharp, pointy leaves led to its nickname. It would certainly puzzle a monkey to climb that tree!

Cocoa tree (*Theobrama cacao*), an evergreen tree that grows to 25 ft (7.6 m) high. Grows in rain forests near the Equator. Large pods grow on the tree. Cocoa beans (seeds) are inside the pods. They are the main ingredient for making chocolate.

Cocoa pods

Rubber tree (*Hevea brasiliensis*), a deciduous tree that grow to 80 ft (24.4 m) tall in cultivation. Originally found in northern South America, it is now grown in many parts of West Africa and in Asia. A milky latex is tapped from the trees to make natural rubber.

Peruvian pepper tree (*Schinus molle*), an evergreen tree that grows in Peru's Andes. Can be 50 ft (15.2 m) tall and with a canopy 33 ft (10.1 m) wide. Its branches droop from the weight of the berries called pink peppercorns. People make cooking pepper with the berries, but the plant's flowers and leaves can be poisonous.

Duckweed (*Lemna obscura*), a fast-growing water plant that is nearly impossible to eradicate. Lake Maracaibo in Venezuela is suffering from the world's biggest duckweed invasion. The plant can double in size every 48 hours.

SOUTH AMERICAN ANIMALS

Giant anteater (*Mymecophaga tridactyla*), a mammal that lives throughout the continent. Can be seven ft (2.1 m) long from the end of its tail to the tip of its very long snout. Has no teeth, but laps up ants and termites all day with its long tongue.

Capybara (*Hydrochoerus hydrochaeris*), the world's largest rodent, is typically 4 ft (1.2 m) long and 1.5 ft (0.5 m) tall. Lives near ponds, lakes, and rivers in northern South America. Can stay underwater up to five minutes—a good way to escape predators such as jaguars and anacondas.

Capybara

Ocelot (*Leopardus pardalis*), a sleek cat that prowls the rain forests at night. Its fur has unique patterns. About twice the size of a house cat—up to 39 in (99 cm) long with an 18-in (46-cm) tail. It climbs trees to hunt for monkeys and birds. Uses its pointy fangs to kill its prey.

Electric eel (*Electrophorus electricus*), a freshwater fish that grows up to eight ft (2.4 m) long. Its body stores electric power that can shock its prey or discourage its predators. It sends out at least 600 volts—five times the power of a standard U.S. electric wall socket.

Hammerhead shark (*Sphyrna lewini*), lives in the temperate and tropical water on the continent's east coast. Adult hammerheads reach 8.2 ft (2.5 m) and weigh 180 lb (81.6 kg). Its head is shaped like a hammer, with eyes and nostrils at the tips of a wide extension. This helps the shark scan for food and home in on its prey.

EUROPEAN PLANTS

Stone pine (*Pinus pinea*), a conifer tree found in Mediterranean coastal areas. Typically grows to 60 ft (18.3 m) tall. This umbrella-shaped tree has a thick, fire-resistant bark and cones that open after being scorched by fire.

Ancient yew (*Taxus baccata*), a conifer tree of the understory throughout Europe. Reaches 80 ft (24.4 m) in height and lives more than 1,000 years. The leaves, bark, and seeds are poisonous.

Sweet chestnut (*Castanea sativa*), a deciduous tree of the mountains and lowlands of southern Europe. It grows to 115 ft (35.1 m) tall with a girth of 7 ft (2.1 m). The glossy nuts grow inside a spiny bur that can puncture skin.

English sundew (*Drosera anglica*), a carnivorous plant of bogs, marshes, and fens. Grows to ten in (25.4 cm) tall. Insects are drawn to its bright red color and the sticky drops, loaded with a sugary substance, covering the leaves. The insects become trapped in the sticky drops and are digested by the plant.

Fly agaric (*Amanita muscaria*), a mushroom native to northern conifer and deciduous woodlands. Grows to eight in (20.3 cm) in diameter. The beautiful bright red mushroom contains a deadly toxin.

EUROPEAN ANIMALS

Alpine chamois (*Rupicapra rupicapra*), a plant-eating mammal of steep, rocky areas in the mountains. Adults are up to 4 ft (1.2 m) long and 2.5 ft (0.8 m) tall at the shoulder. This cousin to antelopes and mountain goats survives in cold alpine habitats and is very agile on mountains.

Eagle owl (*Bubo bubo*), a big bird of prey with bright orange eyes and feathery ear tufts. Its wingspan can reach six ft (1.8 m). It is one of the largest owls in the world and has a powerful, fast flight. Lives in rocky areas, patches of woodland, and open forests.

Saiga antelope (*Saiga tatarica*), a herbivore of southern grasslands. Grows to 4 ft (1.2 m) long and 2.5 ft (0.8 m) tall at the shoulder. Its large nose hangs down over the mouth and gives it a strange appearance.

Wolverine

Wolverine (*Gulo gulo*), a bearlike carnivore of boreal forests and tundra. Adults are about 2.5 ft (0.76 m) long. The wolverine, the world's largest weasel, is a powerful predator and may attack animals many times its size, such as caribou.

Marbled polecat (*Vormela peregusna*), a small carnivore that typically grows to 13 in (33 cm) long. When threatened, it can emit a foul-smelling secretion from its anal scent glands. Lives in shrubby, semi-desert and steppe habitats.

ASIAN PLANTS

Durian fruit tree (*Durio zibethinus*), grows to 130 ft (39.6 m) tall in tropical forests. Its oval fruit can grow to 12 in (30.5 cm) long and 6 in (15.2 cm) in diameter with sharp spines. The fruit can smell like garlic and onions.

Durian fruit

Black bat flower (*Tacca chantrieri*), grows in humid tropical rain forests in China. The black flower is 12 in (30.5 cm) wide with 28-in (71-cm) "whiskers."

Kudzu (*Pueraria lobata*), a climbing, clinging vine native to China and Japan. It will grow over anything in its path. Over many years, it can kill trees and bushes by blocking their sunlight.

Date palm (*Phoenix dactylifera*), a fruit tree that has grown on the Arabian Peninsula for about 6,000 years. Grows to 75 ft (23 m) high. The fruit, called dates, is sweet and chewy. The tree's trunk is used for fuel and timber, and the leaf fibers are woven into rope and baskets.

Cherry blossom tree (*Prunus serrulata*), a small tree, grows to 39 ft (11.9 m) tall in ravines, forests, and on mountain slopes. Its white and pink flowers have become a symbol of spring in many parts of the world.

ASIAN ANIMALS

Sunda flying lemur (*Galeopterus variegatus*), is not a lemur and does not fly. It belongs to an order of batlike animals called Dermoptera, meaning "skin wings." It glides as it leaps between trees. Body length is 26 in (40 cm). Tail length is 10 in (25 cm).

Green peafowl (*Pavo muticus*), bird with show-stopping tail feathers that fan out in brilliant colors. Lives in forests of Southeast Asia. The male is up to nine ft (2.7 m) long, including tail feathers (called coverts) that can average five ft (1.5 m) in length.

Reticulated python (*Python reticulates*), one of the world's longest snakes, found in steamy tropical forests of Southeast Asia. Normally grows to 20 ft (6.1 m) and can weigh more than 300 lb (136 kg). Small individuals feed on rats; larger pythons eat porcupines, monkeys, and wild pigs.

Himalayan jumping spider (*Euophrys omnisuperstes*), a tiny, fuzzy spider that is one of the highest-living animals in the world. Found in the Himalaya at up to 22,000 ft (6,706 m). Finds food by eating insects blown in by the wind.

Firefly squid (*Watasenia scintillans*), a tiny squid that lives hundreds of feet (m) deep in the western Pacific Ocean. Grows to three in (7.6 cm) long, with eight arms and two tentacles with flashing lights that resemble a firefly. When millions of them gather to lay eggs, there is an awesome light show!

AFRICAN PLANTS

Date palm (*Phoenix dactylifera*), a slender tree native to most of North Africa. *For details see Asian Plants*

Umbrella thorn (*Vachellia tortilis*), a tree of savanna and semidry land. It grows to 69 ft (19.8 m). The canopy forms a wide disc, and giraffes and other grazers snack on the leaves at the edges.

Sausage tree (*Kigelia africana*), a flowering tree of the tropics. It grows up to 65 ft (20 m) tall. Long, thick fruits dangle from the treelike sausages. A mature fruit may be 2 ft (0.6 m) long and weigh 15 lb (6.8 kg).

Star Orchid of Madagascar (*Angraecum sesquipedale*), a flower that can grow to 3.3 ft (1 m) across. It has nectar housed inside an 11-in (28-cm)-long spur and is thought to be pollinated by a hawkmoth with a 10-in (25.4-cm)-long tongue.

Jackal food (*Hydnora africana*), a parasitic plant that grows mostly underground. It gets its nutrients from the host plants it grows on. It produces bright red or orange flowers with a strong, foul-smelling odor that attracts beetles that pollinate the flowers.

AFRICAN ANIMALS

African elephant (*Loxodonta africana*), a plant-eating mammal of the savanna and forests. An adult stands 13 ft (4 m) tall at the shoulder and weighs up to 14,000 lb (6,350 kg). The African elephant is the largest land animal. It can eat up to 300 lb (136 kg) of food in a day.

Ostrich

Ostrich (*Struthio camelus*), a large bird of the savanna and deserts. The world's largest bird, it stands nine ft (2.7 m) tall and weighs 350 lb (159 kg). Though an ostrich cannot fly, it can sprint at speeds up to 43 mph (69 kph).

Giraffe (*Giraffa camelopardalis*), a plant-eating mammal of the savanna. An adult grows to 19 ft (5.8 m) tall. It is the world's tallest mammal and grazes on leaves high in trees rather than on grass.

Mountain gorilla (*Gorilla beringei beringei*), a plant-eating mammal of mountain forests. The largest of the apes, an adult stands to six ft (1.8 m) tall and weighs 485 lb (220 kg). Mountain gorillas live in a troop led by a dominant male, called a silverback because of the silver hair on his back.

Cheetah (*Acinonyx jubatus*), a meat-eating mammal of the savanna, dry bush, scrub, and open forests. It stands 3.5 to 4.5 ft (1.1 to 1.4 m) tall at the shoulder. The world's fastest land mammal, a cheetah can go from 0 to 60 mph (96.6 kph) in just three seconds.

Cheetah

AUSTRALIAN AND OCEANIAN PLANTS

Cycads (*Cycas*), a group of palm-like trees related to conifers. They grow in northern Australia, Melanesia, and Micronesia. This group of slow-growing plants is considered a living fossil. Toxic seeds have been detoxified and used as food by Australian Aboriginals.

Cabbage tree (*Cordyline australis*), a tree common throughout farmland, open places, wetlands, and scrubland of New Zealand. It grows up to 65 ft (20 m) tall. The trunk of the cabbage tree is so fire-resistant that early European settlers used it to make chimneys for their huts.

Soft spinifex (*Triodia pungens*), a spiky grass of deserts and rocky slopes of central Australia. It grows to 6.5 ft (2 m) tall. Aboriginal tribes collect the resin and burn it to make a glue for attaching handles to stone axes and spears.

Norfolk tree fern (*Cyathea brownii*), a tree fern of Norfolk Island. It grows to 66 ft (20 m) or more in height. It is the largest tree fern in the world.

Mountain ash (*Eucalyptus regnans*), a flowering tree of the cool, rainy mountains of southeastern Australia and Tanzania. It can grow to more than 300 ft (91 m) tall and is the tallest flowering plant in the world.

AUSTRALIAN AND OCEANIAN ANIMALS

Koala (*Phascolarctos cinereus*), a mammal of eucalyptus woodlands. It reaches up to 33 in

(83.8 cm) in length and weighs up to 20 lb (9.1 kg). This cuddly, bearlike animal is a marsupial, or pouched mammal. The newborn koala is the size of a jelly bean.

Red kangaroo (*Macropus rufus*), a mammal of the deserts and grasslands. The world's largest marsupial reaches 8.5 ft (2.6 m) in length and weighs up to 200 lb (91 kg). A kangaroo can hop at speeds more 35 mph (56 kph) and cover 25 ft (7.6 m) in a single bound.

Inland taipan (*Oxyuranus microlepidotus*), a reptile of desert and scrubland. Grow to about six ft (1.8 m) in length. This fierce snake is considered to be the most poisonous in the world, with venom more toxic than any other species.

Long-beaked echidnas (*Zaglossus*), a group of mammals of rain forests and meadows. They grow to 35 in (90 cm) in length and weigh up to 22 lb (10 kg). These egg-laying mammals are covered with spines and roll into a spiny ball when threatened.

Tasmanian devil (*Sarcophilus harrisii*), a mammal of scrublands and forests. Adults are up to 31 in (78.7 cm) in length and weigh up to 26 lbs (11.8 kg). This mammal is named for its famously fiery temper. It bares its teeth and flies into a growling rage when threatened or fighting.

OCEAN ANIMALS

Arctic tern (*Sterna paradisea*), a small bird that weighs less than 4.4 oz (125 g). Scientists are amazed that some of them fly more than 49,710 mi (80,000 km) from the Arctic to Antarctica. Scientists have attached mini tracking devices to several Arctic terns to follow their routes.

Ascension Island green turtle (*Chelonia mydas*), a turtle that annually migrates from breeding grounds near Ascension Island in the Atlantic to feeding grounds off the coast of Brazil, 1,350 mi (2,173 km) to the west, and back again.

Australian spiny lobster (*Panulirus cygnus*), or Western rock lobster, grows to 12 lb (5.4 kg). Starting life as a small larva close to the coast, it drifts offshore for a distance of up to 600 miles (966 km). Months later as an adult, it migrates in toward the mainland to breed. The lobster usually migrates in masses of many thousands.

Koala

Blue whale (*Balaenoptera musculus*), a marine mammal and the largest animal ever known to have existed on Earth. Adults can grow to 100 ft (30 m) and weigh up to 200 tons (181 t). A blue whale reaches its massive size on a diet of krill. A blue whale can eat up to 4 tons (3.6 t) of krill in a single day.

European eel (*Anguilla anguilla*), a fish of the Atlantic Ocean. The eel grows up to 51 in (130 cm) in length. Adult eels live in freshwater but swim to the Sargasso Sea to lay their eggs. The floating eggs hatch into larvae that drift on ocean currents for about a year before reaching the coasts of North and South America.

Gentoo penguin (*Pygoscelis papua*), populates the Antarctic Peninsula and nearby islands. It gathers in breeding colonies, then migrates on the high seas some 620 miles (998 km) before returning. It can live for up to 20 years.

Gentoo penguin

Short-tailed shearwater (*Puffinus tenuirostris*), a seabird that flies a figure-eight route within the Pacific Ocean. It covers some 20,000 mi (32,187 km), leaving its breeding grounds north of Tasmania in early spring, and spends the next seven months on the wing searching for food.

Wandering albatross (*Diomedea exulans*), a seabird with the largest recorded wingspan of any bird, reaching 11.5 ft (3.5 m) across. It spends most of its life in flight and can travel long distances by riding air currents, barely flapping its wings. Scientists tracked one traveling 3,728 mi (5,965 km) in 12 days.

SKY ANIMALS

American golden plover (*Pluvialis dominica*), has one of the longest migratory paths of any bird. In the spring and summer, it breeds in subarctic parts of Alaska and Canada. Before winter, it flies south to South America. It can grow to 11 in (28 cm), with a wingspan of 26 in (66 cm).

Short-tailed shearwater (*Puffinus tenuirostris*)
  see Ocean Animals
Wandering albatross (*Diomedea exulans*)
  see Ocean Animals
Arctic tern (*Sterna paradisea*)
  see Ocean Animals

Bobolink (*Dolichonyx oryzivorus*), a tiny black-and-white bird, weighing about one oz (28 g). Males have puffy yellow head feathers. It spends summers in North America and migrates long distances to spend winters in South America. A tracking band on one bobolink's foot showed that it flew 1,100 mi (1,770 km) in one day.

INDEX

156

Photo Credits

Key: CI= Corbis Images, DT = Dreamstime, GI = Getty Images, IS = Istock, RH = Robert Harding, NASA = NASA, REX = REX Features, SPL = Science Photo Library, ST = Shutterstock

Cover: Front Cover (UP CTR), offstocker/iStockphoto; (LE CTR), hudiemm/iStockphoto; UPRT), IM_photo/ST; CTR RT TOP), Frans Lanting/National Geographic Creative; (CTR LE), Ammit Jack/ST; (CTR RT LO), Chromatika Multimedia snc/ST; (CTR), LeventKonuk/iStockphoto; (LOLE), sarkophoto/iStockphoto; LORT), akiyoko/ST; (LOCTR), fergregory/iStockphoto; UPLE), dimdimich/iStockphoto; Spine (UPRT), offstocker/iStockphoto; (UP), dimdimich/iStockphoto; (CTR LE), hudiemm/iStockphoto; Back Cover (UPRT), Juancat/ST; (RT CTR), Lumase/iStockphoto; (LORT), RainervonBrandis/iStockphoto; (UPLE), dimdimich/iStockphoto; (UP CTR), offstocker/iStockphoto; (CTR LE), hudiemm/iStockphoto

Front Matter: 1 (UP) offstocker/IS; 2 (UP) Greg Epperson/GI; 2 (R-LO) Andrew Burgess/SS; 2 (CTR-LO) Germanskydiver/DT; 2 (R-LO) Juan Carlos Munoz/Okapia/RH; 3 (UP) Gerry Pearce/SPL; 3 (L-CTR) Peter Giovannini/RH; 3 Ainars Aunins/SS; 3 (L-LO) Wally Herbert/RH; 3 (R-LO) Stu Porter/DT; 6 (UP) ixpert/SS

North America: 10 (LO) Robert Harding Productions/RH; 12 (UP) salajean/SS; 12 (LO) Alexander Raths/SS; 12-1 John Robinson/SS; 12-2 Zhuxi1984/DT; 12-3 Carsten Peter/Speleoresearch & Films/GI; 13-4 Wai Chung Tang/DT; 13-5 Rebecca Picard/DT; 13 (LO) Baloncici/SS; 14 (UP) Alexander Raths/SS; 14 (LO) glen gaffney/SS; 14-1 Martine Oger/DT; 15-2 Phartisan/DT; 15-3 Martinmark/DT; 15-4 michael borders/SS; 15-5 Juan Barreto/AFP/GI; 15 (UP) Englishinbsas/DT; 15 (LO) offstocker/IS; 16 (UP) Philcold/DT; 16-1 Varina And Jay Patel/DT; 16 (LO) Helen Filatova/SS; 17-2 Wild Horizons/UIG/GI; 17-3 Dawn Kish/GI; 17-4 Martinmark/DT; 17-5 Maridav/SS; 18 (UP) Norma Jean Gargasz/RH; 18 (CTR) Alexander Raths/SS; 18 (LO) Baloncici/SS; 18-5 Rinus Baak/DT; 19-1 Crystal Garner/DT; 19-2 Sergio Vila/DT; 19-3 Bonita Cheshier/DT; 19-4 Jeffrey M. Frank/SS; 20-1 Foster Eubank/DT; 20-2 Gelyngfjell/DT; 20-3 Tom Dowd/DT; 21 (UP) Africa Studio/SS; 21 (CTR) Alexander Raths/SS; 21 (L-LO) offstocker/IS; 21 (R-LO) Mihai-bogdan Lazar/DT; 21-4 Marcouliana/DT; 21-5 Czuber/DT; 22 (UP) Rolf Nussbaumer/RH; 22 (CTR) Alexander Raths/SS; 22 (L-LO) offstocker/IS; 22 (R-LO) Andrew Burgess/SS; 22-1 Johnbell/DT; 22-2 David Davis/DT; 23-3 Sekar B/SS; 23-4 Lukas Blazek/DT; 23-5 Matt Jacques/DT; 24-1 Izanbar/DT; 24-3 Tim Stirling/SS; 24-5 Smontgom65/DT; 25 (UP) Outdoorsman/DT; 25-4 Sharon Day/SS; 26 (UP) Alexander Raths/SS; 26 (CTR) Germanskydiver/DT; 26 (LO) Germanskydiver/DT; 26-1 Serghei Starus/DT; 27-2 Mohd Rasfan/AFP/GI; 27-3 Derrick Neill/DT; 27-4 Monkey Business Images/DT; 27-5 Atgimages/DT; 27 (LO) Aprilphoto/SS

South America: 28 (LO) Robert Frerck/RH; 30 (UP) Piccaya/DT; 30-5 Serjio74/DT; 30 (CTR) Baloncici/SS; 30 (LO) Alexander Raths/SS; 30-4 Miragik/DT; 30-3 Oliver Gerhard/RH; 31-1 Philip Lee Harvey/RH; 31-2 Rafa Cichawa/DT; 32-1 Graemo/DT; 32-2 STR/Stringer/GI; 32-3 Padchas/DT; 32-4 Sergio Pitamitz/RH; 33 (UP) Oliver Gerhard/RH; 33 (CTR) Alexander Raths/SS; 33 (LO) offstocker/IS; 33-5 Flip de Nooyer/Minden Pictures/GI; 34-1 Jane Sweeney/RH; 34-2 Pablo Hidalgo/DT; 34-5 Michael Nolan/RH; 35 (UP) Tim Graham/RH; 35-3 Morten Elm/DT; 35-4 Michael Nolan/RH; 35 (LO) Frans Lanting/RH; 36-1 Kjersti Joergensen/SS; 36 (UP) Alexander Raths/SS; 36 (L-LO) Cyberjade/DT; 36 (R-LO) Baloncici/SS; 37-2 Michael Runkel/RH; 37-3 Davthy/DT; 37-4 Jduggan/DT; 37-5 Pete Oxford/Minden Pictures/CI; 38-1 David Myslivec/DT; 38-2 Andoni Canela/RH; 38-3 Vaclav Volrab/DT; 38-4 Puwadol Jaturawutthichai/DT; 39 (UP) Anton Samsonov/DT; 39 (CTR-UP) Baloncici/SS; 39 (CTR-LO) TH Foto-Werbung/SPL; 39 (LO) Alexander Raths/SS; 39-5 Olivier Goujon/RH; 40 (UP) Iakov Filimonov/DT; 40-5 Robert Caputo/RH; 40 (CTR) Alexander Raths/SS; 40-4 Stephen Ausmus/US Dept of Agriculture/SPL 40 (L-LO) Aprilphoto/SS; 40 (R-LO) fivespots/SS; 41-1 Dirk Ercken/DT; 41 (UP) Paul Kennedy/GI; 41-2 Musat Christian/DT; 41-3 Anankkml/DT; 42 (UP) Frans Lanting/RH; 42-2 Peter Groenendijk/RH; 42-5 Peter Groenendijk/RH; 43-1 Sylvie Lebchek/SS; 43-3 Morales/RH; 43-4 Frans Lanting/RH; 44 (UP) Olivier Renck/RH; 44-1 Max Blain/DT; 44-2 Florian Kopp/RH; 45 (UP) Alexander Raths/SS; 45-3 Marco Simoni/RH; 45-4 Stringer/Brazil/Reuters/CI; 45-5 Wolfgang Kaehler/GI; 45 (CTR) Andres Rodriguez/DT; 45 (LO) Aprilphoto/SS

Europe: 47 (UP) Darryl Leniuk/GI; 48 (UP) Werner Dieterich/RH; 48 (LO) Alexander Raths/SS; 48-1 Paffy1969/DT; 48-2 Juan Carlos Munoz/Okapia/RH; 49-3 Vaclav Volrab/DT; 49-4 Juergen Richter/RH; 49-5 Werner Van Steen/GI; 50 (UP) Antonio Cotrim/epa/CI; 50 (LO) Alexander Raths/SS; 50-5 Geoff Robinson/REX; 51-1 Adam Burton/RH; 51-2 Peter Essick/GI; 51-3 Katja Kreder/RH; 51 (UP) AFP/Stringer/GI; 51 (LO) offstocker/IS; 52-1 Patricia Hofmeester/DT; 52-2 Ragnar Th. Sigurdsson/RH; 52-3 Darren Baker/SS; 53 (UP) Juan Carlos Munoz/Okapia/RH; 53-5 Ragnar Th. Sigurdsson/RH; 53-4 Norbert Eisele-Hein/RH; 53 (LO) Felix Lipov/SS; 54 (UP) Karin59/DT; 54-5 Frank Bach/DT; 54-4 Dmitry Kalinovsky/DT; 54-3 Reinhard Dirscherl/RH; 55-1 Smellme/DT; 55-2 Thierry Berrod, Mona Lisa Production/SPL; 55 (UP) Baloncici/SS; 55 (LO) Alexander Raths/SS; 56 (UP) Alexander Raths/SS; 56 (LO) olegganko/SS; 56-1 Pipa100/DT; 56-2 Bildagentur Zoonar GmbH/SS; 57-3 Aleksandr Frolov/DT; 57-4 Joerg Boethling/RH; 57-5 BergeImLicht/SS; 57 (LO) Baloncici/SS; 58 (UP) Eric Isselee/SS; 58 (LO) Alexander Raths/SS; 58-5 Miroslav Hlavko/DT; 59-1 Isselee/DT; 59-2 Mircea Costina/DT; 59-3 Brian Kushner/DT; 59-4 John Cancalosi/RH; 59 (LO) offstocker/IS; 60 (UP) Ljupco Smokovski/SS; 60-5 Ian Cumming/Design Pics/CI; 60-4 Patrick Ward/CI; 61-1 Anthony West/CI; 61-2 Global Warming Images/REX; 61-3 Duncan Andison/CI; 62-1 Juan Carlos Munoz/RH; 62-2 Ruta Saulyte/DT; 62-3 Marco Cristofori/RH; 62-4 Magnus Kallstrom/SS; 63 (UP) Greg Epperson/GI; 63-5 Uli Wiesmeier/RH; 63 (CTR) Alexander Raths/SS; 63 (LO) Aprilphoto/SS

Asia: 64 (LO) AGE/RH; 66 (L-UP) silverjohn/SS; 66 (R-UP) Baloncici/SS; 66-1 Anna Yakimova/DT; 66 (L-CTR) Alexander Raths/SS; 66 (R-CTR) Lambert (bart) Parren/DT; 66-2 Elena Koulik/SS; 67-5 Anatoly Tiplyashin/DT; 67-3 Tony Waltham/RH; 67-4 Ekaterina Pokrovsky/DT; 68 (UP) Alexander Raths/SS; 68 (LO) Joerg Boethling/RH; 68-1 Amos Chapple/GI; 68-2 Ashley Cooper/RH; 69-3 Kaveh Kazemi/GI; 69-4 Dinodia/age fotostock/RH; 69-5 XYZ PICTURES/RH; 69 (LO) offstocker/IS; 70 (UP) Canitk/DT; 70-5 Jake Norton/RH; 70-4 Christian Kober/RH; 71-1 Peter Giovannini/RH; 71-2 Peter Barritt Photography/RH; 71-3 Christian Kober/RH; 72 (UP) Norberto Cuenca/GI; 72 (CTR) Alexander Raths/SS; 72 (L-LO) offstocker/IS; 72 (R-LO) Ailenn/DT; 72-1 Gelia/SS; 72-2 Ilonawellington/DT; 73-3 Dennis W. Donohue/SS; 73-4 Benjamin Wood/DT; 73-5 Stephan Scherhag/DT; 74 (UP) Alexander Raths/SS; 74 (LO) Kira Kaplinski/DT; 74-1 ICHIRO/GI; 75-2 Szczap/DT; 75-3 javarman/SS; 75-4 Jay Beiler/DT; 75-5 Ncristian/DT; 75 (LO) Aprilphoto/SS; 76 (UP) Alexander Potapov/DT; 76 (CTR) Baloncici/SS; 76 (LO) Riondt/DT; 76-1 Mikelane45/DT; 77 (UP) Alexander Raths/SS; 77-2 Lawrence Lawry/SPL; 77-3 Joel Sartore/GI; 77-4 Denise Cottin/DT; 77-5 Hungchungchih/DT; 78 (UP) Annie Owen/RH; 78-1 Miragik/DT; 78-2 Jefri Tarigan/REX; 78 (LO) Donyanedomam/DT; 79-3 Don Mammoser/SS; 79-4 Donyanedomam/DT; 79-5 Heiner Heine/RH; 80 (UP) Baloncici/SS; 80-1 Yongyut Kumsri/SS; 80-2 Paul Souders/CI; 80-3 Pawe_ Opaska/DT; 81 (L-UP) UniversalImagesGroup/GI; 81 (R-UP) Alexander Raths/SS; 81-4 Bill Hatcher/GI; 81-5 ZUMA/REX; 81 (LO) Mario Savoia/SS

Africa: 82 (LO) Gavin Hellier/RH; 84 (UP) erichon/SS; 84-1 Dave Stamboulis/RH; 84 (CTR) offstocker/IS; 84 (LO) Alexander Raths/SS; 84-5 Photovolcanica.com/SS; 85-2 Olivier Goujon/RH; 85-3 Olivier Goujon/RH; 85-4 Mikewaddell446/DT; 86 (UP) Aprilphoto/SS; 86-1 Mark Edwards/RH; 86-4 Gerard Fritz/GI; 86-5 Nigel Bean/Nature Picture Library/REX; 86 (LO) Alexander Raths/SS; 87 (UP) Hedrus/SS; 87-2 Steve Allen/DT; 87-3 Norbert Eisele-Hein/RH; 88-1 Randy Olson/GI; 88 (LO) Dhrupal Jetha/DT; 89-3 David Else/GI; 89-4 De Agostini Picture Library/GI; 89-5 Pal Teravagimov/SS; 90 (UP) Papa Bravo/SS; 90 (LO) Alexander Raths/SS; 90-4 Malcolm Schuyl/Flpa/RH; 90-5 Jocrebbin/DT; 91-1 Sylvain Grandadam/GI; 91-2 Ian Murray/RH; 91-3 Alberto Carrera/RH; 91 (LO) Aprilphoto/SS; 92 (UP) Alexander Raths/SS; 92-1 Pichugin Dmitry/SS; 92-4 shihina/SS; 92-5 Martin Harvey/GI; 93 (UP) Erwin Niemand/SS; 93-2 Gregory Dimijian/SPL; 93-3 Gtw/RH; 93 (CTR) JOAT/SS; 93 (LO) offstocker/IS; 94 (UP) Alexander Raths/SS; 94 (LO) Stu Porter/DT; 94-1 Matej Hudovernik/SS; 95 (UP) Isselee/DT; 95 (CTR) offstocker/IS; 95-2 Seanjeeves/DT; 95-3 Frans Lanting/RH; 95-4 Robin Winkelman/DT; 95-5 Nadezhda Bolotina/DT; 95 (LO) Eastmanphoto/DT; 96 (UP) Eduard Kyslynskyy/DT; 96-4 Vladimir Kindrachov/DT; 96-5 Chicco7/DT; 97-1 Mario Eder/GI; 97-2 BAO/RH; 97-3 BAO/RH; 98 (UP) Alexander Raths/SS; 98 (LO) Norbert Eisele-Hein/RH; 98-1 Last Refuge/RH; 99-2 Shaen Adey/GI; 99-3 David Wall Photo/GI; 99-4 Alexander Nesbit/RH; 99-5 Travel Ink/GI

Australia, Oceania and Antarctica: 100 (LO) Douglas Peebles/RH; 102 (UP) Ulla Lohmann/RH; 102 (LO) Alexander Raths/SS; 102-1 Reinhard Dirscherl/RH; 102-2 Joshua Cortopassi/DT; 102-3 Ongchangwei/DT; 103-4 Bjeayes/DT; 103-5 Michael Runkel/RH; 104 (UP) Nigel Dickinson/RH; 104-5 Gao Jianjun/Xinhua Press/CI; 104-4 Jeff Schmaltz/MODIS Rapid Response/NASA; 104-3 Sam Tinson/REX; 105 (L-UP) Baloncici/SS; 105 (R-UP) Alexander Raths/SS; 105-1 Ulla Lohmann/RH; 105-2 Lucidwaters/DT; 106-1 David Wall/RH; 106-2 Brian Cassey/epa/CI; 106 (LO) Dave Penman/REX; 107-3 Tim Laman/RH; 107-4 Stormcastle/DT; 107-5 Ashley Cooper/RH; 108-1 Tysonv/DT; 108-2 Robert Bayer/DT; 108-3 David Wall/RH; 109 (L-UP) Norbert Probst/RH; 109 (R-UP) Alexander Raths/SS; 109 (CTR) offstocker/IS; 109-4 Michele Westmorland/GI; 109-5 Tim Laman/RH; 110 (L-UP) Alexander Raths/SS; 110 (R-UP) Baloncici/SS; 110 (LO) Auscape/UIG/GI; 110-1 Pornsak Paewlumfaek/SS; 111-2 Mangiwau/GI; 111-3 Alessandrozocc/DT; 111-4 Michael Krabs/RH; 111-5 Ncaimages/DT; 112 (UP) Anan Kaewkhammul/SS; 112 (CTR) Alexander Raths/SS; 112 (L-LO) Baloncici/SS; 112 (R-LO) Pniesen/DT; 112-5 Alan Root/Okapia/RH; 113-1 Morales/RH; 113-2 Thierry Berrod, Mona Lisa Production/SPL; 113-3 Karl Johaentges/RH; 113-4 Gerry Pearce/SPL; 114-1 Will Gray/GI; 114-2 Anders Blomqvist/GI; 114-3 Frans Lanting/RH; 115 (UP) Light & Magic Photography/SS; 115-4 Tui De Roy/Minden Pictures/CI; 115-5 Feathercollector/DT; 116 (UP) Horst Mahr/RH; 116 (CTR) Aprilphoto/SS; 116-4 Christian Goupi/RH; 116-5 Sean Davey/RH; 117-1 WestEnd61/REX; 117-2 Kevin O'Hara/RH; 117 (CTR) Alexander Raths/SS; 117-3 Neale Haynes/REX

Antarctica: 118 (LO) kkaplin/SS; 120 (UP) Wally Herbert/RH; 120-1 Michael Nolan/RH; 120-2 Worldscapes/age fotostock/RH; 120 (L-CTR) Alexander Raths/SS; 120 (CTR) Baloncici/SS; 120 (R-CTR) Sean Mckenzie/RH; 121-5 Gordon Wiltsie/GI; 121-3 Colin Monteath/Hedgehog House/GI; 122 (L-UP) Alexander Raths/SS; 122 (R-UP) Baloncici/SS; 122 (LO) Wally Herbert/RH; 122-1 Volodymyr Goinyk/SS; 122-2 Jonathan & Angela Scott/GI; 123-3 Doug Allan/SPL; 123-4 Graham Neden; Ecoscene/CI; 123-5 Ingrid Visser/RH; 123 (LO) Nobumichi Tamura/Stocktrek Images/GI; 124 (UP) Alexander Raths/SS; 124-1 Michael Nolan/RH; 124 (L-LO) Robert Harding Productions/RH; 124 (R-LO) Aprilphoto/SS; 125-2 Gordon Wiltsie/GI; 125-3 Gordon Wiltsie/GI; 125-4 David Tipling/GI; 125-5 Colin Monteath/RH

Oceans: 126 (LO) Banol2007/DT; 128 (UP) Stuart Westmorland/age fotostock/RH; 128-5 Look67/DT; 128 (L-LO) Baloncici/SS; 128 (R-LO) Fallsview/DT; 129-1 KeystoneUSA-ZUMA/REX; 129-2 Ken Gillham/RH; 129-3 P Rona/OAR/National Undersea research Program/NOAA/SPL; 129-4 Michael Nolan/RH; 129 (LO) Alexander Raths/SS; 130 (UP) Alexander Raths/SS; 130-1 Typhoonski/DT; 130-2 Julie Marshall/GI; 130-3 Shaul Schwarz/GI; 130 (LO) Philip Stephen/bluegreenpictures.com/REX; 131-4 Xiaomin Wang/DT; 131 (UP) Andre Seale/RH; 131 (LO) offstocker/IS; 132-1 J. Henning Buchholz/DT; 132-2 Chriswood44/DT; 132-3 Allen Lindblad/DT; 132 (LO) Alexander Raths/SS; 133 (UP) RichardRobinson/RH; 133 (LO) Aprilphoto/SS; 133-4 Masa Ushioda/RH; 133-5 Tenedos/DT; 134 (UP) Alexander Raths/SS; 134 (L-LO) PhotoStock-Israel/RH; 134 (R-LO) Baloncici/SS; 134-1 Dudarev Mikhail/SS; 134-2 Michael Hutchinson/RH; 135-3 Andrey Nekrasov/RH; 135-4 Galina Barskaya/DT

Sky: 136 (UP) Ambientideas/DT; 136 (LO) Thierry Grun/RH; 137 Graphic of sky, Chris Philpot; 138 (UP) Alexander Raths/SS; 138 (LO) SurangaSL/SS; 138-1 Daniel L. Osborne, University of Alaska/Detlev Van Ravenswaay/SPL; 138-2 Pere Sanz/DT; 138-3 Louise Murray/RH; 139-4 Michael S. Nolan/RH; 139 (L-CTR) Baloncici/SS; 139 (R-CTR) Martine De Graaf/DT; 139-5 Petr Ma_ek/DT; 140 (UP) Stephen Mcsweeny/SS; 140-3 Stephen Dalton/GI; 140-4 Steffen Foerster/SS; 140 (LO) Baloncici/SS; 141-5 Ainars Aunins/SS; 141-1 Dohnal/DT; 141-2 Craig Dingle/GI; 141 (LO) Alexander Raths/SS; 142 (UP) Baloncici/SS; 142-1 Picturecorrect/DT; 142-2 Sergei Remezov/Reuters/CI; 142 (L-LO) Chris Van Lennep/DT; 142 (R-LO) Alexander Raths/SS; 143-3 Douglas Peebles/RH; 143-5 Pytyczech/DT

Games: 144: Top row (Left to Right): TOM GRILL/GI; THOMAS MARENT/Minden Pictures; NIGEL HICKS/Alamy. Middle row (Left to Right): MINT IMAGES/ART WOLFE/GI; MARK BASSETT/Alamy; RUDI VON BRIEL/GI. Bottom row (Left to Right): NOPPAWAT TOM CHAROENSINPHON/GI; STEPHEN DALTON/Minden Pictures; MEEGAN ZIMMERMAN/GI. 145: Top row (Left to Right): FUSE/GI; DUNCAN NOAKES/DT; SKYNETPHOTO/DT. Middle row (Left to Right): EASTCOTT MOMATIUK/GI; MARC PARSONS/ST; ICELAW/DT. Bottom row (Left to Right): BERENDJE PHOTOGRAPHY/ST; FRANCO BANFI/Nature Picture Library; VISUALS UNLIMITED, INC./KEN CATANIA/GI. 146: Top row (Left to Right): BRANDON ALMS/DT; BIDOUZE STÉPHANE/DT; NATAKUZMINA/DT. Middle row (Left to Right): AMMIT/DT; HOTSHOTSWORLDWIDE/DT; SERGEY GALUSHKO/DT. Bottom row (Left to Right); BRIAN GRANT/DT; TAMARA KULIKOVA/DT; IKA66/DT. 147: Top row (Left to Right): PURESTOCK/GI; KEN LUCAS/VISUALS UNLIMITED, INC./GI; INGRAM PUBLISHING/SUPERSTOCK. Middle row (Left to Right): DUFFIE/Alamy; FRED BAVENDAM/Minden Pictures; PHOTONTRAPPIST/GI. Bottom row (Left to Right): CHRIS NEWBERT/Minden Pictures; SHELI SPRING SALDANA/DT; DORLING KINDERSLEY/GI. 148: Top row (Left to Right): BLACKSLIDE/DT; SHIROPHOTO/DT; EGOR TETIUSHEV/ST. Middle row (Left to Right): ZELJKO RADOJKO/ST; GORAN TURINA/DT; NICRAM SABOD/ST. Bottom row (Left to Right): S. DASHKEVYCH/ST; WEBERFOTO/Alamy; ROSALIE KREULEN/ST

End Matter: 152 (UP) Andrew Burgess/SS; 152 (CTR) Vadim Petrakov/SS; 152 (LO) Valentyn Volkov/SS; 153 (UP) Bankolo5/SS; 153 (L-LO) Popova Valeriya/SS; 153 (R-LO) Aaron Amat/SS; 154 (L-UP) Eric Isselee/SS; 154 (R-UP) javarman/SS; 154 (LO) Eric Isselee/SS

Aunt Bertha illustration by Joe Rocco.

Staff for This Book
Priyanka Lamichhane and Amy Briggs,
    Senior Editors
Amanda Larsen, *Art Director*
Bender Richardson White, *Designer*
Kelley Miller, *Senior Photo Editor*
Carl Mehler, *Director of Maps*
Sven M. Dolling and Michael McNey,
    Map Research and Production
Paige Towler, *Editorial Assistant*
Sanjida Rashid and Rachel Kenny,
    Design Production Assistants
Michael Cassady, *Rights Clearance Specialist*
Grace Hill, *Managing Editor*
Joan Gossett, *Senior Production Editor*
Lewis R. Bassford, *Production Manager*
George Bounelis, *Manager, Production Services*
Susan Borke, *Legal and Business Affairs*

Published by the National Geographic Society
Gary E. Knell, *President and CEO*
John M. Fahey, *Chairman of the Board*
Melina Gerosa Bellows, *Chief Education Officer*
Declan Moore, *Chief Media Officer*
Hector Sierra, *Senior Vice President and General
    Manager, Book Division*

**Senior Management Team, Kids Publishing
and Media** Nancy Laties Feresten, *Senior Vice
President;* Jennifer Emmett, *Vice President,
Editorial Director, Kids Books;* Julie Vosburgh
Agnone, *Vice President, Editorial Operations;*
Rachel Buchholz, *Editor and Vice President,* NG
Kids *magazine;* Michelle Sullivan, *Vice President,
Kids Digital;* Eva Absher-Schantz, *Design
Director;* Jay Sumner, *Photo Director;* Hannah
August, *Marketing Director;* R. Gary Colbert,
Production Director

Digital Anne McCormack, *Director;* Laura
Goertzel, Sara Zeglin, *Producers;* Emma Rigney,
Creative Producer; Bianca Bowman, *Assistant
Producer;* Natalie Jones, *Senior Product Manager*

The National Geographic Society is one of the world's largest nonprofit scientific and educational organizations. Founded in 1888 to "increase and diffuse geographic knowledge," the Society's mission is to inspire people to care about the planet. It reaches more than 400 million people worldwide each month through its official journal, *National Geographic*, and other magazines; National Geographic Channel; television documentaries; music; radio; films; books; DVDs; maps; exhibitions; live events; school publishing programs; interactive media; and merchandise. National Geographic has funded more than 10,000 scientific research, conservation, and exploration projects and supports an education program promoting geographic literacy.

For more information, please visit nationalgeographic.com, call 1-800-NGS LINE (647-5463), or write to the following address:
National Geographic Society
1145 17th Street N.W.
Washington, D.C. 20036-4688 U.S.A.

Visit us online at nationalgeographic.com/books

For librarians and teachers: ngchildrensbooks.org

More for kids from National Geographic:
kids.nationalgeographic.com

For information about special discounts for bulk purchases, please contact National Geographic Books Special Sales:
ngspecsales@ngs.org

For rights or permissions inquiries, please contact National Geographic Books Subsidiary Rights:
ngbookrights@ngs.org

Paperback ISBN: 978-1-4263-2044-6
Reinforced library binding ISBN: 978-1-4263-2045-3

Printed in the United States of America
15/WOR/1